JOHN ROSS, CHEROKEE CHIEF

John Neagle, ca. 1848   Oklahoma Historical Society

CHIEF JOHN ROSS (1790–1866)

GARY E. MOULTON

JOHN ROSS
CHEROKEE
CHIEF

THE UNIVERSITY OF GEORGIA PRESS
ATHENS

Copyright © 1978 by the University of Georgia Press
Athens 30602

Set in 10 point Trump Medieval type
Printed in the United States of America
Second printing, 1982

Library of Congress Cataloging in Publication Data

Moulton, Gary E
  John Ross, Cherokee Chief.

  Bibliography: p.
  Includes index.

  1. Ross, John, Cherokee Chief, 1790–1866.   2. Cherokee
Indians—Biography.   3. Cherokee Indians—History.
I. Title.

E99.C5R825   970'.004'97 [B]   76-1146
ISBN 0-8203-0422-0

CONTENTS

PREFACE

I FIRST became acquainted with Chief John Ross of the Cherokees as a historical figure while I attended a class in Oklahoma
history at Northeastern Oklahoma State University, Tahlequah, Oklahoma, the old capital of the Cherokee Nation. Frequently
I walked the very grounds over which Ross had strolled more than a
century before, yet for a long time I felt no spark of interest in either
Ross or Cherokee history. Several years later in a graduate seminar
someone suggested Ross as a major research topic. I soon discovered
that Ross had no adequate biography and, in fact, that a great deal of
his life remained a mystery, especially his private and family life and
his personal finances. Indeed, even large questions in his political
career remained untreated, disputed, or unanswered.

As I explored his life further, I was extremely fortunate that I was
within less than a hundred miles of a vast storehouse of Ross materials. At the Thomas Gilcrease Institute of American History and
Art, I discovered Ross's personal papers, plus the kind assistance of
Marie Keene. Almost as valuable at Gilcrease Institute was the Lester Hargrett collection of imprints which recently has been
catalogued and published under the editorship of G. P. Edwards,
who also lent kind assistance. At the Oklahoma Historical Society I
found, as have so many students of Indian history before me, that
Rella Looney was indispensable for help in tracing the most obscure
documentation in the society's excellent Indian Archives Division.
David Winkles in the Oklahoma Historical Society Library was
especially helpful in tracking down genealogical sources on Ross
through old county histories and Emmet Starr's unpublished Cherokee genealogical notes. At the University of Oklahoma, Jack D.
Haley, assistant curator of the Western History Collections, showed

me a number of courtesies and guided me to important Ross materials. At the John Vaughn Library at Northeastern Oklahoma State University, Helen Wheat cooperated in my search through the library's Cherokee collection.

Ross was a national figure in his day, and many of his letters to leading United States personages are located in collections in other states. Diana Haskell at the Newberry Library traced numerous valuable materials for me in the John Howard Payne Papers, while Nancy G. Boles pointed me to Ross sources in the William Wirt Papers at the Maryland Historical Society.

The historical archives of Georgia and Tennessee maintain Cherokee sources which contain significant Ross correspondence. Ruth Corry at the Georgia Department of Archives and History was helpful, and Jean Waggener of the Tennessee State Library and Archives went out of her way a number of times to do long-distance research and demonstrate that southern hospitality has not declined since Ross's day. To Dr. William McLoughlin of Brown University and Dr. Walter Vernon of Nashville, Tennessee, I owe a special thanks for information and direction on Ross's religious attachments. Dr. Rennard Strickland of the University of Tulsa and Dr. Thurman Wilkins of Queens College kindly loaned me portions of their personal collections of Cherokee material. I was fortunate to meet Penelope Johnson Allen whose knowledge of East Tennessee is matched by a kind and generous heart. She allowed me to copy private Ross materials, some of which had never been used. Elizabeth Tritle of the Quaker Collection at Haverford College pointed me to sources on the Stapler family, while Ernest H. Winter, Jr., of the Alumni Association of Lawrenceville School gave me needed information on the Ross family members who attended the academy during the mid-nineteenth century.

At Oklahoma State University I was blessed with a conscientious, interested library staff. In particular, Heather Lloyd, Dixie Mosier, and Corinne Colpitts deserve thanks for their ready assistance with interlibrary loan material, while Josh Stroman and Vickie Phillips gave me much-needed support in the use of government documents.

I also would like to thank Dr. Theodore L. Agnew, Jr., and Dr. Robert H. Spaulding, Jr., members of the faculty at Oklahoma State University, for their careful reading of the Ross manuscript and for their helpful comments. I especially owe a great deal to my friend and mentor, Dr. LeRoy H. Fischer, who with his own particular blend of encouragement and prodding helped me to master a number of difficult problems, and whose unsurpassed editorial skills made several tedious issues less trying.

I am grateful to my parents, Mr. and Mrs. W. V. Moulton, for their continued encouragement and faith in my efforts. My children, Kim, Russell, and Luanne, merit special recognition for tolerating an absentee father and for trying to appear interested in stories about an ancient Indian chief. I owe so much to Faye—for her constant concern and encouragement that this work be more than an academic exercise. We shared many hours together working toward literary excellence and editorial consistency, but more than that, we shared our lives.

JOHN ROSS, CHEROKEE CHIEF

1

ANCESTRY AND IDENTITY

COMMISSIONER of Indian Affairs Dennis N. Cooley moved in closer to be certain that no words or thoughts would be lost in the interchange with Chief John Ross, the old Cherokee patriarch who lay on a bed before him. Present in that Washington hotel room besides Cooley were other United States officials, all anxious to bring the Cherokee treaty negotiations to a close. The time was April 3, 1866, and Ross, though hovering on the brink of death, had been able to elude the machinations of these men who had worked to sign a treaty with his foes to break the Cherokee unity that he cherished. Commissioner Cooley was the first to speak: "I learn Mr. Ross that you are Seventy five years of age & have served your Nation over fifty."

"Yes, Sir," Ross replied: "I am an old man, and have served my people and the Govt of the United States a long time, over fifty years. My people have kept me in the harness, not of my seeking, but of their own choice. I have never deceived them, and now I look back, not one act of my public life rises up to upbraid me. I have done the best I could, and today, upon this bed of sickness, my heart approves all I have done. And still I am, John Ross, the same John Ross of former years, unchanged."[1]

The life that Ross surveyed in those brief moments was incredibly intricate. Out of the checkered background of white and Indian heritage; a thread of consistency wound its way. Dedication to his people and to a principle had led him once again to Washington to reconstruct his nation on the basis of that singular resolve. The one great aim of his life, the political and social cohesion of his people, was now fixed on the Cherokee Reconstruction Treaty of 1866, and after his death on August 1, 1866, the unity he had sought so long would be restored briefly.

Ross's half-century of leadership spanned an era in which the Cherokees reached the pinnacle of their civilization but were also plunged to the depths of human suffering. To look at his ancestry and his childhood, one would not predict Ross to be a likely leader among the Cherokees. Only one-eighth Cherokee, he spoke the language haltingly, and he never learned its written characters after Sequoyah's stroke of creative brilliance. What tapped him for leadership were qualities that touched the Cherokees' faith—a firm attachment to their ancient lands and a desire to keep united a people formed in untraceable antiquity.

Ross's lineage begins with a remote Scottish figure, William Shorey, and his full-blood Cherokee wife, Ghigooie of the Bird Clan. Little is known and less is certain of Shorey and Ghigooie. He served the British for a time as an interpreter at Fort Loudoun and, because of his fluency in the Cherokee language, accompanied Lieutenant Henry Timberlake and a group of Cherokees to England. During the crossing in May of 1762, Shorey died of "consumption," and whatever evidence might have made him less obscure went with him. The fate of Ghigooie is unknown.[2]

Shorey left behind at least two children, Anne and William. Anne married a Scottish trader, John McDonald. William married a girl named Peggy, and they had at least one daughter, Elizabeth. He also had two other daughters, but it is not likely that they were the children of Peggy. In the 1790s Shorey carried out several military and liaison tasks for his brother-in-law, McDonald. He also must have gained some influence among the Cherokees, for he signed the Cherokee treaties of 1805 and 1806, using his Indian name, Eskaculiskee.[3]

The younger William Shorey died in 1809 and left a verbal will that caused a controversy between his sister Anne and his oldest daughter Elizabeth. Shortly after Shorey's death, McDonald produced a document purported to be a will given orally to Shorey's grandnephew, John Ross, McDonald's grandson. In substance Shorey left the larger share of his estate to his sister Anne. Two Negro slaves were left to Anne and were to pass to John Ross at his grandmother's death. Shorey instructed Anne to care for his two

younger daughters, Lydia and Alcy or Alice, to whom Shorey bequeathed other slaves. To his daughter Elizabeth, who had married a
leading figure in Cherokee affairs, John Lowrey, he left some livestock valued at three hundred dollars. Ross inherited "a part of an
island which is the first below Tellico B[lock] house." This island
was the first of the extensive landholdings Ross eventually would
acquire in Tennessee and Georgia.[4]

Elizabeth Lowrey was not ready to accept this verbal will. She
resisted even to the point of detaining her two sisters who were to be
cared for by Anne. Elizabeth insisted that her father had never mentioned any of the desires purported to be in this will. She thought
that Ross probably had obtained the will when her father was drunk,
that he would never have made such promises sober. Moreover,
Elizabeth emphasized that Shorey's second wife (whose name is unknown) did not accept the will. McDonald felt that Elizabeth
wanted to keep the girls only in order to get more property, and he
also noted that the "wife" had left Shorey many years earlier. Eventually orders from Cherokee Chief Pathkiller and the United States
agent to the Cherokees settled the matter; the decision went largely
in favor of Anne McDonald.[5]

John McDonald, Ross's maternal grandfather, was born in the
Scottish Highlands at Inverness about 1747. Like many Scotsmen,
McDonald was attracted to America by the hope of economic gain
rather than by religious persecution. He arrived in America around
1766 and settled for a time in Charleston, South Carolina. He then
served in a mercantile house in Georgia before being commissioned
for a trading post at Fort Loudoun on the Georgia-Tennessee frontier. Doubtless at Fort Loudoun McDonald met Anne Shorey,
daughter of the interpreter, and in 1769 they married. McDonald
was not content simply to serve as a clerk for another man's profit,
so he joined the next migratory wave of settlers that swept across
the frontier. McDonald settled in the region known as Chickamauga
among the Lower Cherokees, adjacent to the majestic Lookout
Mountain, so reminiscent of his Scottish Highland home. Here, on
November 1, 1770, Mollie, the only known child of John and Anne,
was born.[6]

At the close of the French and Indian War in 1763, the land east of
the Mississippi River came into the possession of the British. The

ruddy and reliable Captain John Stuart, who had worked among the Cherokees during the French and Indian War, was appointed British superintendent of Indian affairs to tribes south of the Ohio River. To the Cherokees he appointed two able representatives as assistants, John McDonald and Alexander Cameron. McDonald continued to live among the Lower Cherokees at Chickamauga, while Cameron worked with the Overhill settlements.[7]

McDonald served in the Revolutionary War as an ensign in the British ranks and as commissary agent for the British troops. In this capacity he proved effective at leading and supplying Indians, qualities that he would cultivate in subsequent merchandising efforts. After the war he settled on the Chickamauga River, carrying on a private trade through Pensacola among the Cherokees with goods bought at Charleston in defiance of Indian trading laws established by the fledgling United States. McDonald's influence with the Cherokees increased, for he dealt with them honestly and spoke their language skillfully. As the three contending powers—England, Spain, and the United States—converged on the Cherokee Nation, McDonald's assistance was sought by each. One American official wrote: "In case of a war with any foreign power, he may be very serviceable, or very dangerous."[8]

In the late 1780s McDonald became connected with the trading firm of Panton, Leslie, and Company. With the advice and assistance of William Panton, McDonald became the first and only agent of the Spanish government among the Cherokees. By June 1792 McDonald was working actively for the Spanish among the Lower Cherokees and receiving a pension of five hundred dollars annually. He was instrumental in getting Cherokee Chief Bloody Fellow to ignore treaties with the United States and to carry on clandestine negotiations with Spanish Governor Baron de Carondelet. Yet, McDonald's active association with the Spanish was short-lived. In early 1793, Governor William Blount of Tennessee received reports that McDonald was friendly to Americans and amenable to accepting a commission. McDonald may have been playing off all three powers. On one occasion he pledged to an American acquaintance: "Believe me Sir I shall never turn Spaniard." He also assured a British official at Detroit as late as 1794 that, though he had been offered a commissary appointment by the Spanish, he had not accepted; yet he continued to draw his five hundred dollar pension until 1798. Nevertheless, by May 1793 he wrote Governor Blount that he would accept an appointment as United States agent to the Lower Cherokees. Blount enthusiastically informed the secretary of war about McDonald, for the governor was ignorant of the Tory trader's connection with the Spanish. Blount considered McDonald particularly able and noted that "he has as much or more, influence with the Lower Cherokees, than any other man who resides among them."[9]

McDonald in 1785 had another opportunity to use his bargaining prowess with Bloody Fellow. Daniel Ross, born in Sutherlandshire, Scotland, about 1760, had been brought to America in his youth and had been left an orphan at Baltimore, Maryland, at the end of the Revolutionary War. Like many young men, he turned to the frontier and in 1785 joined with Francis Mayberry of Hawkins County, Tennessee, to trade for furs among the Chickasaws. Making the usual stop at Setico required of flatboats traveling the Tennessee River, Ross and Mayberry were detained by an incensed band of Bloody Fellow's followers. Ignorant of Cherokee animosities, the two white traders had carried on board their craft a chief whom the Cherokees considered a deadly enemy. Until McDonald intervened, the aptly named Bloody Fellow was ready to massacre the lot. After the Cherokees' hostility had diminished, they asked young Ross to open trade with them. As a result Ross established a trading firm at Setico in the Lookout Mountain valley, probably in connection with McDonald, and within a year had married McDonald's daughter Mollie.[10]

The following years were restless ones for the Ross and McDonald families. In 1788 Daniel Ross moved with his father-in-law to Turkey Town on the Coosa River near present-day Center, Alabama, where he continued to trade with the Cherokees. Two years later, on October 3, 1790, Mollie's third child was born and named John after his grandfather. Daniel and Mollie reared a family of nine children; the two girls who preceded John were Jane and Elizabeth; the other children in succession were Lewis, Susan, Andrew, Annie, Margaret, and Maria. From Turkey Town the families moved to Willstown, one of the largest settlements of the Cherokees, then to Chickamauga, and finally to the northern end of the Lookout Mountain range at present-day Chattanooga. At the base of the mountain near the cool spring of Saint Elmo, Daniel Ross constructed a sturdy log house where he remained until John Ross's manhood. McDonald moved to a house built about 1797, one only about three miles southeast of the Ross house. In a few years, possibly about 1808 after the death of his mother, John Ross moved to the McDonald home and remained there off and on until about 1827. In time the area became known as Rossville, and young Ross continued to make improvements on the two-storied log house which still stands in reconstructed form at Rossville, Georgia.[11]

John Ross's earliest memories were of this home set in the midst of the Cherokees, where Ross observed the folkways of the full bloods who traded at his father's store. As a child Ross was called Tsan Usdi or Little John. According to Cherokee custom, he acquired a different name at adulthood, Kooweskoowe, after some mythological or rare migratory bird. Ross's character belied his name, and his attachment to the Cherokees' native land must have grown with each succeeding year. As a youth Ross favored the ancient dress and customs of his people. At the annual Green Corn Festival, he was reluctant to appear before his young friends in American clothes and stayed behind until his mother let him change to more familiar Cherokee attire.

Ross's American education was not neglected, however. He learned his first lessons while seated near one of the fireplaces of his father's home. Daniel Ross wanted for his children more than a rudimentary knowledge, so he filled his home with the latest American and English newspapers and an assortment of maps and books. One traveler visiting the Ross house felt that he might well have been in England or Scotland rather than the Cherokee wilds. Desiring formal training for his children, the elder Ross in about 1799 hired a private tutor for the youngsters, a certain George Barbee Davis, who guided them through fundamentals before they were sent to private boarding schools. John and his brother Lewis studied for a time with the Reverend Gideon Blackburn at his mission near Chickamauga and later attended an academy at South West Point, now Kingston, Tennessee.[12]

Missionary activity among the Cherokees advanced rapidly in the first decade of the nineteenth century, and the McDonald and Ross families played a part in this modernizing influence. The first significant missionary effort came in 1799, when two Moravian ministers accompanying a wealthy mixed-blood, James Vann, passed through the Cherokee Nation in search of a suitable location for their proposed mission. They visited the McDonald place at Chickamauga but objected to the site, saying that many considered the place "unhealthful." They finally settled on the Vann house at Springplace. In 1816 the Reverend Cyrus Kingsbury came to establish a mission, bringing with him the support of the American Board of Commissioners for Foreign Missions. With the consent of the Cherokee General Council, Kingsbury bought McDonald's site, consisting of about twenty-five acres and his buildings and improvements. The mission was soon christened Brainerd after David Brainerd, a pioneer missionary among the northern Indians. The United States government agreed to pay McDonald five hundred dollars for the location and also to furnish the school with farming equipment and household goods. Brainerd was one of the most successful of the mission stations.[13]

In spite of the Ross family attachment to missionary activity, John Ross was not an early convert to Christianity. His grandmother, Anne Shorey McDonald, frequently attended services at Brainerd, becoming a convert and a mainstay in the congregation, but Ross remained unpersuaded. Like his father and grandfather, Ross was interested in the missionaries, for he understood the advances in education they would bring to the rustic Cherokees, and in later years he often pleaded their cases for use of tribal lands. As a successful planter, he was always ready to supply the missions with corn, and he also was willing to overlook an occasional debt made by the hard-pressed missionaries. Ross eventually was influenced by Nicholas Dalton Scales, husband of his niece Mary Coodey, and by a dedicated circuit rider, John B. McFerrin of the Methodist Episcopal Church, to accept conversion. Ross probably became what the Methodists of the time termed a "seeker," that is, one in preparation for baptism. Formal entry into the Methodist Church came later. Although never deeply religious, Ross maintained an interest in spiritual affairs and remained a Methodist from 1829. He was not a habitual joiner, and although he became a member of the Masons in 1827, it does not appear that he was active there.[14]

During his years at the Kingston academy Ross also received practical knowledge of merchandising. He boarded for a time with Thomas N. Clark, a personal friend of his father and one of the area's leading merchants and planters. Clark also was a friend and advisor to the Cherokees and had several business connections with the tribe. After completing school, young Ross served as a clerk for William Neilson of the Tennessee trading firm of Neilson, King, and Smith. Although Ross engaged in business often during his life, he never seemed content with it. Yet in those early days at Kingston he developed managerial skills that would see him through a lifetime, and he learned the art of personal persuasion so vital to his later political career.[15]

Ross's next business venture was with Timothy Meigs, son of the United States agent to the Cherokees, Return J. Meigs. In late 1813 Ross became a partner in an already thriving enterprise which they now named "Meigs and Ross." This fortunate association brought lucrative government contracts to the firm during the Creek War of 1813–14 when blankets, corn, and other supplies were needed for Cherokee warriors. The partnership seemed to bring their families close together. After Mollie Ross died in 1808, Mrs. Return J. Meigs occasionally would care for the young Ross girls; Elizabeth and Maria became particular favorites of the Meigs family.[16]

After Timothy Meigs died in late 1815, Ross brought his brother Lewis Ross into the partnership, and they were able to continue government contracts. Ross stressed to Agent Meigs on the eve of a marketing trip to Baltimore that he could furnish goods at a lower price than could other local contractors, and that it would be more "satisfactory to the Indians to have such a person as to supply & issue to them as they could confide in." Ross's warehouse and landing became well known among the Cherokees and were sources of supply for the Indians as well as for the United States government. Ross established the landing on the south bank of the Tennessee River and a ferry for the frequent supply and passenger flatboats; the general area soon was known as Ross's Landing, a customary stop for travelers on the Federal Road from Nashville to Augusta.[17]

The Ross store was also a source of supply for Cherokee emigrants going west. It is difficult to determine how long Ross remained in partnership with his brother Lewis, but in 1818 the Cherokees and federal Indian agents were buying goods from "John & Lewis Ross," and the business may have continued until 1827. It also appears that John Ross was connected for a time with his brother Andrew in a merchandising operation at Fort Armstrong, a few miles above Turkey Town on the Coosa River. By the mid-1820s, Ross's increased involvement in Cherokee political affairs and his move to a new home at the head of the Coosa River (now Rome, Georgia) had brought an end to his early merchandising efforts.[18]

After the Louisiana Purchase in 1803, Agent Meigs assumed an extra role as a promoter of removal. The federal government allotted supplies to small parties of Cherokees who would relocate on the western border of Arkansas, where nearly two thousand members of the tribe had settled by 1811. Meigs realized that the threatened conflict with Great Britain endangered contact with the western Cherokees, who were as yet without an agent. Meigs in 1812 commissioned Ross to visit their settlements on the Arkansas River.[19]

Ross may have had an added incentive to visit Arkansas, for he proposed to take charge of a factory on the Arkansas River. The factory system, established by the federal government to gain some control over the large numbers of traders who were entering Indian lands, would license traders through the local Indian agent and authorize trade to selected reliable merchants. Ross seemed to be proposing to Meigs some sort of temporary contract in which he would be paid a thousand dollars per year and a dollar a day subsistence for his work in the West. Meigs and Washington officials were not ready to grant such a contract until they could learn more about the disposition of the western group.[20]

Sometime in early December 1812 Ross left for the country of his western brothers. He carried with him over nine hundred dollars' worth of goods, including such items as calico, gingham, buttons, homespun, and other frontier necessities such as beaver traps, shotguns, and butcher knives. Ross was accompanied by John Spears, a mixed-blood Cherokee interpreter, an old full-blood, Kalsatee, and Peter Esquebell, a Spanish-speaking servant. The group arrived at Huntsville on the Tennessee River in mid-December after what Ross described as a "very disagreeable voyage." Before reaching Huntsville, Ross exchanged his less seaworthy flat-bottomed boat for a keelboat purchased for sixty dollars from Isaac Brownlow. About forty miles below Fort Massac, located at the confluence of the Tennessee and Ohio rivers, the Ross party was stopped by a group of white men who swore that if any Indians were on board they would kill them. Only a short time before, three Indians had indeed been killed, and these men sought further bloodshed. Ross informed them that his companions were Spaniards and had Esquebell speak a few words as proof. The men galloped off, but Ross cautiously sent Kalsatee by land to join them at Fort Massac.[21]

Ross reached Fort Massac on December 30 and picked up more supplies sent out the year before under Samuel Riley, the interpreter for Meigs. It seems that Riley had gone only as far as Fort Massac before turning back after hearing of earthquakes some miles below on the Mississippi River at New Madrid. Ross reported that some tremors still could be felt a short distance below Fort Massac. With the added supplies Ross now carried over $2,200 worth of goods for the western Cherokees. A portion represented money owed the Cherokee settlers for the 1811 annual payment, but the greater part would serve to maintain friendship with the frontier Indians. Ross and his band departed Fort Massac on January 1, 1813, but were able to travel only four miles owing to winds which nearly flooded their boat. The remainder of the trip was almost as adventurous as the first part, for the boat apparently wrecked, and a march of some two hundred miles across land was required to reach their destination.[22]

Ross arrived home in April, and within a few months the Cherokees were embroiled in a conflict with a hostile faction of upper Creeks. Ross noticed divisions among the Creeks in July 1813 when he visited several Creek towns. Certain Creek chiefs sent messages to Meigs through Ross, informing the agent of their tribal rebellion and calling for his support for those Creeks loyal to the United States. Ross offered his services to gather intelligence for Meigs. Shawnee Chief Tecumseh had convinced a dissident Creek band that Indian nations should band together against the inevitable conflict with whites. When war broke out between the United States and Great Britain, these bellicose Creeks, the "Red Sticks," seized the occasion to make raids on lonely white settlements. Influential agents like Colonel Meigs and prominent Cherokees like The Ridge (soon to be known as Major Ridge) were able to persuade the lower Creeks and Cherokees to align with the United States against the onslaught of the Red Sticks.[23]

Ross entered military service in October 1813 as an adjutant in Captain Sekekee's company of mounted Cherokees with the rank of second lieutenant under the command of Colonel Gideon Morgan, Jr. Morgan's first attempt to lead his troops into battle proved unsuccessful, as the engagement they sought at Tallashatchee was resolved by advance forces before their arrival. On November 18 Morgan linked his band of Cherokees with the Tennesseans under Brigadier General James White and they pushed to the Creek town of Hillaby. As the town had just sent a peace envoy to General Andrew Jackson, the Creeks were not prepared for an attack. Yet White ordered an assault, and the town was devastated, with no losses counted on the American side. There was little glory in this gratuitous violence.[24]

In late January 1814 General Jackson began to build his forces at his Fort Strother headquarters on the Coosa River below Turkey Town. The Creek Indians, who challenged Jackson in the southern arena of the War of 1812, had massed a force of nearly 1,200 warriors at Horseshoe, a bend of the Tallapoosa River, fifty miles of hard marching from Jackson's troops. Jackson hoped to drive them from their well-entrenched position by combining Tennessee militiamen with regulars from the Thirty-ninth Regiment and Cherokee volunteers. The Cherokees were nominally led by Pathkiller, but Colonel Morgan was the active commander of the Cherokee regiment.[25]

In the leisurely fashion of nineteenth-century warfare, Lieutenant Ross was enjoying a furlough at his Chickamauga home when on March 2, 1814, he was plunged back into active service. That evening Ross hastily wrote Colonel Meigs: "I have this moment received by Express a letter from Colo. Morgan dated Ft. Armstrong 1st March intimating that he had just recd. marching orders & would march this morning for Fort Strother. All those who wish to signalize themselves by fighting & taking revenge for the blood of the innocent will now step forward. . . . my brother & myself will set off on the 4th or 5th."[26]

By mid-March Jackson's forces had reached their maximum strength of nearly five thousand men. Jackson's strategy was to make an intense frontal attack on the fortified Creeks at Horseshoe Bend, while supporting units cut off escape by canoes that the Red Sticks had ready on the shore. Ross was among Major General John

Coffee's cavalry who crossed the Tallapoosa downstream from Horseshoe Bend. Jackson found the Creeks behind a well-constructed breastwork that would subject advancing forces to a heavy crossfire. He decided to bombard the Creeks with relentless artillery fire. After nearly two hours of ineffective cannonade, the restless Cherokees could wait no longer. The Whale and two other anxious warriors plunged into the river and reached the opposite shore, where The Whale was wounded and unable to return. The other two started back with canoes intended for the Creeks' escape. These canoes were quickly filled with Cherokee warriors who engaged the Creeks from the rear, as other comrades returned with more canoes to bring reinforcements. Jackson, realizing the significance of this rear assault, broke through the breastwork and took the Creeks by storm. Jackson later called the result a "carnage"; nearly eight hundred Creeks lay dead. The Americans had twenty-six killed with one hundred six wounded; the Cherokees had eighteen killed with thirty-five wounded. Thus the Creeks' ability to resist was broken at Horseshoe Bend.[27]

It is doubtful that Ross made that daring plunge with The Whale and his companions. On occasions in later life when he had opportunity to mention the Creek War, he never spoke of his personal exploits, but he testified readily to the courage of The Whale. Two weeks after the Horseshoe Bend engagement, Ross ended his brief military career. Perhaps he contemplated the obvious leasons: no Indian tribe could withstand the superior military power of the United States, and the result of armed resistance was annihilation.[28]

Ross was not completely absorbed in business activities and military exploits during these years. In 1813, probably between April and October, he married Elizabeth Brown Henley, known more commonly by her Cherokee name, Quatie. Quatie's background remains a mystery. Some sources say she was a full-blood Cherokee of the Bird Clan, while others contend that she was the daughter of Thomas Brown, a mixed-blood who owned the ferry at Moccasin Bend on the Tennessee River. The best evidence suggests that she was the daughter of a Scottish trader and the sister of Judge James Brown of the Cherokees, thus a mixed-blood but with a stronger Cherokee line than Ross. Quatie was born about 1791 and first married a certain Henley by whom she had at least one child, Susan, who lived with John and Quatie until 1827, when she married Ross's nephew, William Shorey Coodey.[29]

John and Quatie had six children. One died at birth; the others lived well into adulthood. The boys, James McDonald (1814–64), Allen (1817–91), Silas Dinsmore (1829?–72), and George Washington (1830–70) were all born in the Cherokee Nation east of the Mississippi River. All of Ross's sons served with the Union during the American Civil War, and James was a casualty of that conflict. Of all the children, Allen probably was closest to his father. Silas was named after the United States agent to the Cherokees, while George was named after the president most admired by the Cherokees. Jane (1821–94), the only daughter to live, was educated at the Moravian Female Academy at Salem, North Carolina.[30]

Quatie likely had little impact on Ross's life. As a rising star in Cherokee political affairs, Ross made yearly treks to Washington. Quatie did not accompany him and she may have been an invalid during the 1830s. Often these journeys kept him away from his home and family six months of the year; yet no letters to Quatie exist. Numerous letters to other members of the family remain; one may suppose that she did not read English, and certainly Ross did not write Cherokee easily, if at all. Even more surprising, Ross never mentioned her in more than a half-century of active correspondence. The one occasion on which he noted her existence was in his last will when he listed her merely as the mother of his children. She died on February 1, 1839, near Little Rock, Arkansas, while on the Trail of Tears, scarcely mourned and largely forgotten.[31]

The youth and early manhood of Ross do not seem to provide the active ingredients for a life of dedication to a people with whom he had a fairly remote relationship. People around his father's store and his childhood friends were probably more often Cherokee than white; yet Ross's education and superior opportunities were quite unlike those of the children of that remote area. Ross had to overcome several liabilities to gain acceptance among the tribe. His short Scottish stature was so dissimilar to the typical warrior type that it must have been a handicap, as was his incapacity with the native Cherokee tongue. Perhaps he chose the Cherokee path because he found among this people a ready avenue for personal advancement. Full commitment to the Cherokees may not have come until the mid-1820s. But by then he had caught the vision of his Cherokee kinsmen and modeled his life after their standards of loyalty to their homelands. Persuaded to the Cherokees' concept of unity, Ross affirmed his Cherokee identity.

2

POLITICAL APPRENTICESHIP

THE qualities that Ross displayed in the Creek War, his education and enterprise, and his willingness to accept responsibility marked him as a natural leader. He was propelled into the political arena partly by his own inclinations and partly by the needs of the Cherokees as they were pushed into more frequent encounters with their land-hungry neighbors. The Cherokees did not want another leader who would accommodate the whites and barter away their lands for profit. They needed someone who understood the white man's game of treaty-making yet was committed to their cause. Over the next decade and a half the Cherokees had numerous opportunities to observe Ross in a variety of political positions, and they found him more than adequate for their emerging needs.

Ross's first political assignment came in late 1815 when problems that had plagued United States–Cherokee relations for a number of years demanded settlement at Washington. Return J. Meigs obtained permission from the War Department to accompany the Cherokee delegation which included Ross, John Lowrey, John Walker, Major Ridge, Richard Taylor, and Cheucunsenee. Of all the delegates Ross alone used the English language with any degree of fluency; thus he was the key member in written negotiations. The aging Pathkiller instructed delegates on the major issues: settlement of boundary disputes, ownership of a small tract of land in South Carolina, white intrusions on Cherokee lands, claims of Cherokees for property destruction during the Creek War, and establishment of iron works and smith shops in the ore-rich Cherokee Nation. (It was becoming increasingly clear to the Cherokees that they must learn the use of the white man's iron tools and agricultural implements.[1])

Since Indian delegations were not frequent at the capital in the early years of the United States, leading members of Washington society sometimes feted Indian dignitaries. Newspapers listed the Cherokees as "men of cultivated understanding" and lauded their arrival in early February 1816, but the delegates quickly turned to political deliberation. Carefully they brought before President James Madison the recommendations of Chief Pathkiller and the Cherokees. On the problem of white intruders, they received speedy redress through Secretary of War William H. Crawford, who ordered Meigs to remove the offending persons immediately, using military force if necessary. One by one other major issues were taken up. The president responded positively to the request that the Cherokees receive compensation equal to that obtained by white citizens for damages to their property by military forces incurred during the Creek War. Madison considered their request for iron works premature, however, and suggested that they continue to rely on their agent for these supplies.[2]

After the deliberations with the president, Meigs addressed the delegates on the major outstanding issue. He suggested that between the Cherokees and Creeks boundary questions might be settled by ceding the disputed lands to the United States. In this way, the Cherokees would have a ready ally in case of war and a buffer between themselves and possible enemies. He encouraged their trust in the president, "as I know that he will never do injustice in any transactions." The delegation remained adamant concerning the boundary, however, stressing that the Creeks had no right to relinquish the lands through a treaty with General Jackson. The delegation did consent to an American public road through Cherokee lands for communication purposes only. To a request that the Cherokees cede additional lands, the delegation promised to take the issue before the tribe.[3]

Toward the end of March 1816 the major issues had been resolved, and two treaties were signed on March 22. The first dealt only with the tract of land which the South Carolinians had desired and which the Cherokees ceded for five thousand dollars. The second treaty concerned the boundary question and several lesser points, including a Federal promise to pay for damages done during the Creek War.[4]

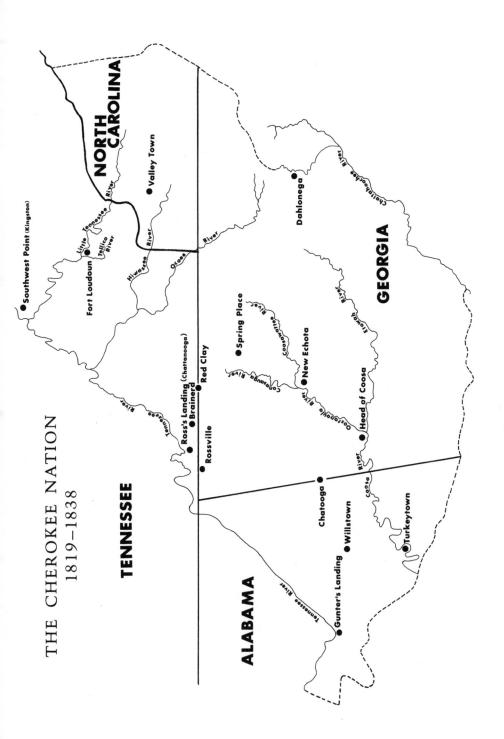

THE CHEROKEE NATION
1819–1838

NORTH CAROLINA

GEORGIA

TENNESSEE

ALABAMA

Southwest Point (Kingston)

Fort Loudoun

Valley Town

Dahlonega

Little Tennessee River

Tellico River

Hiwassee River

Ocoee River

Spring Place

New Echota

Head of Coosa

Conasauga River

Coosawattee River

Coosa River

Etowah River

Oostanaula River

Chattahoochee River

Ross's Landing (Chattanooga)

Brainerd

Red Clay

Rossville

Tennessee River

Chatooga

Willstown

Turkeytown

Gunter's Landing

Coosa River

Tennessee River

Tennesseans were disturbed that a tract of land they considered theirs by right of bloody contest had been casually given to the Cherokees at Washington. It must have been especially painful to that proud Tennessean Andrew Jackson to be ordered to serve as one of the commissioners to buy back the land he thought fairly won by the sword, but he worked out an agreement with his usual dispatch and with the aid of "presents" to the willing signers. In the treaty, concluded on September 14, 1816, the Cherokees ceded nearly 1.3 million acres for an initial sum of $5,000 with an annuity of $6,000 over the next decade. This settlement was noticeably boycotted by several leading Cherokees on the grounds that it was made with a small clique representing only a minor faction of the tribe.[5]

Ross was not present during these negotiations, for after his return from Washington he occupied himself with personal and business affairs. During April 1817 he worked out contracts with Meigs to supply U.S. military forces in the Tennessee area and was quickly on his way to Baltimore to purchase goods from the trading firm of Talbot Jones. Although Ross took an occasional assignment for the Cherokees, he was not yet fully committed to a life of public service. So it was as somewhat of an observer that he returned to the Cherokee Nation in time to witness one of the grander attempts of the United States commissioners to gain Cherokee lands.[6]

The Cherokees had hardly recovered from the earlier land transaction when on June 20, 1817, a new commission gathered at the agency just relocated at Calhoun on the Hiwassee River. Jackson led the commission, accompanied by General David Meriwether of Georgia and Governor Joseph McMinn of Tennessee, and they quickly made their purpose known. They sought a cession of land to compensate the United States for the lands occupied by the western Cherokees and the removal of the entire tribe to the West for an equal exchange in Arkansas. The Cherokees were stunned. Yet by this ruse Jackson was able to secure an extraordinary treaty in July 1817 over the protests of sixty-seven of the most influential chiefs. Again the use of well-placed bribes and circumspect negotiations with a small unauthorized faction had enabled the commissioners to get their way—with such success that no monetary compensation was included in the treaty provisions.[7]

The Cherokees had hoped to prevent such treaties by creating in May 1817 a bicameral system with increased powers. Assembled at Fortville, Cherokee Nation, the leading men had created a "standing committee" of thirteen men to transact political business, but only with the consent of the whole Nation. In time this group became an effective force for Cherokee advancement and security, but the National Committee, as it came to be called, hampered Jackson little in the summer of 1817. On September 3 the National Committee convened and passed a resolution bitterly denouncing Jackson's various maneuvers of the year before.[8]

Under the provision of the Treaty of 1817, the United States had agreed to supervise and aid in the removal to Arkansas of all Cherokee settlers who wished to go. McMinn remained in the Cherokee Nation to oversee the removal and distribute the promised supplies. The summer months of 1818 were busy for McMinn, as he used every means to convince and cajole Cherokees to remove. His final estimates were that over five thousand had left, but Cherokees contended the number was closer to thirty-five hundred. With his work completed among those willing to move, McMinn asked that a council of the Cherokee Nation be convened in November 1818. On the eve of this council, Ross assumed the position of president of the recently created National Committee and was active in the council proceedings. In the course of this meeting, McMinn offered an indemnity of one hundred thousand dollars for Cherokee removal, but was refused. He then proposed double that amount, to be paid in installments, but this ploy was also rejected. Ross sent the Cherokees' most vigorous protest to be published in the North Carolina *Raleigh Register* to expose McMinn's methods and to demonstrate the determination of the Cherokees to remain on their lands.[9]

The Cherokee leadership decided to renew negotiations at Washington in order to obtain clarification of the recent treaties and to complete the execution of the ambiguous Treaty of 1817. Led by Charles Hicks, the delegation of twelve included John Ross and his brother Lewis. Before their departure from Knoxville on January 1, 1819, McMinn had succeeded in bribing at least two of the delegates and had reached partial success with two more, but he seems not to have tempted Ross.[10]

Secretary of War John C. Calhoun asked the Cherokees to transfer a portion of their land (from within the limits of Tennessee and Georgia) in proportion to the estimated number of their nation who had emigrated to Arkansas. Another cession was to come from the Alabama area, and the proceeds from land sales there would be used to set up a trust fund for Cherokee schools. However, the Alabama cession would not be counted as a land contribution for the Cherokees who had already emigrated. Calhoun completely skirted the delegation's most vexing question, whether the lands left them would be guaranteed as a "permanent and lasting home without further cessions." He merely noted that as they increasingly took on the ways of the white man, far less land would be necessary for them. The Cherokees strongly disagreed and stated that "comfort and convenience . . . requires [sic] us to retain our present limits."[11]

The major provisions of the treaty, signed on February 27, 1819, contained the points expressed by Calhoun together with several clarifying articles, the third of which spelled out in some detail what had been only suggested in the 1817 treaty. Because of the advancement made by some of the Cherokees, especially some of the more prosperous mixed-bloods, provisions were made so they could receive a reservation of 640 acres with a view to becoming citizens. Some of these allotments were reservations "for life," which would pass to the children of the reservee in fee simple title; others were given in fee simple title directly.[12]

Ross's reservation was laid off to include "the Big Island in Tennessee River, being the first below Tellico," which was the island left to him by his great uncle, the younger William Shorey. At the time of the negotiations, John Williams, a senator from Tennessee, informed Calhoun that the Tennessee congressional delegation was not opposed to any of the reservations except Ross's. "If his is ratified," Williams said, "it will have a most pernicious influence on future negotiations with the Cherokees. Under my present impressions I will resist the ratification of the treaty with a reservation at Tellico Island for Jno. Ross." In later years Ross received severe criticism from Cherokee dissidents for his reservation, as many who opposed him contended he was less a Cherokee for having once contemplated removing from the limits of the Nation and becoming a United States citizen. Ross, however, always contended that he never actually lived on this land and in truth had no thought of taking citizenship. Ross also acquired land in east Tennessee for speculation about that time. In November and December 1820 he purchased 415 acres, paying one quarter of the total value, $725.75. The land varied in price from $2 to $28 per acre.[13]

While the delegation was in Washington in March 1819, Ross became involved in a dispute with one of his colleagues, John Walker. Walker had received special consideration in the Treaty of 1819, for he obtained two 640-acre reservations, one for his dwelling and ferry and another to include his grist and sawmill. It seems that Walker was attempting to acquire a third. Since he had received a $500 bribe from McMinn, heated words had passed between him and Ross. The evening before the delegation left Washington, Ross stayed up unusually late to complete some unfinished correspondence, when John Martin, a fellow delegate, stopped in to recount his evening of entertainment. Walker suddenly burst into the room and attacked Ross with a knife, inflicting a slight shoulder wound before Martin could separate the two. The incident was kept from other members of the delegation, and the two men seem not to have spoken of it again.[14]

Ross did not return to Cherokee Nation with the other delegates but spent some time in Baltimore attending to business affairs. He reached home just at the time of President James Monroe's visit to Brainerd Mission in the early summer of 1819. Ross mentioned the president's trip in a letter to a friend and expressed hope that missionary efforts would make Americans aware of the potential in the Indian race. While Ross acknowledged that the Cherokees were only newly exposed to white civilization, he firmly believed that "the seed of education must be sown and replenished by the mists of patience perseverance ... when it has taken root & sprouted it would ultimately bear down the old growth of natural Habits & customs and finally root it out."[15]

On the Arkansas border the recently settled Cherokees had been in constant conflict with the neighboring Osages, and the missionaries discovered instances of captured Cherokee children being sold into slavery by the Osage tribe. One such child was recovered by the missionaries and named Lydia Carter after her benefactor, but her brother had been taken by some white men into Alabama. The missionaries convinced Agent Meigs to send a party to rescue the boy, and he asked Ross to assume the task. Ross traveled to Mobile in September 1819 and recovered the child only shortly before the boy was to be placed on the slave market. The missionaries named the child John Osage Ross, and he was adopted by Ard Hoyt, an American Board missionary, and placed at Brainerd School, where later he was baptized.[16]

Like any young political apprentice, Ross sometimes had to accept unrewarding tasks. One such chore involved leading the Cherokee light horse company to remove intruders on Cherokee lands. Commander Ross was given the unenviable job of removing these white settlers, then burning their crops and improvements. Cherokees were used initially because General Andrew Jackson declared he had no troops to spare, but perhaps because of Ross's vigorous work, Jackson discovered he did have adequate reserves after all. So Ross by mid-1820 was relieved of the odious task. In connection with his legislative duties, Ross served as clerk to Pathkiller, carrying out various missions for him and for Associate Chief Charles Hicks that took him to all parts of Cherokee Nation on financial and political matters.[17]

Because of the various land cessions and the questionable methods by which treaties had been made over the years, the Cherokees attempted in 1820 to strengthen the changes adopted in 1817. The bicameral legislature known as the General Council was now formally composed of the National Council and the National Committee, and a principal chief and an assistant were named. The Cherokee Nation was divided into eight districts with a judge, marshal, and local council assigned to each; from these districts, representatives to the National Council and the National Committee were chosen. Salaries for the national officers were stipulated; Ross as president of the National Committee received $3.50 a day when the legislature was in session. Within two years the Cherokees had the opportunity to test this new system.[18]

The reconstructed Cherokee government met in October 1822; with a flush of power and an exaggerated sense of independence they passed a resolution "declaring unanimously . . . to hold no treaties with any Commissioners of the United States to make any cession of lands, being resolved not to dispose of even one foot of ground." Signed by Ross and fifty-eight other members of the Cherokee legislature, this declaration was forwarded to Meigs who was shocked by the "rash resolution." Thinking it may have been devised by some young radicals, he advised Charles Hicks: "It will not do to commit the government of your highest concerns into the hands of your young men."[19]

In April 1802 the state of Georgia had signed an agreement with the United States government ceding the immense area of land that she claimed on her western border; at the same time the United States agreed to work out the extinguishment of Indian title to all lands within Georgia boundaries as early as could be "peaceably obtained, and on reasonable terms." Georgians considered the United States delinquent in the bargain, especially after the Cherokee Treaty of 1819 providing that the federal government would grant citizenship and permanent land ownership to selected members of the tribe. Georgians decided to move for their own protection and sent representatives to the Cherokees to hurry the removal process. President Monroe, feeling the obligation to fulfill these promises, appointed a commission to meet with the Cherokees.[20]

Duncan G. Campbell and James Meriwether, appointed commissioners to the Cherokees in June 1822, arrived in the Cherokee Nation in the early summer of 1823, eager to begin negotiations. They suggested meeting in August at Taloney, some distance east of the Cherokee capital, called Newtown at the time, and located at the junction of the Conasauga and Oostanaula rivers; the Cherokees insisted on a September meeting at their capital. If a meeting was to be held in spite of the Cherokees' reluctance, they wanted at least to decide the time, the place, and the extent of the discussions. The commissioners were angered by Ross's allusions to international law, when he pointed out that he knew "of no instance of Ministers or Commissioners, to a foreign Court, persisting in selecting a spot remote from the Seat of Government to which their embassy was directed." Campbell and Meriwether considered for a time going on with the meeting at Taloney, but McMinn recognized the impropriety of such a move, and the commissioners acquiesced. In January 1823 Meigs died, and the active, ever-present McMinn, following prearranged instructions from Washington officials, took the colonel's place; in the Cherokees' estimation a worse choice could not have been made.[21]

Because of heavy spring rains the General Council of 1823 did not convene until the first of October. Discussions eventually got underway when the Cherokees quickly rejected Georgia proposals for Indian land cessions. To the Georgian contention that the Cherokees actually had more land than "intended by the Great Father of the Universe," the Cherokees replied that they were unaware of the intentions of the "*Supreme Father* in this particular." Campbell and Meriwether became more frustrated as they used what they considered historically sound arguments based on previous treaties but were thwarted at every turn by the canny Cherokees. The basis of the Cherokee arguments centered on the "fixed and unalterable determination . . . never again to cede *one foot* more of land."[22]

Not content with negotiations on this level, the commissioners stooped to Machiavellian measures so successfully adopted by McMinn and hired a Creek, Chief William McIntosh, to bribe the leading Cherokees. McIntosh surely realized that Ross had been a principal block to negotiations for every Cherokee document was sealed with his florid signature. Perhaps he thought Ross, a new member of the Cherokee National Committee, susceptible to corruption. During the meeting McIntosh passed a note to Ross which read in part: "If the chiefs feel disposed to let the United States to have the land part of it, I want you to let me know. I will make the United States commissioners give you two thousand dollars, A. McCoy [clerk of the National Committee] the same and Charles Hicks $3000 for present [sic] and nobody shall know it." McIntosh had $12,000 in all to be used by Ross in the most advantageous manner, exclusive of the $7,000 he had already promised. The outraged Ross told his associates of the note, and at their suggestion he rose in the session the next day, October 24, 1823, to address the assembly: "It has now become my painful duty to inform you that a gross contempt is offered to my character as well as to that of the General Council. This letter which I hold in my hand will speak for itself, but fortunately the author of it, has mistaken my character and sense of honor."[23]

McIntosh was dismissed from the meeting in disgrace and within six months was brutally murdered by members of his own tribe. The incident raised Ross's prestige considerably and, when a decision was made to send a delegation to Washington to settle the matters brought up by Commissioners Campbell and Meriwether, Ross was chosen by an overwhelming majority. Accompanied by Major Ridge, Elijah Hicks, and George Lowrey, Ross served as correspondent, interpreter, and principal negotiator.[24]

The delegates arrived the first week in January 1824. After a meeting with President Monroe, Calhoun, and Secretary of State John Quincy Adams, in which they passed pleasantries without official pronouncements, the Cherokees retired to the tedious task of correspondence assumed by the able, articulate Ross. They referred first to the negotiations of the past winter and insisted it was still their decision to surrender no more land. They requested Congress to clarify the Compact of 1802 with Georgia so as to end further attempts to acquire Cherokee lands, and they also suggested that the United States possessed an extensive territory in the Floridas that could be used to compensate Georgia. The delegation reminded Calhoun that "the Cherokees are not foreigners, but original inhabitants of America . . . and that the limits of their territory are defined by the treaties which they have made with the Government of the United States."[25]

To these overtures Calhoun could only ask the Cherokees to be sensible and he left them with three choices: "remain . . . exposed to the discontent of Georgia and the pressure of her citizens," cede their lands for others beyond the Mississippi River, or accept individual ownership of lands with a view to future citizenship. The Cherokee delegates knew that in truth Calhoun offered them only the option to remove, which they would not accept. They declared that even if the United States were to offer "an extent of territory twice as large west of the Mississippi, as the one now occupied by the Cherokees east of that river, or all the money now in the coffers of your treasury," the Cherokees still would refuse.[26]

Calhoun eventually advised the Georgians that conferences with the Cherokees had reached a stalemate. When the Georgia congressional delegation in a heated note accused Monroe of bad faith, the president with the advice of his cabinet drew up a message to Congress in which he examined the Compact of 1802. He reasoned that the security of the Cherokees would be promoted if they would retire to the western border, and in a final inconclusive statement he left to the decision of Congress what measures, if any, should be taken. Ross also responded to the Georgians' claims in a petition to Congress in which he reviewed the state of negotiations, again insisting the Cherokees would never cede their lands or remove "to the barren waste bordering on the Rocky Mountains."[27]

The Cherokee delegation also attempted to get the thoroughly disliked McMinn removed as agent. A popular man in Tennessee, McMinn had served the constitutional limit of six successive years as governor before taking assignments to the Cherokees; he was somewhat less admired among the Indians. Within a month after their arrival, having made no headway in settling their disputes over the removal question, the Cherokee delegates asked that McMinn be dismissed for "want of confidence." They also attributed ingratitude to McMinn, who had lived among them as a youth but had forgotten the Cherokees' kindness. Nevertheless, Calhoun seemed satisfied with McMinn, and he remained at his post until his death the following year.[28]

The delegation was angry that McMinn had brought white families into the Cherokee Nation in violation of Indian intercourse laws. These white men were living on grounds of the agency which the Cherokee delegation insisted belonged not to the federal government but to the tribe. Ross arranged that McMinn could cultivate the lands he needed but could not receive title to them, and could not move white families there. What infuriated the Cherokees was that McMinn had allowed a white tavern keeper, James Cowan, and the trading establishment of McGhee and McCarty to be located on the agency site. A year later, after McMinn's death, the new agent, Hugh Montgomery, broached the subject. He was disturbed that the area was so crowded, for in addition to Cowan, McGhee and McCarty, Lewis Ross had acquired a reservation in that area, and the subagent, James G. Williams, also was there. When the Cherokees suggested he move to New Echota, Montgomery refused, saying that the people in the vicinity did not keep the Sabbath, and that there were too many drunks there.[29]

The delegation also petitioned for the still unpaid $1,000 annuity from the Tellico Treaty of 1804. The surprised Calhoun denied that any such treaty existed, but the Cherokees produced the document. With a certain amount of chagrin, the secretary found the treaty, and the Senate approved the annuity payment in May 1824. The Cherokees also requested compensation of six percent per annum for the use of their lands by the government, but it appears they never received this.[30]

After a six-month stay in Washington, members of the delegation took up the few remaining points of their mission. On other matters they were not so successful. They were greatly disturbed that the annuity to be given under the Tellico Treaty of 1804 would be paid on the basis of the 1819 treaty; that is, one-third to the Arkansas Cherokees and two-thirds to the eastern Cherokees. They saw in this a portent for future problems, for if the government could pay money to different sections of the Cherokees, then it might pay it to individuals rather than to the Cherokee Nation. Nor were they paid for their bill at Tennison's Hotel, as the government had not requested their presence.[31]

Ross returned home in late June 1824 to find the country in a desperate condition owing to a prolonged drought and the raging specter of smallpox. After four brief months with his family, he turned again to his duties as president of the National Committee. The General Council held its annual meeting the latter part of October, passing a number of laws dealing with the Cherokee light horse companies, miscegenation, and duties of various minor officials. The Cherokees also discussed procedures for a census "of the manner of living and the state of agricultural improvements"; evidently the findings were to be used to illustrate the Cherokees' progress to answer demands for removal.[32]

Ross led another group to Washington in 1825. They had as little luck on the objectives of their mission as the delegates of 1824. The Cherokees renewed their request for the interest on the twenty thousand dollars due them from the Tellico Treaty of 1804. Commissioner of Indian Affairs Thomas L. McKenney was willing to pay this amount once he had deducted the claims of various white traders in the Cherokee Nation, amounting all together to nearly sixteen hundred dollars; the remainder would be divided between the eastern and western Cherokees. Ross and the eastern band of delegates worked out a compromise with their western brothers in which they asked the United States to hold one-third of the money in trust until a joint meeting of the United States and the Cherokee Nation could be arranged to work out a settlement for the remainder. The money deducted for the traders was for the tax the Cherokee Nation had levied on such individuals in 1824. Although the tax had the sanction of several leading jurists, McKenney deducted the amount from the annuity payment in order to reimburse the traders.[33]

Another point of contention was the issue of lands reserved under the Treaty of 1819. Several of the reservees had been forced off their lands without compensation, while white settlers made improvements on these lands and enjoyed the benefits. Further, the acting agent, James G. Williams, had added unauthorized names to a list of reservees who had surrendered their claims, many of whom had no thought of releasing their lands. The delegates also brought reports of further intrusions on their Georgian enclave. They were incredulous when McKenney asked if they were willing to surrender those lands. Ross referred the commissioner to their communications of the preceding year, and to a question of their competency to negotiate such matters, he replied: "We have full authority in saying that those sentiments remains [sic] the same."[34]

Before leaving Washington, the Cherokee delegates sent a complimentary communication to the incoming president, John Quincy Adams, and gave him a "retrospective view of the History and true causes in the downfall, degradation and extinction of certain Tribes." To assure that their earlier communications had not been lost upon the former secretary of state, they reminded him that "a removal of the Cherokees can never be effected," and they looked forward to the time when their tribe could merge with the United States. The latter idea fit nicely with the new president's own wishes.[35]

Ross returned in time for a special council of the Cherokees in June 1825. Thinking the reorganization of the Cherokee government in 1820 would not be sufficient to stave off land-hungry whites, the General Council passed on June 25 an "Article of Fixed and Irrevocable Principle by which the Cherokee Nation Shall be Governed." Lands were to be held in common, but improvements were the exclusive property of the citizens. Annuities also were to be public property, stored in the Cherokee National treasury, then at Fortville, Cherokee Nation. Chiefs or citizens of the Cherokee Nation no longer had the right to dispose of common property; only with the consent of the General Council could acts of a public character be authorized. With Ross still president of the National Committee, the regular General Council convened in October 1825 and met for nearly one month, passing over thirty pieces of legislation. Significant among these was the provision for laying out the recently established capital of New Echota. Divided into a hundred town lots of one acre each, the capital would contain a public square and national buildings. Ross appointed three commissioners to lay out the city and superintend public construction.[36]

The demands of political office convinced Ross that he should move to a more central location among his people; this difficult decision was made in the spring of 1827. Ross left his property at Rossville to Nicholas Dalton Scales, a Methodist minister and husband of Ross's niece, Mary Coodey. Scales also took over Ross's business enterprises at the nearby landing in partnership with Pleasant H. Butler. Ross moved his family to the new location, "Head of Coosa," where the Oostanaula and Etowah rivers merge to form the Coosa. There Ross committed himself to the life of a planter and tied his fortunes even more closely to the fate of the Cherokees. Within three miles of Major Ridge's home and business, and only thirty miles from New Echota, Ross was in easy reach of all the leading men of the nation. On these grounds, Ross buried an infant child and his father, Daniel Ross, under one of the post oak or ash trees that dotted the area.[37]

At Coosa, Ross built a comfortable two-storied house seventy by twenty feet. The weather-boarded home included a basement and was topped with an ash shake roof. A porch ten feet high ran the length of the front and on either end were tall red brick chimneys. The interior was given a light and open feeling by the twenty glass windows, while four fireplaces lent warmth. Set a short distance from the house was a kitchen, while farther away other buildings dotted the grounds: workhouses, smokehouses, slaves' quarters, stables, corn cribs, a smith shop, and a wagon house. One of the outlying cabins also was used for regular and well-attended Methodist church services. Circuit riders made Head of Coosa a frequent stop, and the Reverend Nicholas Dalton Scales occasionally led the Sabbath meetings. Ross's five fields around his residence varied in size from fourteen to seventy-five acres and in quality from cleared and fenced land to unimproved acreage. These lands totaled nearly one hundred seventy acres, not including five small lots of undetermined measurement. On the grounds were fruit trees of several varieties, and by the mid-1830s Ross counted one hundred seventy peach, thirty-four apple, nine pear, five quince, and five plum trees. Ross also owned a ferry on the Coosa River yielding an annual income of one thousand dollars and valued at ten thousand dollars. Within two years after his move, Ross was serving as federal postmaster for the Coosa area, and by the 1830s Ross had nearly twenty slaves and was one of the wealthiest men in Cherokee Nation.[38]

Ross's move to Coosa not only showed a deeper attachment to Cherokee affairs but also presaged his rise as a leading figure in the Cherokee Nation. During Ross's early adulthood, two chiefs were prominent in the Cherokee Nation—Pathkiller and Charles Hicks. Pathkiller remained as chief until 1827, but in many ways was merely a figurehead after the Creek War. Hicks became the real power and was the first transitional figure in Cherokee history. With a sure knowledge of English, he served occasionally as interpreter for Meigs and accumulated a stock of English books. Although his writing was rough and his penmanship atrocious, his correspondence shows a grasp of political parlance. Hicks further embraced the white man's ways when he became an early Moravian convert. During the first decade of the nineteenth century, Ross had served as clerk and confidant to Hicks and Pathkiller. The year that Ross moved to Coosa, Hicks began to tutor him in the oral traditions of the Cherokees; through Hicks, Ross gained greater understanding of the full-bloods. Missionary Daniel S. Butrick noticed the relationship of Ross and Hicks: "Mr. Ross is rising highly in the opinion of the Nation. He is not in point of influence inferior to any except Mr. Hicks. These men walk hand in hand in the Nation's Councils and are the hope of the Nation."[39]

In December 1826 Hicks and Ross answered several questions that Cherokee Agent Montgomery had brought up for the annual meeting of the Cherokee General Council. Hicks had prevented the state surveyor of Georgia from laying out a canal to connect two rivers on Cherokee lands. Since Governor George M. Troup was prepared to call out the state militia, President Adams requested Montgomery to negotiate a settlement, but Ross and Hicks followed the wishes of the National Council and refused the application. Ross was incredulous when Montgomery informed him in the same communication that a sum of money from the annual Cherokee payment had been given to the western Cherokees. This contradicted the arrangement made with McKenney just nine months earlier in regard to the annuity left unpaid from the 1804 treaty. The money amounted to nearly seven thousand dollars, and the agreement had been for the United States to hold it in trust. Ross felt strongly that the money actually belonged to "the Cherokee nation," and that the western Cherokees had voluntarily withdrawn from that nation.[40]

In 1817 and in 1820 the Cherokees had restructured their government to ensure wider participation in tribal affairs and closer supervision of treaties with the United States. Cherokee efforts to strengthen their government culminated in 1826 with the calling of a constitutional convention. Ross, representing the Chickamauga District, served as president of the convention. The document produced in July 1827 was strikingly similar to the United States Constitution.[41]

The first articles of the constitution dealt with the right most sacred to the Cherokees: to hold their lands inviolate against the encroachments of the federal government and surrounding states. The remaining articles defined the power and responsibilities of the executive, legislative, and judicial branches of the government, and a miscellaneous article included references to individual rights and to amendment procedures. A bicameral system was formally established retaining the familiar National Committee with two members from each district and the National Council composed of twenty-four representatives. Elections were to be held in August, and the yearly sessions of the General Council—the legislature composed of the National Committee and the National Council— were to be on the second Monday in October. The executive power was vested in a single individual called the principal chief, who was to be a natural citizen and at least thirty-five years of age. Members of the General Council were to be elected every two years, and that body was to select the principal chief quadrennially. The principal chief was given veto power over legislation, but his negative could be overridden by a two-thirds majority in the General Council.[42]

The Georgia legislature refused to recognize the Cherokee constitution and demanded that it be disallowed by the federal government. That body also accused the United States of having violated the Compact of 1802 by not procuring the lands of the Cherokees; the Georgians went so far as to contend that their state government had the right to "extend her authority and laws over her whole territory, and to coerce obedience to them from all descriptions of people, be they white, red, or black, who may reside within her limits." The Georgia governor and the state's congressional delegation likewise demanded that the constitution be overturned.[43]

Commissioner of Indian Affairs McKenney had only a slight understanding of the Cherokee constitution but thought that it ought not to be encouraged, fearing it might "operate independently of our laws." Other American officials took the same view, warning the Cherokees that the document had raised a clamor in neighboring states and that it would not change the relationship between the United States and the Cherokee Nation. Washington officials viewed it as merely "regulations of a purely municipal character." Ross referred them to the document itself and noted that the relations of the two governments had not changed.[44]

In January 1827 the aged Pathkiller died, and two weeks later Ross's close friend and mentor Charles Hicks also died. Ross as president of the National Committee and Major Ridge as speaker of the National Council now held the principal offices in the nation. During the interim before new principal and assistant chiefs were chosen, they would guide the tribe. The period of Ross's apprenticeship was closed.[45]

Ross had learned a number of lessons in his first fifteen years of political training. On several trips to Washington, he had gained vital experience in negotiation and had mastered the intricacies of treaty-making. Ross had met the leading men of his day—Monroe, Adams, Calhoun, and Jackson—men who would play a significant role in the coming struggles of the Cherokees. More important, he had found these men to be fallible, pushed and pulled by personal and political considerations, men who would compromise and bargain. Indeed, Ross recognized that the Cherokees could use these same techniques to secure their just rights. The next decade would prove the worth of these lessons.

3

THE GEORGIAN THRUST

THE Cherokees had scarcely recovered from the shock of the death of Chiefs Pathkiller and Charles Hicks when United States commissioners required major political decisions of them. John Cocke, the leader of the commissioners, had arrived in New Echota in July 1827, had witnessed the selection of the constitutional convention delegates, and had been received warmly by Major Ridge and Ross as a comrade-in-arms from the Creek War. Cocke found the Cherokees "disorganized and confused" and thought the chances good that a land cession might be obtained. Ross, as president of the National Committee, and Major Ridge, speaker of the National Council, served as the interim government until the General Council met in October 1827. The past decade of experience and the solid advice of his political mentor Major Ridge made Ross an even match for this new Federal team.[1]

Cocke joined his fellow commissioners, George L. Davidson and Alexander Gray, at the Cherokee Agency, Calhoun, Tennessee, in mid-August, and they issued a circular asking the Cherokee assembly to meet them there on September 18. When the commissioners gathered, they were met by only a dozen Indians, none of any significant rank, and they learned that Ross and Ridge considered their invitation undiplomatic because the commission had appointed a time and place for the meeting without consulting the Cherokee leadership. Ross, however, invited the three men to meet the General Council at the next session in October, at which time the hospitality of the Cherokee Nation would be extended to them. The commissioners, however, remained at the agency and insisted on negotiations there.[2]

Ross and Ridge had remembered Cocke's July visit somewhat

differently from the commissioner's version. As the three were old acquaintances, the earlier meeting at New Echota had been quite amicable, but the statesmen did not recall Cocke's mention of an official appointment. Cocke, however, felt he had adequately negotiated for the September meeting in July. Again Ross, attempting to bridge the misunderstanding, offered a meeting at New Echota in October, insisting that it was the logical and customary place for meeting United States officials. The commissioners accused Ross of using "all his influence with the nation to thwart the views of the United States" and of trying to keep the nation uninformed of the purpose of the commissioners. Such accusations and inducements were of little avail in arranging a meeting on agency grounds, so Cocke, Gray, and Davidson forwarded their requests to the Cherokee General Council. When they proposed to purchase five hundred thousand acres of Cherokee land in North Carolina and to construct a canal connecting the Hiwassee and Conasauga rivers, Ross reiterated the General Council's pledge not to "dispose of one foot more of land." Not content with one attempt at negotiation, the United States also sent Major Francis W. Armstrong into the Cherokee Nation the following summer with identical proposals. His mission was as thoroughly unsuccessful.[3]

In the fall council of 1827 William Hicks, son of the late Chief Charles Hicks, had been elected to fill out the term of the deceased Pathkiller, and Ross had been assigned the post of second principal chief. In a joint message to the General Council the following October, Ross and Hicks pointed to the recent accomplishments of the Cherokees and then attempted to deal with some of the needs of the tribe. They proposed the erection of a national academy, anticipated for a number of years, and recommended overseers for public elections and inspectors to ensure high academic standards for their mission schools. The greater part of the message, however, answered the allegations of Georgians who defamed Cherokee constitutional government and made thrusts at Cherokee territory.[4]

The chiefs noted that Georgia based its claims to Cherokee lands on discovery, conquest, and compact. To the first point they answered: "Our ancestors from time to time immemorial possessed this country, not by a 'charter' from the hand of a mortal king, who had no right to grant it, but by the will of the king of kings." During the previous summer, in an effort to carry out the Compact of 1802, the United States had sent James Rogers, a western Cherokee, to gain the favor of the eastern band and to offer inducements for the surrender of their lands. In order that his glowing descriptions of the West might not be suspect, Rogers traveled as a confidential agent of the federal government, but he failed to fool his eastern brothers, and the new chiefs recommended that a petition be sent to the United States government asking that the Compact of 1802 with Georgia be carried out in some manner other than a cession of Cherokee lands.[5]

The message of Ross and Hicks was later carried in both Cherokee and English across the five-column width of the recently created Cherokee national paper, the *Cherokee Phoenix*. The beginnings of the newspaper can be traced to untiring efforts of an illiterate Cherokee mixed-blood, Sequoyah (George Guess), to create an alphabet, eventually perfected about 1821. Soon the Cherokee Nation was reading the scriptures and inspirational tracts in its native tongue through a system that could be mastered by an illiterate Cherokee in only a few days.[6]

Once the system was perfected, it was immediately adapted to reach the Cherokees concerning public issues. A tour of the United States by Elias Boudinot (who later became editor of the newspaper) and the philanthropy of the mission societies made the bilingual national press a reality, and the General Council leased land and a building to house the press and office. Samuel Worcester, the American Board missionary at Brainerd Mission, went to Boston in 1827 to purchase the press and type faces and suggested *Cherokee Phoenix* as the name for the weekly. Ross took an active hand in these affairs. Worcester consulted with him on the purchase, and the press was forwarded to New Echota in Ross's name. The first issue of the *Cherokee Phoenix* was published on February 21, 1828, and carried a prospectus in which Boudinot promised to print the laws and public documents of the nation, the manners and customs of the Cherokees, and interesting news of the day.[7]

In the chiefs' first annual message, Ross and Hicks expressed the hope that the public would patronize the newspaper. They were concerned as to the use of the paper and warned against the "admission of scurrilous productions of a personal character, and also against cherishing sectarian principles on religious subjects." Because the press was to be public property, it was to be as "free as the breeze that glides upon the surface." However, the *Cherokee Phoenix* was not blessed with freedom from financial burdens, and from the start was mired in monetary problems. Boudinot felt that his annual salary of three hundred dollars was insufficient, and he was on the verge of resigning as editor in November 1829 unless he could obtain an assistant and a raise in pay. He may have been discouraged because the printer received a larger salary than he. Ross took the editor's plea before the General Council and pledged that if the assembly would not pay the increase, he would pay it personally rather than see the venture fail. The General Council assented to the raise in pay and also to the hiring of an assistant for the newspaper.[8]

According to the provisions of the Constitution of 1827, the principal chief of the Cherokee Nation would be elected for the first time in 1828 by a ballot of the General Council and every four years thereafter in the same manner. Ross and Hicks were nominated for the leading post, and when the vote was taken Ross was the overwhelming choice by a margin of thirty-four to six. George Lowrey was elected assistant principal chief, while Major Ridge was elevated to the post of counselor. Other General Council business included the selection of a delegation to handle Cherokee affairs in Washington. Ross recommended Richard Taylor, Edward Gunter, and William Shorey Coodey as delegates. The General Council requested that Ross accompany the delegation, and he agreed to do so.[9]

Ross departed for Washington with his associates around the first week in January 1829, and they settled in Williamson's Hotel. One of the first subjects they brought before the federal government was Cherokee displeasure at the conduct of their agent, Hugh Montgomery, whom the delegation wanted replaced by Thomas C. Hindman, a friend of the Cherokees and a relative of Lewis Ross. They charged that Montgomery had allowed whites to live in the Cherokee Nation, that he took possession of a farm some one hundred miles from the agency on Cherokee land in direct contradiction of Cherokee and United States laws, and that he had not fully prosecuted suits against white intruders. Even though the delegation delivered testimony from Thomas L. McKenney, Commissioner of Indian Affairs, whose statements were in basic agreement with the accusation that Montgomery had been deficient in his duties, the appeal for a new agent was denied.[10]

Ross's greatest concern in 1829 was with Georgia's decision to extend its laws over the Cherokees. On December 20, 1828, the Georgia legislature, on the advice of Governor John Forsyth, added a large portion of the Cherokee territory to the state and declared that its laws extended to that region—to whites immediately and to Indians after June 1, 1830. Ross appealed to the federal government for relief but received from Secretary of War John H. Eaton only a historical recitation on the relations of the Cherokees with the United States. Eaton concluded his essay on a note of little promise to the beleaguered Cherokees: "No remedy can be perceived, except . . . a removal beyond the Mississippi, where, alone can be assured to you protection and peace."[11]

Ross and his colleagues turned next to Congress, outlined their grievances, and noted the act of the Georgia legislature which would deprive them of their basic rights. Ross emphasized the right of the Cherokees to regulate their own affairs and vigorously protested the extension of the Georgia laws. Ross and the delegation departed from Washington in late April of 1829, doubtless feeling their four months of work especially barren since the short congressional session had not allowed time to consider the Cherokees' petition.[12]

Georgia was not alone in its attempts to crowd the Cherokees off their lands. Under President Andrew Jackson, who had been elected within a month of Ross's election as principal chief, the federal government also pursued an energetic policy of Indian removal. In a treaty signed with the western Cherokees on May 6, 1828, Washington officials provided that efforts would be made to convince the eastern Cherokees to emigrate. In this regard Montgomery was to step up his efforts at recruiting emigrants, and by November of 1829 he had convinced some five hundred Cherokees and their blacks to move west. Furthermore, the Jackson administration, seeing a crisis in Indian affairs, commissioned William Carroll, governor of Tennessee, and John Coffee, a Georgia military and political figure, to secure acceptance of removal. Secretary of War Eaton realized only too well that the old methods of negotiations were useless, and advised the commissioners to do away with the traditional "talk" before an assembly of the natives and to take their propositions to the chiefs and leading men on a personal and intimate level.[13]

Carroll arrived in the Cherokee Nation on the morning of August 13, 1829, and after visiting Agent Montgomery, he met Lewis Ross who lived adjacent to the agency. Two days later he visited Chief Ross and other leading men of the Coosa vicinity. Carroll exhausted every argument at his disposal in a dozen private interviews, but at last resorted to the traditional method of a "talk" before an assembly of the leading men. This too proved useless. Coffee did not arrive until Carroll had concluded his fruitless bargaining, but he soon discovered what Carroll also was to confirm: the Cherokees were confident that Congress would intervene and prevent the states' encroachments. Carroll found Ross and his political associates considerate and attentive but firm in their intent to remain in their ancestral lands.[14]

Georgia reached for every pretext to extend its control over more Cherokee lands. Governor Forsyth renewed the controversy over the Creek-Cherokee boundary and found a ready audience at Washington. John Coffee again was detailed to the Cherokee Nation to settle the dispute. Nor did the intrusions into Cherokee lands diminish, for the aggressive attitude of the Georgia legislature merely encouraged its trespassing citizens. Agent Montgomery insisted that it would take a military force to keep intruders out, which the Jackson government would not permit, viewing such a move as an infringement on states' rights. Ross was especially bitter when Montgomery insisted that he could not remove intruders since he was unsure whether the land actually belonged to the Cherokees. Before the General Council, Ross confessed, "there is no place of security for us, no confidence left that the United States will be more just and faithful towards us in the barren prairies of the west, than when we occupied the soil inherited from the Great Author of our existence."[15]

The General Council again decided to send representatives to Washington to continue to resist Georgia's maneuvers. Ross instructed them to petition Congress in regard to the unanswered petition of the preceding year. They were to draw on the annuities if extra funds were needed. Ross kept in close contact with the delegation to learn of its progress and to give information of events in the Cherokee Nation which might be useful.[16]

One episode in February 1830 greatly agitated the Cherokees and put a new complexion on Georgian incursions. The leading men of the nation were becoming more upset at the United States' official disregard toward intruders on Cherokee lands, and Ross therefore delegated Major Ridge and a party of about fifty Cherokees to dislodge the greedy pioneers and to burn their possessions. In early February Ridge set about his task and having removed the squatters dispersed his men to return home. A group of incensed Georgians gathered a band of about twenty-five men and went in pursuit of Ridge and his party. Four of Ridge's band remained behind and, drunk, were captured by the whites, who brutally beat them and left exposed to die a Cherokee called Cheewoyee. The Cherokee delegation at Washington complained of such barbarous acts, and the federal government quickly detailed troops from Fort Mitchell, Alabama, "to stay any acts of hostility." The Cherokees were likely less than elated when these orders made no provisions to remove white intruders who were the source of their troubles.[17]

Ross also informed the delegation of new intruders on Cherokee lands—gold diggers. In July 1829 gold had been discovered in northeastern Georgia on Cherokee lands, and the resulting stampede attracted lawless people from throughout the southern frontier region. Ross had contacted Montgomery several times concerning these growing invasions, but he found the agent apathetic and reluctant to act. In truth, Montgomery probably never had the power to remedy these injustices. Ross believed the United States should pay for the intrusions of the gold seekers and asked that the Cherokee delegation in Washington petition President Jackson. As was the case with other petitions to him, the Cherokees had little hope of success. During the summer of 1830, Governor George R. Gilmer of Georgia issued proclamations to prevent Indians as well as whites from digging gold in the Cherokee Nation, but threats and proclamations proved little hindrance to white gold seekers.[18]

The summer of 1830 was a portentous period for the Cherokees for two other reasons. President Jackson openly declared to the Cherokees his intention not to interfere in the exercise of state sovereignty; the Cherokees must prepare to abide by such regulations as the surrounding states might issue. In this regard, the president suspended the method then in use of registering small bands of Cherokees for removal, awaiting the decision of the tribe for a general migration. The federal government also changed the system of paying annuities to the Cherokees. Up to that time, it had been the policy to pay yearly allowances to the constituted tribal authorities, but the new method would pay the annual distributions to individual Cherokees. Ross opposed both these measures, which were clearly intended to withdraw the only source of Cherokee revenue and force removal to the West. He recounted the obligations of the United States to the tribe and noted that "the territory of the Cherokees is not within the jurisdiction of Georgia, but within the sole and exclusive jurisdiction of the Cherokee nation." On the annuity question, Ross understood that the money would amount to only about forty-six cents per individual, but that the loss of these funds would deprive the Cherokees of the necessary finances to promote their case effectively before the United States government. Furthermore, the withdrawal of the money would dash many of Ross's dreams for Cherokee advancement.[19]

Ross called a special meeting of the Cherokee General Council in July 1830. He noted that the delegation which had recently returned from Washington reported its petitions to Congress unsuccessful, and he therefore suggested that the Cherokees turn to the judicial branch of the United States government to secure their rights. The General Council authorized Ross to institute legal proceedings in the Supreme Court of the United States and the courts of Georgia in order to determine the question of sovereignty. Ross conveyed his faith to the General Council and concluded that "in the appearance of impossibilities, there is still hope."[20]

Ross probably became convinced that the Cherokees must turn from their customary arguments when Congress passed Jackson's Indian removal bill in May 1830. In his first annual message, Jackson had proposed that land west of the Mississippi be set aside for the Indians. Although he recognized that the choice of removing belonged to the red men, Jackson insisted that those who stayed must submit to state law. The removal bill was one of the most hotly contested issues of the Twenty-first Congress, and sectional and party interests were as much involved as the moral issue of Cherokee rights. The opponents of the removal bill used as their basic ammunition a series of essays printed in the *National Intelligencer* under the signature of "William Penn," in reality Jeremiah Evarts, a guiding figure of the American Board missionaries and a stalwart friend of the Cherokees.[21]

The sectional nature of the bill was clearly evident during congressional debates, for the leading opponents of the bill were northern men, Theodore Frelinghuysen of New Jersey, Peleg Sprague of Maine, and Henry Storrs of New York, while southerners who spoke loudly in its favor included Hugh L. White of Tennessee and John Forsyth and Wilson Lumpkin, both of Georgia. The debates touched on the whole range of Indian history but centered on the issue of state sovereignty. Southern supporters accused opponents of the bill of hypocrisy, since they had long before driven unwanted Indians from their domain. Southerners further insisted that removal actually would be in the best interests of the Indian. The bill passed the House of Representatives by the narrow margin of five votes in late May 1830.[22]

Not all frontier and southern congressmen voted for the bill, and to one Tennessean who opposed Jackson's policies, Ross remarked: "Cupidity and Avarice by sophistry intrigue and corruption may for a while prevail—but the day of retributive justice must and will come, when integrity and moral worth will predominate and make the shameless monster hide its head." Ross expressed these thoughts to David Crockett and added several comments on Jackson's Indian proposals: "I have known Genl. Jackson from my boyhood—my earliest and warmest friends in Tennessee are generally his advocates—during the late war I held a rank in the Cherokee regiment & fought by his side . . . but it is with deep regret, I say, that his policy towards the aborigines, in my opinion, has been unrelenting and in effect ruinous."[23]

Ross nevertheless remained optimistic throughout the difficult year of 1830 and tried to bolster the sagging spirits of the Cherokees on every public occasion. In private conversation he also showed a positive disposition and admitted to his missionary friend Elizur Butler that his "hopes of success were never greater." Ross's reasons for hope were scant, as Georgia and the federal government continued pressure for removal. In a circular letter to the southern Indian agents, Secretary of War Eaton depicted those chiefs who opposed removal as oppressive tyrants who permitted no opinion but their own. He further emphasized Jackson's earlier decree that if the Indians would not accept the offer of the United States to remove, then they simply would come under the jurisdiction of the several states. The first example of this policy came when Cherokees as well as white intruders were dislodged from the gold regions of the Cherokee Nation. Within a short time federal troops were taken out of the nation altogether, a sure invitation for avid gold hunters, but when Ross requested some explanation, Montgomery replied that he could give no reason except that Ross must come to expect the federal government to withdraw its protection.[24]

The political possibilities of the Indian question were not lost on Jackson's opponents, and under the influence of Jeremiah Evarts several prominent National Republicans, including Daniel Webster and Ambrose Spencer, suggested that the Cherokees hire legal counsel for their defense. They hoped to reduce Jackson's power in the North—especially in Pennsylvania where the Quaker vote was crucial—and to impair the South's sacrosanct state sovereignty. The Cherokees turned to former Attorney General William Wirt, who though not an avid opponent of Jackson was capable and sympathetic to the Cherokees. Oddly enough, Wirt was a relative of Governor Gilmer, but he made no headway in personal appeals to that Georgian.[25]

Wirt took up the Cherokees' case in June 1830 and prepared a brief centering on what he considered the vital question, the right of Georgia to extend its laws over the Cherokees. Wirt concluded that the Cherokees composed a sovereign nation and that their laws and lands could not come under Georgia's sway. More important, this interpretation allowed original jurisdiction to the Supreme Court. Ross rushed the opinion to the *Cherokee Phoenix* printer and distributed it widely among United States officials. Ross and Wirt had hoped to enlist some of the leading figures of the day but were unsuccessful in getting their first choice, Daniel Webster, so Wirt chose another associate, John Sergeant of Pennsylvania. Since the Cherokees were not receiving their annuities, they were severely

short of funds; Ross therefore made frequent promises of the faith-
fulness of the Cherokees in fulfilling their pledges as he forwarded
small amounts of money to Wirt and Sergeant.[26]

In December 1830 Ross took the next step in an intricate legal
procedure. With the business partner of Major Ridge, George M. Lav-
ender, Ross set out on December 20 to serve officials of the state of
Georgia with a notice that the Cherokees would bring suit against
them the following March. One week later they handed the document to Governor Gilmer at Milledgeville. The message apprised
him that the Cherokee counsel would appear before the United
States Supreme Court on March 5 to seek an injunction to restrain
the state from enforcing its laws in the Cherokee Nation.[27]

The Cherokee case came up for hearing in the famous case, *Cherokee Nation* v. *Georgia*. Wirt already had attempted to get Chief
Justice John Marshall's opinion on Wirt's interpretations of similar
cases, but Marshall had declined. Wirt must have been somewhat
cheered when Marshall revealed that his private sympathies were
with the Cherokees, and that many of the leading legal thinkers of
the day considered the United States Supreme Court the constitutional arbiter. Yet on March 18, the last day of the session, the court
refused to consider the case, declaring that it did not have jurisdiction. Marshall skirted the alternatives offered him by the Cherokees
and the state of Georgia: that the Indians were either foreign or subject nations. Rather the chief justice held that the Cherokees were in
a special position as "domestic dependent nations" and were wards
of the United States. Marshall, however, did leave a hint for future
actions, suggesting the issue of property rights could get the case
before the court.[28]

Cases before the Georgia courts were as unsuccessful as attempts
before the federal judiciary. Of the seven lawyers retained by Ross,
only three seem actually to have done effective work: Thomas G.
Barron, David Irwin, and Edward Harden. The remaining four—
William H. Underwood, Samuel Rockwell, William Y. Hansell, and
Thomas W. Harris—spent most of their time badgering Ross about
their fees. Harris even had a Cherokee arrested for nonpayment and
the other three eventually defected to Ross's opposition.[29]

In mid-April of 1831 Ross set out to explain to his people the decision of the United States Supreme Court and the general state of

Cherokee national affairs. He found among them a "unanimity of sentiment" to remain in their cherished homeland. Montgomery accused Ross of deceiving the Cherokees by telling them that the Supreme Court had decided in their favor, but it is more likely that Ross was deceived. The Cherokees continued to receive assurances from leading American political figures—Henry Clay, Daniel Webster, and Theodore Frelinghuysen—that their cause was just and that they could win. Ross even hoped that Jackson's cabinet changes in 1830 might presage a new era in Cherokee–United States relations. If Ross was guileless in 1831, he assured Wirt that if the issue were decided against them, "it would be extreme folly to believe that the Cherokees could again be duped into Confidence of the good faith of the U.S."[30]

The Cherokees had gained the sympathy of a wide audience of humanitarians, many most energetic in their defense. The zealous attitude of the resident missionaries attracted the attention of the Georgians, and in the Georgia legislative session of 1830 several measures were passed to deal with such malcontents. In addition to suspending the Cherokee General Council and courts, the legislators set a deadline of March 1831 for all white residents on Indian lands to be licensed and to swear to support the government of Georgia or suffer four years at hard labor. They also created the Georgia Guard to protect the interests of the state.[31]

The Georgia Guard was essentially an anti-Indian military unit, but it was also used in carrying out legislative decrees. Late on Saturday evening, March 12, 1831, the guard descended on the home of Isaac Proctor, an American Board missionary, and hurried him away to a nearby public house. The next morning the guard arrested Samuel A. Worcester at New Echota. Upon their claims that they were authorized agents of the federal government, the missionaries soon were released. President Jackson disallowed these claims, however—even to the point of taking away Worcester's postmastership—and then the group was arrested again. In September a state court convicted eleven captured missionaries of violating state law and prescribed the maximum sentence of four years at hard labor. All but Worcester and Elizur Butler accepted pardons. The released missionaries hurriedly made plans to leave Georgia, and many took up stations among the western Cherokees. The significance of the Georgia court decision was not lost on Ross, who informed Wirt of the decision and asked what effect it would have on the Cherokee case if the missionaries were released. Ross also was concerned about the personal welfare of Worcester, Butler, and their families, and he told Mrs. Butler of his great interest in her family's well-being, insisting that she not hesitate to ask for his help. Ross also contributed to a fund to enable the two wives to visit their husbands at Milledgeville where they were detained.[32]

The Georgia action toward the missionaries was Wirt's great opportunity to return the Cherokees' case to the Marshall court. Although it was not clearly a property rights question, Marshall used the case of *Worcester* v. *Georgia* as a pretext to examine all Cherokee treaties, and in a wide-ranging interpretation observed that the Cherokees never had yielded their sovereignty. Marshall also reasoned that it was the responsibility of the United States to preserve and protect the tribes in their native lands. The court delivered its opinion on March 3, 1832, demanded the release of Worcester and Butler, and declared all Georgia Indian laws unconstitutional. Even without Jackson's alleged statement that Marshall would have to enforce his own decision, the judgment would not have been valid until the court ruled a second time. Supreme Court Justice John McLean, sympathetic to the Cherokee cause, was pessimistic and despite the decision suggested that the Cherokees work for statehood. The argument over execution of part of the decision became moot when the missionaries accepted pardon under Georgia law. B. B. Wisner, secretary of the American Board, informed Ross that Worcester and Butler would "stay further proceedings," as the Board thought it inexpedient to prosecute further. It must have been disheartening to Ross when Wisner also suggested it might be best for the Cherokees to accept the terms of the federal government and move west.[33]

Georgians were not satisfied with merely intimidating white men among the Indians but hoped that they could divide the Cherokees, thus making them more vulnerable to removal. Governor Gilmer, in an attempt to create distrust of the Cherokees in power, sent Colonel John W. A. Sanford among the tribe to ascertain Ross's Cherokee parentage and to determine the extent of his influence on the full-blood majority. To Gilmer's certain satisfaction Sanford reported that "the *native* Indian has but little part . . . in the administration of their government but that its affairs are managed *exclusively* by those who are so remotely related to the Indian, as gives them but slender claims to be classed among that people." Ross's white opposition constantly alleged that he ruled the Cherokee Nation with an iron hand, that he left the average Cherokee little freedom under his despotic regime, and that most Cherokees would gladly remove if out from under his grip. Missionaries closely acquainted with Cherokee affairs denied these allegations, and Worcester once asserted that "individuals may be overawed by *popular opinion*, but not by the *chiefs*. On the other hand, if there were a chief in favor of removal, *he* would be overawed by the *people*."[34]

A minor crisis was provoked by a Georgia legislative act which suspended assembly of the General Council, setting punishment for attending such meetings at four years of hard labor. As the October General Council for 1831 approached, the legislators were apprehensive, and Elias Boudinot confided to Ross that several members would resign rather than attend the New Echota meeting. Ross was reluctant to change the constituted place of meeting but called for an early gathering at his home to discuss the issue. Against the judgment of Ross, who was reluctant to set a precedent in breaking Cherokee constitutional statutes, the combined National Committee and National Council voted to meet outside the limits of Georgia, in a rough clearing near Chatooga, Alabama. Further, the General Council appointed John Martin, John Ridge, and William Shorey Coodey to go to Washington as delegates and decided that future meetings would be held at Red Clay in the Tennessee portion of Cherokee lands. Ross advised the delegation to remind the president that the Cherokees would never willingly move west of the Mississippi River. The delegation also was to call for payment in the traditional manner of the delinquent annuities and to keep Ross informed of its progress.[35]

As Georgians became impatient for Cherokee lands, there were repeated instances of violence. Ross himself came close to losing his life, possibly because the land-hungry intruders knew that he was the greatest obstacle to their success. On the evening of November 30, 1831, Ross was visiting in the home of Major Ridge with his brother Andrew when someone shouted for him. Ross described the caller as "a tall gaunt figure," a certain white man named Harris who said he was looking for a horse thief who may have used Ross's ferry the preceding evening. Ross said he had not seen the man and Harris departed. Ross then decided to consult with his nephew William Shorey Coodey before Coodey left for Washington the next day. Andrew Ross and Chief Ross talked as they rode along the path toward Coodey's place and were unaware that Harris had slowly drifted behind them. Suddenly Harris shouted, "Ross, I have been for a long time wanting to kill you." Without looking back, Ross quickly wheeled his horse and galloped off as shots rang out; fortunately none hit the mark.[36]

The Cherokee delegation of the winter of 1831–32 was as unsuccessful as the earlier ones, and its pessimistic report called for much soul searching. Ross set aside July 19, 1832, as a day of prayer and fasting. A special meeting was called later that month by Ross to obtain the full report of the Washington delegation's work and to hear of the success of Ridge and Boudinot in their tour of the East in search of funds to bolster the diminished treasury. At the meeting, the critical matter of the coming election in August was also discussed. Inasmuch as Georgia law prohibited such elections and the Georgia Guard stood ready to enforce these decrees, the General Council decided to set up a provisional government which would continue with the same chiefs, legislative members, and executive council until peaceful elections could be resumed. The General Council also had to deal with new propositions from the federal government delivered by a special agent of Secretary of War Lewis Cass.[37]

Elisha W. Chester had received his commission as a special agent to the Cherokees in May 1832 and arrived in the Cherokee Nation the first week in June. Ross called Chester's visit "rather uncouth," for he earlier had espoused the Cherokee cause and even was legal adviser to Worcester and Butler. After meeting with Ross and others of the tribe and noting their opposition to removal, Chester still thought he had a good chance to negotiate for a removal treaty, and he advised Cass that there was a good prospect of success and asked how long it would take commissioners to get to the Cherokee Nation to sign a treaty. Success may have seemed imminent to Chester because he carried from Cass a seventeen-point proposal; the provisions seemed especially inviting. The lands in the West to be given the Cherokees would be guaranteed them "forever without the boundaries of any State or Territory." The Cherokees would have complete self-government and the right to appoint an agent to live in Washington to oversee their rights. The United States would pay the expenses of the removal, which could be accomplished under their own supervision, would provide subsistence for one year after removal, and would establish an adequate annuity for the relinquished lands and improvements. The remaining items gave the Cherokees adequate recompense for their losses and even provided for a selected few to remain if they would accept citizenship and take up reservations.[38]

To similar propositions Ross had once remarked: "Were the President to send his Agents into the frontier countries of Georgia with similar instructions to enroll Georgians, instead of Cherokees, I have no doubt they would be more successful." Chester was no more successful than earlier proponents of removal. Ross initially delayed the commissioner's address by demanding his credentials, but ultimately the General Council decided to have no direct communication with him at all and addressed its answer to Secretary of War Cass through Montgomery. The reply was that the "true sentiments of the Cherokee people remains the same."[39]

At the October 1832 General Council, Chester again pressed his suit, but Ross barely listened to him, advising him that a delegation had been appointed to attend to Cherokee business in Washington. The Cherokees still naïvely looked for the Supreme Court to sustain them and even hoped that Henry Clay might win the election of 1832 and reinstate their rights. In his annual message to the General Council, Ross suggested that the Cherokee Nation might lose its national character by removal and that former treaties with the United States would be dissolved, a serious threat to Cherokee independence. Ross also noted that surveyors had described the Arkansas area as an "extensive prairie badly watered" with only "corpses of wood." That winter Ross headed a delegation to Washington staunchly opposed to removal.[40]

Ross and his companions arrived in Washington the first week in

January 1833 and settled at the Indian Queen Hotel but, perhaps knowing that the federal government would not pay their expenses, soon transferred to the less luxurious Brown's Hotel. After an interview with reelected President Jackson and Secretary of War Cass, Ross put the Cherokee case in writing. Recounting Chester's visit, Ross explained that in spite of the dilemma which the Cherokees faced before the "*array* of *oppressive* power," they were "unshaken in their objections to a removal west of the river Mississippi." Cass discovered only one hope for the harassed Cherokees—removal. Ross also brought up the question of annuities: for the past three years the Cherokees had not received the annuities, which had been placed at a United States branch bank at Nashville, Tennessee, until the Cherokees accepted them individually. Cass's final reply was terse and to the point—the president's views remained unchanged. The delegates had one more brief meeting with President Jackson before they departed, but there was no progress.[41]

During 1832 and 1833 the Cherokee Nation began to face dissension within its own ranks. John Walker, Jr., a Ross opponent, had been displeased with the results of the General Council in 1832 and had intimated to Montgomery that if the United States would guarantee his expenses, he would get up a delegation to Washington that would discuss the subject of removal. Walker approached some of the leading Cherokee men with the idea and although he was refused by most of them, he did convince a few to follow him to Washington where his actions were vigorously protested by the legitimate delegation. Ross assured his followers not to worry about Walker's conduct and noted that the conflict was no longer between the Cherokees and the United States, but (because of the decision in *Worcester* v. *Georgia*) between Georgia and the federal government. Walker's failure was not a true gauge of Cherokee sentiments toward removal, however, and the few men he approached probably were opposed more to Walker than to his ideas.[42]

Sometime in 1832 the intelligent and influential John Ridge began to have doubts about the efficacy of the Cherokees' unrelenting decision to remain in their native lands, and bit by bit he influenced Major Ridge, his father, and Elias Boudinot, his cousin. Boudinot, the erudite editor of the *Cherokee Phoenix*, expressed his distaste for what he considered Ross's arbitrary methods by resigning his post, giving as his reasons the decision of the United States Supreme Court, the want of funds, the conflict of views between himself and the "authorities of the nation," and his health. Boudinot did not share the general Cherokee elation in the Worcester decision, for he knew too well the power of President Jackson. What ultimately persuaded Boudinot to quit the enterprise was Ross's growing belief that "the toleration of diversified views" in the paper would create "fermentation and confusion" and in the end prove disastrous to the nation. Ross insisted on *"unity of sentiment and action for the good of all,"* even to the extent of muzzling the press. The General Council appointed Ross's brother-in-law, Elijah Hicks, as editor, and Boudinot's opinions were effectively suppressed.[43]

The Ridge faction, as these dissidents came to be called, believed sincerely that the only salvation for their people lay in moving beyond the sphere of white influence. They hoped, however, that their views could be expressed through regularly constituted channels, and at this point they had not entirely abandoned their faith in Ross. John Ridge wrote Ross at Washington in 1833 to explain how the Cherokees were "robbed & whipped by the whites almost every day," and then implored: "I have the right to address you as the chief of the whole Cherokee Nation, upon whom rests, under Heaven the highest responsibility—and well being of the whole people; and I do trust that you will return as I know you are capable of acting the Part of a statesman in this trying Crisis of our affairs. . . . We all know . . . that we can't be a Nation here, I hope we shall attempt to establish it somewhere else! *Where*, the wisdom of the nation must try to find."[44]

On his return from Washington, Ross called an extra session of the General Council to report the delegation's work. At the rain-soaked Red Clay Council Ground, Ross reported to the assembly that President Jackson had offered the Cherokees a treaty with a two million five hundred thousand dollars' allowance for their lands, which he raised to three million dollars provided the Cherokees supervised their own removal. Ross counter-proposed to Jackson that the federal government buy out those who invaded Cherokee lands and let them emigrate westward. Ross also intimated that the delegation members had been offered a bribe of eighty thousand dollars to induce them to sign a treaty. Ross noted further that Elbert Herring, the Commissioner of Indian Affairs, had promised to remove intruders from "the assailed parts of your country." Ross may have read too much into this statement, for he thought he detected a change of heart in Herring. Ross's opponents were not deceived; rather they thought it a plot to bluff the full-bloods. During the summer of 1833 the cold reality of Jacksonian policy was revealed anew when Ross received word that the president would entertain no Indian audience in the coming year. Herring belatedly explained that the "assailed parts" were Cherokee lands in Tennessee and North Carolina—states which had not extended their jurisdiction over the Cherokees.[45]

By the middle of 1833 Ross sensed the growing power of his opposition and sent letters to his friends in several districts to bolster loyalty. He assured his people, "I shall never deceive you and that so far as my feeble talent and ability will permit it shall be exerted solely with the view of promoting the welfare and happiness of the whole people." Lest the appeal of the Ridges be too strong, he warned: "A man who will forsake his country . . . in time of adversity and will co-operate with those who oppose his own Kindred is no more than a traitor and should be viewed—and shunned as such."[46]

The regular General Council met in October 1833, and Ross spoke briefly on October 15. He reiterated his confidence in the good faith of the United States in spite of four years of what he viewed as a "temporizing and oppressive course of policy." The chief struck his familiar theme of unity and commented on the division developing among his people: "On all important questions, when a difference of opinion arise in regard to their rights and interests, the sentiments of the majority should prevail. . . . The duty of the minority to yield, and unite in the support of the measure, this is the rule of order, sanctioned by patriotism and virtue; whilst a contrary course would lead to faction, confusion and injury." The General Council commissioned Ross and four other Cherokees to go to Washington and to call upon the federal government to pay over to the Cherokee national treasurer thirty-five hundred dollars out of the annuities in order to meet their expenses. Just before their departure, Cherokee Agent Montgomery informed Ross that the delegation's expenses would be met only if they had the authority and intent to form a treaty upon President Jackson's principles. Ross therefore left for the capital city with little hope of getting the annuities. Perhaps he also realized that the chances were equally slight that injustices to the Cherokees would be rectified.[47]

Ross had become chief of the Cherokee Nation during an era of large alteration in the traditional way of life. His election demonstrated the shift in Cherokee custom; the tribe now looked to leaders who possessed the white man's skills. Internal modification had pushed aside the clan system in favor of familial relations; the code of personal vengeance had been replaced by an intricate legal apparatus, while literacy and Christianity had changed the vision of the primitive full-bloods. Yet the partial adoption of white civilization did not diminish Cherokee reverence for their land, and despite their numerous "advancements" the increasing threat of the loss of their homeland was extremely painful. Ross had mastered the necessary political techniques and possessed genuine qualities of leadership, but, more important, he had assumed the Cherokees' instinctive love for their land. His legal maneuvering and political prowess had diverted the Georgian thrust temporarily, but internal dissension and external pressure had weakened his effectiveness. Ross may even have added to the creeping discontent of the Ridge followers, for had he viewed them as a loyal opposition rather than an unpatriotic threat to unity, he might have stifled their growth. As it was, he forced them to search for avenues outside the Cherokee political system to voice their objections. In the end Cherokee factionalism, state sovereignty, and federal executive power eroded the once solid Cherokee foundation.

4

CHEROKEE IMPASSE

FACTIONALISM increased rapidly over the next two years. The cleavage widened as the Ridge faction became more convinced that Cherokee salvation lay in removal only, while the Ross party was just as firmly set on remaining in the homeland. Internal disruptions were inflamed by federal agents who used the Cherokee rift to further their aims. As Ross traveled to Washington in 1834, he had only vague notions of the consequences of Cherokee difficulties; neither had he contemplated what extraordinary proposals for settlement he would have to make in coming months.

Ross and the delegation soon confirmed their apprehensions that President Jackson's attitude was still securely set on Indian removal, though he did allow a brief meeting on February 5. The next day Ross presented Secretary of War Lewis Cass with a written statement of the delegation's mission, a statement that included references to Ross's concern over the reports of Benjamin F. Currey. Currey had been appointed as emigration agent to the Cherokees after impatient Georgians had insisted that Jackson renew the removal process which the president had halted earlier awaiting a mass migration. Currey also served as a discreet intermediary to the Ridge faction and was an alert and often uninvited guest at all Cherokee gatherings. His reports of the May 1833 meeting of the Cherokees had been especially derogatory to Ross, and he had praised the protreaty faction.[1]

The written statement also reminded Cass that the decision of the federal judiciary had never been adequately enforced in regard to Cherokee property rights. Cass's terse reply brought a note from the Cherokee representatives offering further concessions; the delegates suggested that a portion of the Cherokee land be ceded for the use of Georgia, with the understanding that the United States would then effectively protect the Cherokees on the remainder. Although this plea was directed to Jackson, the delegation received only brusque replies from Cass.[2]

At this point, Ross felt compelled to propose extraordinary measures. Conceding that the Cherokee Nation was just emerging from a "natural state of man," he proposed nonetheless to cede a portion of their territory to satisfy Georgia and then to "enter into an arrangement, on the basis of the Cherokees' becoming prospectively citizens of the United States." The crucial point for Ross was whether the Cherokees could maintain a separate identity of some sort, and he promised that "the Cherokee people will never consent to sell their freedom, nor dispose of their heritage in the soil which moulders the bones of their ancestors." Feeling they had given their ultimate concessions, the Cherokee delegates were astonished, after a month-long wait, to receive from an administration underling a curt rejection. Ross turned to the Senate with a petition on Cherokee grievances, but it lay unread in the southern-dominated Committee on Indian Affairs. Other vexing problems were taken before the Jackson administration with as little success.[3]

Occasionally Ross met other Indian delegates in Washington and discussed with them their common hopes and problems. In the winter of 1834 Ross addressed a Seneca delegation in haunting language:

We have been made to drink of the bitter cup of humiliation; treated like dogs; our lives, our liberties, the sport of whitemen; our country and the graves of our Fathers torn from us, in cruel succession: until driven from river to river, from forest to forest, and thro a period of upwards of two hundred years, rolled back nation upon nation, we find ourselves fugitives, vagrants and strangers in our own country, and look forward to the period when our descendants will perhaps be totally extinguished by wars, driven at the point of the bayonet into the Western Ocean, or reduced to . . . the condition of slaves.[4]

Ross's work was hampered by a rival delegation of Cherokees in Washington in 1834, and its presence probably drove him to concede more than he felt the Cherokee Nation would accept. A disgruntled portion of the tribe had gathered at the Cherokee agency shortly after Ross's departure, elected William Hicks as chief, and commissioned a group to secure a treaty for removal. Upon Jackson's demand for more substantial members of the tribe, this protreaty delegation was altered to include Major Ridge, David Vann, and Elias Boudinot in addition to the original appointees, Andrew Ross, T. J. Pack, James Starr, and John West. Thus Ross was opposed by two relatives—Andrew, his brother, and Pack, a distant cousin. The protreaty faction was not without its own internal dissensions; Andrew wanted to sign a treaty under any circumstances, while Ridge and Boudinot could not accept what they considered the extremes of either of the Rosses, so they withdrew from further discussions.[5]

The Ross delegation presented to Secretary of War Cass a protest against the recognition of any unauthorized delegation. The protest, purportedly signed by thirteen thousand Cherokees, was turned over to the Department of War and then examined by Andrew Ross and his delegation. They found many duplicate names plus signatures of white men, Creeks, and women, children, emigrants, and even those who favored emigration. Ross conceded certain errors but said they were made by oversight and not by intent, and he added, "We have perceived an inclination on the part of (at least some of them) the officers of the Government to discredit every statement." Certainly the federal government could not deny that a majority of the tribe was opposed to this self-made delegation, and Chief Ross was astonished when former Secretary of War John H. Eaton informed him that he had been appointed as President Jackson's commissioner to treat with the Cherokees and that "a treaty was in progress."[6]

Andrew Ross and his colleagues, claiming to represent some eighteen hundred Cherokees, signed a treaty with Eaton on June 19, 1834. The treaty ceded all the Cherokee lands east of the Mississippi for an annuity of twenty-five thousand dollars for twenty-four years, various other sums for Cherokee improvements and education, and the western lands. Supplemental articles contained two interesting points: Andrew Ross was to receive a thousand dollars for a "turnpike road," and "ardent spirits" were to be allowed into the Cherokee Nation when carried by a Cherokee. The treaty died in the Senate for want of the necessary two-thirds majority.[7]

Ross returned to the Head of Coosa about the first week in August 1834 and found that his home and fields were advertised in local

Georgia newspapers for public sale, a common occurrence among the Cherokees. As early as 1831 Georgia had ordered that the Cherokee domain be surveyed, and the next year surveyors laid out the area in ten counties. In 1833 the state granted all Cherokee lands within its claimed jurisdiction to local citizens in a grand lottery. Although Ross was able to remove one eager squatter when he took his case, *John Ross and Others* v. *Clyatt and Others*, before the Floyd County court, he realized that these greedy claimants could be delayed only temporarily. This was evident when Governor George R. Gilmer, although failing to get a recalcitrant area judge impeached, easily nullified his decisions.[8]

The Red Clay Council Ground again reverberated in August 1834 with the sounds of tramping Cherokees coming to hear their chief. John Ridge, present during the meeting, was incredulous as he listened to Ross explain the terms the delegation had offered at Washington. Ridge believed that Ross had attempted to falsify several concessions the delegation had proposed to President Jackson, especially the provision for eventual amalgamation with the Union.

In outlining his work in Washington to the Cherokee people, Ross did not always speak with candor. He lightly passed over the proposition for uniting his tribe with the United States, saying such an event was remote and need not even be considered. He failed to clarify that he had actually advanced such terms at the capital city. Emotions ran high during the troubled session. At one point Thomas Foreman, an ardent Ross supporter, made a heated speech in which he accused Major Ridge of hypocrisy, saying that he had gone around the country telling the people to love their land and then had gone to Washington to give their lands away. Foreman's rhetoric caught the feeling of the crowd, and at one time an excited Cherokee was even heard to whisper, "Let's kill him." A petition was presented for impeachment of Major Ridge, John Ridge, and David Vann for favoring removal. The impeachment charge was laid aside, however, to be decided at the October General Council meeting.[9]

Foreman's outrage at Major Ridge's position was indicative of Cherokee factionalism. Andrew Ross had been home only a couple of weeks when he discovered plans for his murder and for the murder of T. J. Pack. The meeting in August was further roused by the sensational news that John Walker, Jr., a protreaty advocate at Washington the year before, had been shot and killed. His father Major Walker accused Ross and his followers of instigating the murder and threatened Ross's life. The elder Walker may have wished he had succeeded in killing Ross while they were in Washington in 1819. So real did threats and rumors seem that friends guarded Ross that night, and he returned home at the end of the General Council under escort. Members of the Ridge family also considered themselves in danger and took precautions. When news of this threatened violence reached President Jackson at the Hermitage near Nashville, he was so infuriated that he instructed Hugh Montgomery to notify Ross that he would be held personally responsible "for every Murder committed by his people on the emigrants." Ross found it hard to believe that Jackson would assume such powers over the Cherokees, since treaties bound the United States to protect "the whole Cherokee Nation," not any particular branch or faction.[10]

Ross expressed to the Ridges his concern over the growing violence. He met Major Ridge in September to discuss their mutual concern over rumors that Ross was to be assassinated by Ridge adherents. Major Ridge also wanted confirmation of reports that a certain Thomas Woodward was designated by Ross to carry out threats on the Ridges' lives. Ross, of course, denied these allegations and emphasized that it was "high time all such mischievous tales should be silenced." Ross himself was slow to listen to such rumors, as he still believed in the honesty of Major Ridge, who had been his friend for so many years. The chief also emphasized to John Ridge his sincere wish that "partyism, should be discarded. Our country and our people—should be our motto."[11]

The problem of Cherokee annuities never had been adequately settled since the federal government withdrew the funds in June 1830 on the pretext that they had to be paid to individual Cherokees. An arrangement made by federal officials in March 1834 allowed the Cherokees to determine a method to distribute the money. Montgomery prescribed that a vote should be conducted on October 1, 1834 at the Cherokee agency with emigration agent, Benjamin Currey, as supervisor. Currey hoped that the site would enable the Indians to be "unawed by any of the pretended Chiefs or their spies." Ross wanted to have a clerk and interpreter from Cherokee ranks, but Currey objected, determined that Ross would have no chance to sway voters. Currey vented his wrath in a personal diatribe against Ross, alleging that he betrayed the interests of the Cherokees in order to line his own pockets. In spite of this, the final tally showed 388 in favor of paying the annuity funds to Ross, with only one opposed. Currey suggested to the Office of Indian Affairs that the annuities still not be paid, saying that the election was a hoax and that the Cherokee national treasurer was not a legitimate authority since no elections had been held since 1830.[12]

After the polling at the Cherokee agency, Ross returned to Head of Coosa to prepare his annual message for the General Council at Red Clay within two weeks. Ross indicated his pleasure at the people's decision on the annuity question and his hope "that the day of retribution will . . . come, when reparation for wrongs done . . . will be made . . . to our suffering people." In recounting the events of the past year, he concluded that there was "no alternative left the nation . . . but to persevere in the peaceable course of asserting & maintaining our clearly acknowledged rights." Ross had two great fears concerning the course of the federal government: the frustrations and sufferings of the Cherokees in a removal to the West, and the probable change in the relations between the tribe and the United States which would diminish Cherokee rights even further. The chief wanted the Cherokees to press their case anew.[13]

At the meeting of the Cherokee General Council in October 1834 Currey tried to implement the removal treaty signed in June by Andrew Ross and his band. To John Ross's expression of shock that Currey should even display the fraudulent treaty, Currey replied to Ross and his "fallen government," that they could not expect better terms. The General Council resolved never to accept the treaty and appointed Chief Ross and four other antitreaty men as delegates to Washington.[14]

Currey thought Ross's object was to try to outlive the Jackson administration. Ross certainly was getting that advice, for one of the lawyers employed by the Cherokees suggested that when Indians were turned out of their homes, they should stir up excitement which might cause Vice-President Martin Van Buren concern over his chances in Ohio, New York, and Pennsylvania for election to the presidency. Ross completely ignored this sort of advice.[15]

The Cherokee delegation to Washington in the winter of 1834–35 appealed to President Jackson on a number of points. Ross appealed to Jackson's humanity in behalf of Cherokees who were losing their homes in the Georgia land lottery. Adept mixed-bloods like Ross had been able to stay the greedy Georgian hand for a time by legal maneuvering, but primitive full-bloods had been readily turned out. The delegation, thinking the controversy over annuity payments settled, expected to receive expense money while in Washington. When Ross asked if the delegation would be reimbursed, Secretary of War Cass reportedly replied, "If you make a Treaty on the terms proposed, yes—not otherwise." Ross retorted that the delegates were "prepared to pay their expenses but not to sell their consciences."[16]

Ultimately Ross presented what he must have considered the most extreme concession: that the Cherokee Nation grant the United States an extensive portion of its territory. From their once vast domain, the Cherokees would retain only a remnant along the borders of Tennessee, Georgia, and Alabama, plus a small tract in North Carolina. They in return would expect the United States to guarantee their remaining lands without restriction of ownership and to protect them from intruders. Ross, feeling it only just that the original inhabitants of these lands be granted the same privileges that European immigrants had obtained, also anticipated United States citizenship for Cherokees. Secretary Cass replied that "nothing short of an entire removal" would remedy their difficulties.[17]

Because a rival delegation led by John Ridge and Elias Boudinot was also present in Washington, Ross and his colleagues were driven to desperation. Fearing that the United States Senate might be more amenable to Ridge's terms than toward Andrew Ross's earlier proposal, Ross moved ahead with exaggerated propositions. He suggested that the United States pay the Cherokees twenty million dollars for all their lands east of the Mississippi River and protect the tribe from incursions for five years by which time the Cherokees would resettle. Also, the federal government would reimburse the tribe for all losses sustained in violation of former treaties and would pay an indemnity for claims under the Cherokee treaties of 1817 and 1819. Ross reiterated, nevertheless, that no amount of money could induce the Cherokees to leave if they felt that they could be adequately protected by the federal government in their homelands.[18]

On the morning of February 18, 1835, members of the Ross faction seated themselves around the office of Secretary of War Cass, hoping to work out verbally what written communications would not yield. Although Jackson had considered Ross's terms financially extravagant, Cass had reopened negotiations when Ross reminded him that the president often had remarked that "he would grant us as liberal terms as the Senate . . . would be willing to allow." Cass asked the delegation to put its terms in writing, and he stepped out of the room as the group discussed the issue. When Cass returned, Ross gave him the decision "to abide [by] the award of the . . . Senate . . . and to recommend the same for the final determination of our nation." Cass agreed and assured them that the president would "go as far as the Senate." Cass also agreed to make available minutes of the Senate proceedings. Ross and his associates retired, confident that the Senate would justify their trust.[19]

But the Senate did not accept Ross's propositions. In spite of petitions and entreaties to old friends in the Senate, the sum for removal was set at five million dollars. President Jackson, triumphant, was then ready to deal with Ross on the basis of the chief's pledge, at least as he and Cass interpreted the pledge. Opinions then and now differ on Ross's promise. Ross was a strict constructionist on the Cherokee constitution which forbade anyone to make treaties independently without the Cherokee Nation's consent. Ross wanted to see the whole record of the proceedings of the Senate as Cass had promised in their meeting on February 28, but the Secretary of War now refused and would hear no further pleas. At another private meeting Cass intimated that Jackson might even enter into a treaty with the Ridge faction, but he promised that the President would move with "a just regard . . . [for] individual rights." Ross pledged to take the treaty to the Cherokee Nation and to comply with every promise that had been made.[20]

Ross's defeat was bitter, and he reached out blindly in other directions. He asked a friend, Baron Friedrich Ludwig von Roenne, Chargé d'Affaires of Prussia, to give him a letter of introduction to the Mexican Chargé d'Affaires in Philadelphia, J. M. de Castillo y

Lanzas. Ross recounted to Roenne the "unparalleled oppression which have been heaped upon the Cherokee people" and thought it "desirable to explore some of the provinces of Mexico . . . for settling a Colony within its sovereign jurisdiction." In mid-March of 1835 Ross met Lanzas in Philadelphia and presented him with the Cherokee constitution and other documents to illustrate the tribe's state of advancement. Ross spoke of the "caprice and whim of power" which necessitated a Cherokee removal, and of possible arrangements for migration to Mexico, provided the Cherokees could obtain full rights of citizenship. Ross insisted that if some plan could be worked out, the Cherokees must not be settled in the midst of colonists from the United States. Ross's propositions came out of anguish and despair and, whether answered or not, were never acted upon.[21]

Ross's return to the Cherokee Nation in spring 1835 was a melancholy affair, for creeping Georgian incursions finally had reached his home. Although Colonel William N. Bishop, head of the Georgia Guard, attempted to reach Ross in Washington to inform him that he had put the legal claimant to the chief's property in full possession of his home, fields, ferry, and improvements, Ross did not receive this message while in Washington and traveled home unaware of his family's plight. Arriving about ten o'clock one evening, Ross dismounted and ordered his horse put up. To his astonishment he found himself a stranger in his own home and his family turned out. He paid the arrogant occupant for the care of his horse and departed in search of his family. Ross eventually moved across the Tennessee border near the Red Clay Council Ground. There, half a mile south of Flint Springs, Ross established Red Hill as his residence, where he lived until 1838. In a rough-hewed log house of barely two rooms, the chief shared the common sufferings of his people.[22]

Members of the treaty faction received kinder treatment. Governor Wilson Lumpkin of Georgia informed Elias Boudinot that he would ask Colonel Bishop to delay the grant for his lands and improvements, and the seizure of Major Ridge's house and ferry was held up while he was in Washington "doing all in his power to effect a negotiation." Emigration Agent Currey was ready even to use the military to protect Major Ridge's property, and the Georgia legislature ruled his ferry immune from seizure. Conversely, intimidation and bribery were used against recalcitrant Cherokees. Currey warned Lewis Ross that his property on the agency grounds would be seized if he used his influence to prevent acceptance of the treaty.[23]

According to the usual custom, the returned delegation called a meeting of the Cherokees to explain the proceedings in Washington and set the gathering for the second Monday in May. Ross was somewhat surprised then to learn that Currey had called a private meeting of Cherokees at John Ridge's farm home, Running Water. Knowing that the intent of the meeting was to reopen the question of the method of paying annuities, Ross balked, for he believed that the question had been settled the year before. Nevertheless, Currey went ahead with his meeting at Running Water. The meeting lasted only two days, and Currey felt that Ross had convinced the mass of Cherokees to stay away.[24]

The Cherokees assembled at the Red Clay Council Ground on May 11, 1835. Nearly one thousand were present, and they signed a protest against Currey's actions. Ross explained that his propositions were rejected by the president and then touched only lightly on his actual promises. Ross was accused by Currey of negligence and deceit and of omitting significant portions of the Ridges' treaty proposals. Ross had dwelt mainly on his familiar themes of "unanimity of sentiment & action" and had used strongly worded phrases about the Ridges' collusion with the Jackson government. John Ridge felt that Ross was duping ignorant Cherokees and that few understood the measures the treaty party had worked out.[25]

During the summer of 1835 a new figure strolled across the Cherokee stage, the Reverend John F. Schermerhorn. Imbued with a sense of missionary zeal, the "devil's horn," as the antitreaty Cherokees called him, was appointed commissioner with Governor William Carroll of Tennessee to make final treaty arrangements for removal. Ross appealed both to Schermerhorn and Currey to meet the Cherokees at either Red Clay or the Cherokee agency grounds, but they refused, and Ross therefore sent out runners. Within ten days more than twenty-five hundred Cherokees had gathered at Running Water, hoping to settle the annuity question.[26]

The scheduled assembly opened on July 20 with a prayer by the native preacher, John Huss, and the singing of a hymn in Cherokee, accompanied by the somber notes of fife and drum of the Georgia Guard stationed nearby. After Currey's introductory remarks in which he implied that Ross was deluding the people, Ross rose to defend himself. "I am not a party man . . . [in] what I have done," he emphasized, "I have been actuated by a desire to promote the best interests of my people. I have no enmity to Mr. Ridge." John Ridge then took the opportunity to declare, "It is long since I have been accustomed to hear such language from him [Ross]." Ridge acknowledged his differences with Ross but stressed that he also had been moved by a sense of duty to his people. Calling for a reconciliation between Ross and Ridge, Schermerhorn concluded the speeches and asked to present a plan for harmony on the next day. By the time speech making had ended it was quite late, and debate on the annuity payment had not even begun. After two motions, one for individual payment and another for the traditional lump-sum allotment, the meeting was forced to recess until the next day.[27]

While the Cherokees slept Schermerhorn had workers construct a pulpit-like stand to be used at the next day's proceedings. When the commissioner was about to take the stand that morning, Ross interrupted him, suggesting the vote be completed first. Schermerhorn, seeing this as a ploy to finish the vote and then have the Cherokees drift away during his talk, insisted on going ahead. Ross yielded, and Schermerhorn began his address. Although Schermerhorn's secretary considered the commissioner's talk "excellent" and took notes on five or six sheets of paper while the Indians listened with "great gravity and serious attention," another observer noted that anxious Cherokees idled about during the three and one-half hour speech on President Jackson's sincerity and the liberal articles of the projected treaty worked out with Ridge and Boudinot. Again, the voting could not be completed. On the third day, July 22, the issue was settled when 2,225 Cherokees voted against the motion for individual payment, and only 114 supported it. Major Ridge immediately proposed an amendment to the resolution for lump sum payment so that none of the money would be used to pay legal fees. The Ridge faction used this as a pretext to gain sympathy for their cause by a number of speeches, but the amendment was withdrawn, and the motion was quickly passed by acclamation. Lieutenant M. W. Bateman, the regional disbursing agent, then turned over the annuity funds to the Cherokee treasurer.[28]

Reporting these events, Schermerhorn declared that Ross had an "uncontrolled sway over the Indians," and that the Cherokees were dictatorially "drilled equal to a Swiss guard, *to do only what they were bidden.*" Nevertheless, the commissioner was not adverse to arranging treaty settlements with this alleged tyrant. Near the close of the meeting, he inquired if Ross had appointed a committee to meet with him and Governor Carroll, and when Ross said no, Schermerhorn requested that members of the two factions join him at the Cherokee agency on July 29. Ross declined, saying that the people were tired and hungry, and that the consensus of Cherokee leaders was not to meet the commissioners again until October.[29]

Discouraged by the discord at the meeting, Ross hoped to work out some accord with the Ridge faction without the interference of designing whites, and he asked Major Ridge and his son John to attend a special meeting in order to restore "brotherly confidence and harmony," a conference "purely Cherokee, and composed of a chosen few." On the morning of July 31, the two Ridges with 20 of their followers reined their horses at the chief's gate. Ross rose from his breakfast table to welcome the guests and asked as many as could get in to share his morning meal. They passed the day in pleasant conversation, but nothing was said of the difficulties. In fact, distrust and disharmony actually grew more intense. Many Cherokees questioned Ross's motives for meeting with the Ridges, and rumors spread that Ross had joined the treaty faction.[30]

The breach between Ross and the Ridge faction widened when the Cherokee national press was seized in August 1835. Stand Watie, sometime editor of the *Cherokee Phoenix* and younger brother of Elias Boudinot, joined the notorious Georgia Guard and confiscated the press, types, books, and paper. The seizure occurred only hours before wagons sent by Ross arrived to remove the press to the Red Clay area for its protection. Ostensibly, the Ridge faction intended to reinvigorate the moribund paper by making it an open forum. When Ross complained of this outrage, Currey did nothing but throw unwarranted accusations at the chief. He even suggested that the press belonged to Boudinot, since he had financed its continuation through a fund-raising tour in the East, but even later when both parties requested the press returned, Currey would not accede, and the press was never recovered.[31]

John Howard Payne, essayist, poet, playwright, and composer, probably best known for his sentimental "Home, Sweet Home," drifted into Cherokee affairs at this time somewhat by accident. On a tour of the United States to promote subscription to a projected literary magazine, Payne passed through Georgia and heard that Ross possessed manuscripts by Charles Hicks that described the Cherokee oral traditions. He was eager to meet Ross, about whom he had heard numerous and contradictory stories. "I found Mr. Ross a different man, in every respect, from what I had heard him represented to be," Payne wrote some unknown correspondent, and further described Ross as

of the middle size, rather under than over . . . he is mild, intelligent, and entirely unaffected. I told him my object. He received me with cordiality. He said he regretted that he had only a log cabin, of but one room to invite me to, but he would make no apologies. . . . From a visitor, I afterwards learned how the principal chief of so many thousands happened to live in such discomfort. The story contains the story at this moment of the whole nation. . . . It was . . . hard conduct which had driven the principal chief to one of the humblest dwellings in his nation.[32]

Ross convinced Payne to stay for the October General Council where he could learn firsthand from some of the ancient members of the tribe the long and melancholy history of the Cherokees. Payne awoke the day before the meeting to view the spectacle of Cherokees streaming by Ross's home enroute to the nearby Red Clay Council Ground: "The train halted at the humble gate of the principal chief: he stood ready to receive them. Everything was noiseless. The party, entering, loosened the blankets which were loosely rolled and flung over their backs, and hung them, with their tin cups and other paraphernalia attached, upon the fence. The chief approached them. They formed diagonally in two lines, and each, in silence, drew near to give his hand."[33]

On the first day of the General Council, October 12, 1835, Ross delivered his annual message and reiterated many of the points he had made at the May meeting. In regard to the United States Senate's action on the amount to be given for Cherokee lands Ross was specific. Since President Jackson had merely requested that the Senate Committee on Indian Affairs bring up the question, he had led the Senate to believe that he actually had nothing formal to submit. Under these circumstances, Ross believed that the action of the Senate was "nothing more than a mere expression of opinion, which cannot be obligatory on the President." Moreover, the resolution of the Senate was not official and Ross felt that there was "no committal on the part of the delegation," nor were the Cherokees obligated by the Senate's action. The assembled Cherokees vigorously disapproved the Senate's resolution, so another Cherokee delegation was appointed to go to Washington. Ross closed the meeting with his characteristic challenge: "Let us be united . . . and leave a character on the page of history that will never dishonor the name of the Cherokee nation."[34]

The remainder of the council was spent in taking up various propositions offered by Commissioner Schermerhorn. William Carroll, Schermerhorn's associate commissioner, had been in the Cherokee Nation only at the late July meeting, which Ross did not attend, and confessed that his rheumatism was so painful that he could not participate in future negotiations. His ailments did not hamper his work with the Tennessee legislature, for he secured acts to extend the laws of Tennessee over the Cherokees and to prevent the tribe from settling on the state's domain. The General Council rebuffed Schermerhorn's petitions for a hearing, so the indignant commissioner produced a manufactured document which discredited Ross and the mixed-blood Cherokee leadership. The drift of his arguments was that Ross and his supporters had somehow renounced their claim to Cherokee citizenship when they accepted the terms of the Cherokee treaties of 1817 and 1819. Ross would in later times find it necessary to answer these recurrent charges, but at this point he simply termed Schermerhorn's address "irrelevant and ungracious."[35]

In explaining Schermerhorn's aggressive actions toward Ross, the preacher's biographer revealed that the commissioner viewed his confrontation with Ross in cosmic dimensions. He actually saw Ross as the "Devil in Hell." Moreover, Schermerhorn's desire for success was prompted by his hope of attaining a personal reward from the Jackson administration, perhaps a government position in the future Indian state.[36]

During the October session, Ross asked for a meeting of the two factions to work out the accord he had sought in July. Five men of the Ross faction met with a like number from the Ridges' group, and they agreed to "bury in oblivion all unfriendly feelings, and act unitedly in any treaty arrangements with the United States." This apparent harmony resulted in the appointment of twenty men to work out the difficulties between the United States and the Cherokee Nation, either on the Red Clay Council Ground or at Washington. Of the twenty, Ross and sixteen others were from the antitreaty faction, while John Ridge, Elias Boudinot, and Charles Vann represented the treaty party. The proportion of men within the committee was supposed to be roughly equivalent to the strength of their adherents.[37]

Commissioner Schermerhorn saw an opportunity for success and arranged to meet with the ad hoc committee on the afternoon of October 27, 1835, at Red Clay. He presented an elaborate set of proposals carefully worded with occasional blank spaces for negotiating monetary claims, but this bargaining piece contained only slight modifications from the earlier one negotiated with the Ridges and still retained the standard sum of five million dollars. The committee questioned Schermerhorn about his activities and his proposed treaty. Members of the committee were willing to overlook the inadequacy of his credentials, which came from the secretary of war rather than the president; they would waive the objection that he represented only half of the commission appointed, and they even were willing to disregard the fact that his credentials allowed him simply to negotiate a treaty and not to sign one. In fact, all these objections could be relaxed, and they would even forget Schermerhorn's unpleasant remarks about Ross and other mixed-blood council members. But the articles of this treaty, they asserted, had "no real variation from those against which the Cherokee Nation have already openly and formally protested." Schermerhorn's treaty lay unsigned, but the resilient commissioner advised Ross that he would proceed with the prearranged council at New Echota in December. "If the Cherokee people refuse the terms of a treaty," he warned, "on their own heads must rest the consequences."[38]

On Saturday evening, November 7, shortly before midnight, as Ross and John Howard Payne sat peacefully at the Red Hill cabin, a band of about twenty-five armed Georgia Guards burst in and arrested the two men. The rough intruders hastily gathered up what public papers they could find and, when the leader, a certain Sergeant Young, began to riffle through Payne's personal belongings, the poet protested. "Hold your damned tongue," Young sneered and struck him across the face. The Georgia Guards then carried their prisoners through the night in a torrent of rain some twenty-four miles to the Old Moravian mission at Springplace within the chartered limits of Georgia. Payne must have thought it ironic that as they rode along, one guard hummed the tune of "Home, Sweet Home." During the days ahead Ross and Payne began to gather clues as to the cause of their arrest. Payne was believed to be an abolitionist, perhaps a French spy, and Ross was accused of impeding the census of the Cherokees; often the names of Colonel Bishop and Major Currey were heard in the background.[39]

After a brief meeting with Bishop and a longer interview with John Ridge, who had discovered their plight, Ross was released on November 16. Ross may have partially bought his freedom when he wrote Governor Gilmer of Georgia, implying that nothing could really be settled until a delegation with sufficient powers reached Washington, and promising as leader that "no exertion shall be wanting on my part to favor its adjustment." Payne was released four days after Ross. Although both Payne and Ross were convinced that Currey and Schermerhorn were the instigators of the plot, it seems more reasonable to assume that the Georgia Guard simply possessed an exaggerated sense of power.[40]

The harmony which had bloomed in October began to fade in November. Boudinot resigned his appointment as a member of the bipartisan delegation—perhaps because he knew the Washington negotiations with Ross as leader would fare no better than the interviews with Schermerhorn, or perhaps because he had more definite plans. He alleged that Ross had expanded the delegation in disregard of the compact which called for only nineteen members. Actually

Ross appointed another member on the insistence of some Cherokee citizens who felt themselves underrepresented and only after the approval of the General Council. John Ridge became incensed when publications appeared in the *Knoxville Register* over Payne's signature recounting his imprisonment and including a plea entitled "The Cherokee Nation to the People of the U. States." In this polemic Payne embraced so entirely the sentiments of the Ross faction that Ridge thought it had been prepared at Ross's suggestion. Ridge found the tract "diametrically opposite" his views and asked that his name be withdrawn as a member of the delegation. Ross countered that his views were not set on any fixed course and that Payne had written the account based on his own impressions. Ridge must have accepted these explanations, for he remained a part of the delegation and journeyed on to Washington.[41]

Shortly after his departure, Ross received a note from Currey enclosing correspondence from Secretary of War Cass and Commissioner of Indian Affairs Elbert Herring. Cass wrote that it would be "utterly useless . . . for the proposed delegation to come here." Moreover, Cass told Schermerhorn: "It is out of the question to attempt to make an arrangement with a part of the nation. You will therefore relinquish any such expectation." Both Ross and Schermerhorn paid little heed to Cass's letter; Ross with a number of other delegates departed for Washington on December 2, 1835, while Schermerhorn prepared for the meeting at New Echota to be held on December 21.[42]

Ross sought in his propositions to the federal government in 1834 and 1835 some alternative to a general Cherokee removal. Always acknowledging the backward condition of his people, he nevertheless made the extraordinary proposal of United States citizenship for the tribe, a step admittedly ahead of its time. In more moderate offers, Ross followed the will and direction of the Cherokees as well as his conscience, but he occasionally left his people too uninformed of Washington proceedings to make intelligent decisions. Moreover, Ross did not follow through on promises made at Washington to recommend the proposal treaty to his people after the Senate concurred with Jackson. The chief was perhaps concerned with the disruptive situation the Cherokees would have faced had he gone with

Andrew Ross's scheme in 1834 or the Ridges' plan in early 1835. Leaderless but still resisting removal, the Cherokee Nation would have fallen an easy prey to every whim of Georgia or the federal government. Ross's resistance to removal was surely not motivated by a desire for personal gain. Having been driven from his home, deprived of his fields and ferry, unable to secure the Cherokee Nation's annuities, threatened by his own people, intimidated by federal officials, and even imprisoned by the Georgia Guard, Ross must have felt his course of action profitless. Service must have been part of his motivation. Yet he was challenged by members of his own faction when he sought harmony with the treaty proponents at the same time that he was blamed for acts of violence by resisters to removal. Within the next few weeks Ross's opponents sealed the fate of the Cherokee Nation by signing a document which became the dividing wedge so dreaded by the chief.

5

THE TREATY OF
NEW ECHOTA

THE REVEREND John F. Schermerhorn, turned federal commissioner, had a preacher's penchant for proselyting, but during his six-month sojourn in the Cherokee Nation he could count barely one new soul solidly converted to removal. He was further distressed that he was recalled at the very moment when he felt he could achieve glory by completing a removal treaty. The commissioner already had sent out a notice for the Cherokees to meet with him and his fellow commissioner at New Echota on the first day of winter in 1835. With Ross in Washington, the commissioner saw a chance to effect a treaty, despite general Cherokee opposition and official orders to the contrary. The ever-ailing Tennessee governor William Carroll again failed to arrive, but neither this nor anything else deterred Schermerhorn.[1]

Major Ridge and his close-knit supporters arrived at New Echota December 19, and the bulk of protreaty troops gathered three days later. The meeting convened on December 22. In the following two days Schermerhorn addressed the assembled Cherokees "in his usual style, only a little more so," as one Ross adherent put it. Benjamin F. Currey, the federal emigration agent, was reading the proposed treaty when the roof of the house caught fire, and the gathering quickly scattered. One pro-Ross bystander thought the fire "emblematical of the indignation of Heaven at the unlawful proceedings within." Nevertheless, the reading of the treaty was completed, and Currey suggested appointing a committee to discuss its terms. A committee of twenty was designated, which included Ross's principal opponents—Major Ridge, Elias Boudinot, John

Gunter, Archilla Smith, and the chief's brother, Andrew. On December 28 the assembled Cherokees were not surprised to learn that the committee had concurred with the suggested treaty, and these same men were elected by the assembly to close the settlement. Also, a committee of thirteen was delegated to carry the completed document to Washington. On the evening of December 29 the committee reconvened, and according to a Ross supporter, "About midnight, the fatal act was committed."[2]

On the day the New Echota group assembled, Chief Ross was enroute to Washington. He had stopped briefly at Salem, North Carolina, to visit his daughter Jane, who had recently enrolled at the Moravian Female Academy. On January 2 the Ross delegates presented their credentials and requested an interview with Secretary of War Lewis Cass and President Jackson. At a private interview with Cass four days later, they learned that the president would not increase the offer of five million dollars, that no individual reservations would be allowed, and that all financial stipulations would be paid to individual Cherokees and not to tribal authorities. At a meeting the next day the Ross contingent met with Jackson, who implied that the group could present propositions to the government which would be considered and acted upon. In a few days what had seemed an amicable beginning would sour.[3]

About January 12 or 13 Ross received word of Schermerhorn's "Christmas trick." Unaware of both the signers and the significance of this treaty, the Ross delegation issued only a mild protest to Secretary Cass. Soon after the removal delegates arrived in early February they wrote Ross informing him of the New Echota proceedings and enclosing a copy of the treaty. Hoping that they could work out an agreement with Ross as they had been instructed by the federal negotiators, they appealed to him to assist in ratifying the treaty. The tone of the correspondence was moderate and sincere, but the treaty faction was firm in its resolve to go ahead with the New Echota bargain. Ross never answered this appeal, feeling that to answer it would, in a sense, be formal recognition of the treaty party and an indirect sanction for its acts.[4]

Ross quickly realized the full import of the document and, when a Cherokee messenger brought a protest against the New Echota treaty signed by some three thousand Cherokees, there was no question on the subsequent course of the delegation. Ross forwarded this protest to Secretary of War Cass. Surprisingly, the signatures of both John Ridge and Stand Watie were attached to the accompanying letter. Shortly these two treaty advocates showed their true sentiments, however, by joining their relatives and signing their names to the alleged treaty. To purge themselves further, Ridge and Watie attacked Ross for what they termed his self-perpetuating and dictatorial reign. Ross's response was to criticize the younger Ridge's action, "his fourth entire revolution in politics within as many months: varying as often as the moon, without the excuse of lunacy for his changes." Moreover Ross discovered the warm reception earlier displayed by the federal government quickly cooled. Commissioner of Indian Affairs Elbert Herring wrote that "you are laboring under extreme misapprehension in believing that you have been recognized by the Department as the duly constituted representatives of the Cherokee Nation." Herring believed their misunderstanding arose from the courtesy of Cass and Jackson. Ross probably knew that it was not his lack of understanding, but Jackson's ignorance of the bargain Schermerhorn had made.[5]

Ross sent word to George Lowrey, assistant principal chief, to call the Cherokees together to protest the Schermerhorn treaty. Currey, the federal emigration agent, had thought the Indians fairly well satisfied with the treaty, and he advised Commissioner Herring that he could "date their [the Cherokees'] late dissatisfaction with the receipt of letters from that stubborn & perverse Chief Ross & his coadjutors." Whether Ross had this kind of power or not, the National Committee and National Council convened at Red Clay in the bitter cold weather of February 1836 and passed a resolution protesting the work of the unauthorized New Echota gathering. Rushed to Ross by loyal followers who had canvassed the Cherokee Nation and obtained over fourteen thousand signatures, the document was presented to Secretary of War Cass in late February. Ross also exhibited several letters of persons acquainted with the New Echota proceedings. Schermerhorn had estimated the assembly at from three hundred to five hundred persons, but the tally on the only vote taken on the treaty had been seventy-five for and seven against. Most Cherokees had not attended, since the leading men had admonished them to stay away.[6]

The treaty that Schermerhorn concluded at New Echota was similar to the one which had been rejected by the Cherokees in May and again in October of 1835. The principal provision, including the supplemental articles demanded by Jackson, was that the Cherokees would receive five million dollars for their lands east of the Mississippi in exchange for the lands guaranteed the western Cherokees in 1828 and 1833. From that amount, five hundred thousand dollars was deducted for an additional tract of land of eight hundred thousand acres, the so-called Neutral Lands. The United States agreed that the lands as listed in the treaty would never be included within the jurisdiction of the United States without Cherokee consent. Two articles were struck from the document at Jackson's demand. These clauses had allowed Ross to designate selected Cherokees for preemption rights and provided payment for the claims of the reservees under the treaties of 1817 and 1819; these provisions would be separate from the normal evaluations. Perhaps Major Ridge and other treaty supporters had hoped to gain Ross's acquiescence with these provisions, but Jackson insisted on total removal, so the offending passages were deleted. In the place of preemptions and reservations, six hundred thousand dollars was allotted to pay for Cherokee treaty claims.[7]

Ross and his fellow delegates worked vigorously against these terms. Several drafts of objections in Ross's handwriting illustrate the development of his thought. At one point he contemplated a description of the long train of Cherokee–United States negotiations dating from the first treaties. In another draft he listed several general objections and then took the treaty apart article by article to demonstrate its unfairness and inadequacy. What he finally presented to the United States Senate the day after debates began on March 7, 1836, was one of the most elaborate protests ever sent to Congress by the Cherokees. It detailed events which had led to the signing of the New Echota treaty and demonstrated the malfeasance of Schermerhorn and Currey. The delegation declared emphatically that the Senate should not ratify "a treaty made without their [the Cherokees'] authority, false upon its face, and against the known wishes of the nation." The antitreaty delegates closed their remarks "resting upon the sacred rights of the Cherokee Nation, so often recognized and solemnly guarantied on the faith of treaties, the delegation now appeal to the sympathies, the honor, good faith, and magnanimity of the United States . . . the destiny of the Cherokee people [is] in the hands of the American Senate."[8]

Ross and his associates were not alone in questioning the validity of the Schermerhorn treaty. Major William M. Davis, who had been appointed as an enrolling agent for emigrating Cherokees in 1831, had observed Schermerhorn's tactics through 1835 and 1836. Davis declared himself an impartial friend of both Cherokee factions and of Jackson's supporters. He had served Jackson in Kentucky and fought beside him at New Orleans in the War of 1812. Davis considered Schermerhorn's appointment "a most unfortunate selection" and his policy a "series of blunders first to last."[9]

While some of the accusations he made were vigorously denied, two charges made by Davis were never adequately refuted. Schermerhorn's meeting at New Echota was carried out without the confidence, advice, or consent of the regularly constituted authorities of the Cherokee Nation, and, had he had even double his estimate of five hundred persons, it still would have been an illegal body carrying out an unauthorized act. Schermerhorn also took his treaty to the valley towns in North Carolina and, although he prepared a barbecue feast in the midst of those hungry hill people, only two came, and they out of curiosity. More important, Davis's charge that Schermerhorn had used his influence to drive a wedge between the factions and that he had aided Currey in fomenting discontent between Ross and his opponents was singularly correct.[10]

The antitreaty delegates during this time were diligently attempting to secure the annuity payment, partially because it would give them recognition as constituted representatives. More important, the delegation was hard pressed for funds, and even its sympathetic creditors were demanding payment. The treaty faction did not face such embarrassments, for each member of the delegation received about twelve hundred dollars to meet his Washington expenses. Two appeals finally brought an answer from the Office of Indian Affairs. Commissioner Herring reminded Ross and his colleagues that their presence in Washington was in defiance of the president's "express prohibition." He further stated that the year's annuity distribution had not been determined by the Cherokee Nation in a vote, and that this stipulation would have to be met before the money could be paid. Ross protested this "useless and temporizing course," but numerous appeals brought no answer.[11]

A petition to Congress ultimately gained a response from Herring, who acknowledged that about a thousand dollars was due the eastern Cherokees from an improper payment to the western band, but even this amount was not paid, and he insisted that the regular annuity would have to be brought up for another election. One significant outgrowth of the petition, however, was that Congress appropriated the twenty-years' interest which had accrued from the Cherokee Treaty of 1804, not ratified until 1824.[12]

When the New Echota treaty finally came before the Senate, it did not engender the kind of debate which the Indian Removal Bill had produced. Henry Clay of Kentucky introduced a resolution which would have negated the treaty, but his amendment was rejected. The narrowness of the vote convinced the protreaty Senate faction to marshal its forces for the final poll. The final vote on the treaty was taken May 18, 1836, and, with two senators absent, the tally stood at thirty-one for approval and fifteen opposed—only one vote more than the necessary two-thirds majority to bind the pact. The vote did not divide on the same sectional lines as had the congressional debates on the Removal Bill of 1830. Senator Thomas Hart Benton of Missouri declared that the free states' votes actually secured for the South a treaty which would convert "Indian soil to slave soil." Since fourteen free state votes "precisely balanced and neutralized the slave state negatives," Cherokee considerations again had been caught in the morass of regional and slavery issues.[13]

Ross still held out hope that the House of Representatives would reject the treaty by refusing to appropriate the money, but this did not happen. Ross may have been unduly encouraged by some members of Congress to expect that the treaty would not be sanctioned. There were even hints that he had received money from some members to sustain the delegation during its stay in Washington. The treaty was signed by President Jackson and proclaimed on May 23, 1836. The Cherokees had two years to remove to their new western homes.[14]

The majority of the delegation had returned to the Cherokee Nation after the Senate vote, but Ross remained to observe the action of the House of Representatives and to work out his objections to the New Echota treaty in a full statement to be published in a pamphlet and distributed in the East. Written in the form of a letter to an unnamed, curious friend who had inquired why Ross's name was not attached to the treaty, Ross spoke to an audience of easterners who he felt were unaware of the treaty's impact. He insisted that it did not possess the advantages to the Indians unwary easterners might imagine. In fact, Ross emphasized, because of the terminology in the treaty the Cherokees might well find themselves in a similar predicament again. The treaty did not guarantee the Cherokees permanent rights to the lands, but what further frightened Ross was the use of the phrase "such land shall *revert* to the United States" in reference to their western lands. Ross saw in this a sinister maneuver to eventually take western Cherokee lands. The unidentified inquirer also asked why Ross's name was included as the head of a committee to evaluate Cherokee claims against the United States in relation to removal. In fact Ross's name had been added to Schermerhorn's treaty without the chief's knowledge or sanction. When the committee was formed, not only Ross but all the anti-treaty men who were named in the New Echota document refused to serve, so their places were filled by members of the Ridge faction.[15]

In the address Ross took up in some detail the recurring charge that he actually had no rights as a Cherokee because he had once accepted a reservation with a view to becoming a United States citizen. Ross insisted that the reservation was *"special"* and *"untrammelled by conditions."* The Treaty of 1819 provided that the intended reservee was to give notice to the agent that he planned to live there. Ross's notice to Meigs in 1819 was that he proposed to "occupy and enjoy permanently" his reservation, not "reside" on it, and in truth he never lived on the land and never left the Cherokee Nation. This was in accordance with the discussions on that treaty in Washington in 1819. Ross also had to face charges that the reservation in question was not his alone but belonged partially to John Watts who, along with other members of the treaty party, accused Ross of depriving him of his property. Watts, however, had been one of the early emigrants under the Treaty of 1817 and, according to its provisions, had relinquished all rights to lands east of the Mississippi. In the Treaty of 1819, Ross was given exclusive rights to his reservation.[16]

Ross returned to the Cherokee Nation and Red Hill; sometime after his arrival home, he called for a General Council on September 15, 1836, at the Red Clay Council Ground and invited the Ridges and members of their faction to the meeting. That date was chosen in order to compete with the meeting the Ridges had earlier called and set for September 12. Knowing that they would have no chance of any sizable gathering in competition with Ross, the Ridges postponed their meeting. Ross also invited Brigadier General John E. Wool, who had been placed in command of United States troops in the Cherokee Nation. Wool was to prevent hostilities that might arise in reaction to the treaty. He found that duty far from pleasant and hoped that the Cherokees soon would be moved beyond the reach of white men "who, like vultures, are watching, ready to . . . strip them of every thing they have or expect from the Government of the United States."[17]

Laboring under ambiguous orders, Wool met Ross about August 20, 1836, at Athens, Tennessee, and acquiesced in the chief's request for a Cherokee General Council, although Wool was careful to warn Ross of the president's disapproval. Wool's belief that "no good will result from it" was overruled by his knowledge that Ross "whenever he pleases, can unite the whole nation, at least a large majority, in a war against the United States." In fact, Wool had become so convinced of Ross's pacifism that he discharged volunteer troops on the eve of the General Council meeting. Wool seems to have been partially swayed by Ross's captivating personality and later was censured for permitting the General Council session. He eventually requested transfer from the Cherokee post. The ever-circulating emigration agent, Currey, missed the gathering but expressed disapproval of Wool's actions, maintaining that "had I . . . been present & had control of the troops Mr. Ross & his pretended authorities . . . would now be in confinement." Nevertheless, Wool won the gratitude of the Cherokees for his "honorable course . . . and . . . gentlemanly deportment."[18]

At the General Council meeting resolutions were passed declaring, in the best southern tradition, the New Echota pact "null and void" and unenforceable. Ross and several comrades also were dispatched again to Washington but were instructed first to proceed to the Cherokees west of the Mississippi so that in concert the two groups might overturn the treaty. Just prior to the delegation's departure, Wool delivered an order from the Department of War that no delegation would be received at Washington on the subject of modifying the treaty of 1835.[19]

Under provisions of the New Echota treaty, a committee was to evaluate Cherokee property before the federal government paid claims to emigrating Indians. Although Ross was included in the treaty as a member of this committee, he never served, and the group was composed generally of treaty party men. Governor Wilson Lumpkin was called out of retirement from his home in Athens, Georgia, and reluctantly accepted appointment with Governor William Carroll of Tennessee as United States commissioners to settle the Cherokee claims. Lumpkin had to suspend operations for a time and did not actually begin his work until December 1836 when a replacement for Carroll, who had been plagued with recurring ailments, arrived. During the interim, the appraising went ahead, and Ross's property was one of the early claims evaluated. Ross probably had not intended that his properties at Red Hill and Head of Coosa be appraised. One of the chief's anxious overseers, however, permitted the valuation. Ross's opponents saw this as a subtle acceptance of the inevitable execution of the treaty. Boudinot charged that by this act the chief fully assented to the treaty. Ross probably had come to believe that the treaty eventually would be enforced, but he now was working for some modification of its provisions. Ross's property valuations at Red Hill and Head of Coosa came to $23,665.75, making him one of the five wealthiest men in the Cherokee Nation, a distinction he shared with his brother Lewis and his old friend Major Ridge.[20]

Before Ross and his fellow delegates left for the West, letters had gone out to the western superintendent, William Armstrong, to arrest Ross if he tried to "incite opposition to the treaty." Ross met with little trouble there, however. Having retorted to Commissioner of Indian Affairs C. A. Harris in regard to Ross, "*I know with whom I have to do,*" Armstrong did not really know what to do with him and conveniently found himself busy with affairs at nearby Fort

Gibson. Ross and the eastern delegation arrived about November 20, and a meeting of the western Cherokee legislature was called for December 8. Apprised of the order for his arrest, Ross paid it little heed and continued visiting friends while awaiting the time of the meeting. The western Cherokee legislature met and passed resolutions opposing the "instrument purporting to be a treaty" and appointed a delegation to accompany Ross to Washington to work for a "final adjustment of the Cherokee difficulties."[21]

The joint delegation traveled by way of the eastern Cherokee Nation, as some of the western members wanted to see their old homes again. Ross had looked forward to a few days of relaxation at Red Hill but after only a night and parts of two days with his family, Ross received a note from his brother Lewis saying, "There is nothing more certain than you will be arrested if you remain a day at home." He advised his older brother "to put out from home tomorrow morning, and cross the Highwassee at Pattons ferry . . . and get to Athens without delay." The prospect of arrest was not exaggerated, as Lewis well knew, for he had been released from confinement only recently himself. As one of the Cherokee committee that was to manage Cherokee finances, Lewis had gathered with other members in order to settle the treasurer's accounts preparatory to his departure for the West. Late that night several of Wool's troops surrounded Martin's home, arrested those inside, and seized all the public papers. Wool soon released the Cherokees but kept the papers for a longer time, insisting that ex-Governor Lumpkin and the Cherokee claims evaluation committee needed them.[22]

From Red Hill Ross traveled to Knoxville, Tennessee, where the delegates purchased horses; bad roads made travel by stage impossible. They rode from Knoxville to Salem, North Carolina, where Ross visited Jane and where they were warmly received by the sympathetic Moravian missionaries. Improved roads allowed them to travel the remainder of the way by stage, and they arrived in Washington about February 9. At the capital the delegation discovered that a joint endeavor was no more productive than earlier meetings in altering the New Echota pact. Several notes passed between the Cherokees and the executive department, but no recognition or audience was obtained.[23]

In March 1837 Martin Van Buren, the "Red Fox" of Kinderhook, political protégé and personal choice of Jackson, was inaugurated as president. Ross and his associates sent a petition to the new president through his secretary of war, Joel R. Poinsett, setting forth two propositions—that new negotiations be initiated to settle United States–Cherokee relations and that the New Echota treaty be submitted to the whole Cherokee Nation in legislative session. Although Poinsett rejected their propositions he did consent to a personal meeting at which the Cherokees posed a disturbing question: What would be the action of the government if the Cherokees did not remove at the expiration of the two-year limit? Poinsett was not prepared to say, but the query must have been provoking. The delegation found the new administration amenable on past disputed issues, and for the first time in several years the Cherokees were able to receive their annuities without elections and entreaties. Realizing the influence of the delegates, Commissioner of Indian Affairs Harris renewed the annuity payment, hoping to conciliate them and to "forego their opposition to the execution of the treaty."[24]

During April 1837 Ross made a tour of the East, specifically to Philadelphia and New York. Ross probably visited John Howard Payne on this excursion, for the chief was working on another manuscript and, as Payne had assisted him with earlier addresses, he may have sought the poet's literary advice again. Payne may have introduced Ross to Job R. Tyson, the "Gentleman of Philadelphia" to whom the pamphlet was addressed. In the pamphlet Ross questioned the authority of the federal government to negotiate with a minor faction of the tribe but, more important, he noted precedents for negating Indian treaties that had been unfairly made. Although such reversals had the sanction of precedent and the endorsement of former Commissioner of Indian Affairs Thomas L. McKenney, when McKenney suggested reconsideration to Poinsett two years later in 1839, Poinsett replied: *"Colonel McKenney, Mr. Van Buren will never consent to undo anything that General Jackson has done."* Ross returned to Washington toward the end of April and before departing brought up several unsettled points with Poinsett, which were simply laid aside.[25]

During December 1836 Benjamin F. Currey had died, and Brigadier General Nathaniel Smith had taken his place as superintendent of emigration. Even during Ross's absence Smith was aware of the chief's influence as emigration increased or declined according to the tone of Ross's letters. Friends spread the news of his activities at Washington, and even nominal successes brought emigration registration to a standstill. Ross was back at Red Hill by the end of May and quickly sent out circulars calling a General Council for July 31 at the Red Clay Council Ground.[26]

Most federal officials in the Cherokee Nation at that time were positive that Ross would use the General Council to protest and vilify the New Echota pact. Wilson Lumpkin, still serving as the Cherokee claims evaluating commissioner, observed Ross's moves and found him a "very reserved, obscure and wary politician," the "Master Spirit" of opposition to the treaty; but Lumpkin was unable to discover any overt act that might legally incriminate the chief. As soon as the circulars were widely spread, emigration enrollment dwindled appreciably, but Brigadier General Smith was as unsure as Lumpkin why and did not know whether to blame what Ross said or merely his presence. Actually, there was some question whether Ross even could hold the General Council meeting, since Wool's General Order Number 74 had expressly forbidden further councils. The order was explicit that "even at the hazard of actual hostilities . . . they will be promptly repressed." Wool, however, had found his duties so distasteful that he had requested and received transfer, and Colonel William Lindsay was appointed to replace him in May 1837.[27]

Ross met Lindsay on June 22 at the Cherokee Agency, and the colonel, informing the chief that he felt compelled to follow Wool's earlier orders, vetoed the proposed General Council. Ross assured Lindsay that the purpose of the meeting was to report the work of the delegation recently returned from Washington. Ross seemed prepared to proceed in spite of Lindsay's orders, but a week before the scheduled meeting the colonel received a directive to allow it. Federal leniency was prompted partly by a desire to place another spokesman before the Cherokees to advocate acceptance of the treaty.[28]

Ross spoke to the General Council on August 3 and gave a detailed account of his mission to Arkansas and to Washington. Contrary to what he had promised Lindsay, the message showed distinct opposition to the treaty and he drifted into a description of the coun-

try to the West, which he considered "impossible for the whole nation to settle down in . . . permanently, with any reasonable hope of
enjoying prosperity and happiness." The next day John Mason, Jr.,
arrived in the Cherokee Nation as a special emissary of the federal
government and requested permission to speak to the General
Council on August 7. Mason's instructions were to use mild and
persuasive terms with the Cherokees, but to express firmly the intention of the government to carry out the terms of the pact.[29]

Mason traveled with George W. Featherstonhaugh, an English
naturalist whom he had met near Spring Place, North Carolina, and
invited to the General Council. On the stagecoach ride from Spring
Place to Red Clay, the Englishman observed "fine fat deer bounding
across the narrow wood road with their magnificent antlers. The
quail, too, were numerous, and the young birds large. The soil being derived from the lower Silurian limestone is very fertile, and
certainly I never saw heavier Indian corn than in two or three
settlements we passed." At the council ground they met Brigadier
General Smith and, after tea, they walked around the Red Clay
region. Featherstonhaugh took in everything and left a narrative:

There was a copious limestone spring on the bank of the stream, which gave
out a delicious cool water in sufficient quantities for this great multitude.
What contributed to make the situation extremely picturesque, was the
great number of beautiful trees growing in every direction. . . . Nothing
more Arcadian could be conceived than the picture which was presented;
but the most impressive feature, and that which imparted life to the whole,
was an unceasing current of Cherokee Indians . . . moving about in every
direction, and in the greatest order . . . their turbans, their dark coarse, lank
hair, their listless savage gait, and their swarthy Tartar countenances, reminded me of the Arabs from Barbary.

Featherstonhaugh, hearing stories of the amorous adventures of
Commissioner Schermerhorn, found that the slightest mention of
the Cherokee term for devil's horn set the Cherokee women to gig-
gling.[30]

Featherstonhaugh was especially impressed by the arrangements
for feeding this multitude. Upwards of fifteen head of cattle were
slaughtered every day, and twenty-four families were engaged in
cooking the provisions for the crowd of nearly three thousand. At
the center was Ross, the "sole director," who paid about three hundred dollars a day to furnish the necessities. Ross invited the Eng-

lishman to dine at Red Hill on August 6, where at noon the several guests were "taken to a room, upon the table of which a very plentiful dinner, singularly ill-cooked was placed. Neither our host nor his wife sat down to eat with us, the dinner, according to Cherokee custom, being considered to be provided for the guests. . . . I was helped to some meat, but could not tell what it was, or whether it passed for roast or boiled. It was afterwards explained to me that it was pork, first boiled in a pot with some beef, and then baked by itself afterwards."[31]

Mason delivered his address on August 7, horns and public criers announcing him. He stood under a stand near the General Council house while the hapless Cherokees listened gravely in the pouring rain. Although the Indians were attentive, the address seemed to make little impression on them; Ross called the speech a "Compound of the sweet and tartish." The next month Mason was back in Washington reporting his impressions of attitudes which he found decidedly opposed to removal "till they see the Federal bayonet on the fatal 23rd of May next levelled against the breast of the Cherokee." Mason was somewhat awed by Ross's power but clearly recognized that

with all his power, Ross cannot if he would change the course he has heretofore pursued, and to which he is held by the fixed determination of the people. . . . Were he, as matters now stand, to advise the Indians to acknowledge the treaty, he would at once forfeit their confidence, and probably his life. Yet, though unwavering in his opposition to the treaty, Ross's influence has constantly been exerted to preserve the peace of the country . . . opposition to the treaty on the part of the Indians is unanimous and sincere . . . it is not a mere political game played by Ross for the maintenance of his ascendancy in the tribe.[32]

The remainder of the Red Clay General Council was taken up in preparation of resolutions against the New Echota treaty and in the appointment of another delegation to attend the coming session of Congress. At Washington Ross later would find Mason an overly optimistic ally and the delegation's work unrewarding. As the October General Council had been dispensed with, the Ross deputation set out for Washington on September 12 on horseback and, after a short visit at the Moravian Academy at Salem, North Carolina, they traveled to the capital.[33]

The New Echota pact must have been especially difficult for Ross

to accept, for he arrived in Washington in early 1836, probably prepared to negotiate some sort of removal arrangement. With John
Ridge and Stand Watie as members of the delegation, Ross would
have been compelled to make concessions, if only to maintain
Cherokee unity. Certainly the discrepancy between the five million
dollar allotment set by the Senate the year before and Ross's bid for
twenty million dollars could have been adjusted, for Ross was no
unbending arbiter but a practical politician long accustomed to
compromise. Yet when faced with a ready-made document signed
by a small coterie of his opposition and administered by federal officials who had repeatedly assailed him, Ross set himself rigidly
against removal. The Jackson administration, weary of Ross's yearly
delaying tactics, welcomed the treaty, legally tainted as it was,
while Congress, caught in sectional controversies, narrowly assented. Even though Ross discovered more amiable associates
among the Van Buren administration, he announced no new plan
and merely maintained his intransigent course. The next year would
call for extreme concessions as he exerted his energies to undo the
treaty's harsh conditions.

6

YEAR OF DECISION

MEMBERS of the Ross delegation appointed for the 1837–38 congressional term at Washington desperately prepared for a final stand against the New Echota pact. They faced an ominous deadline of May 23, 1838, the time set for completion of Cherokee removal.

The delegates arrived in Washington in early October 1837 and on Saturday October 7, they presented their credentials to Secretary of War Joel R. Poinsett, who invited them for an interview the following Monday. A few days later they met with President Van Buren but, perhaps because of the presence of former Governor John Forsyth of Georgia, now a congressman, no important business was discussed. At another meeting Poinsett solicited the aid of Chief Ross in bringing the Seminole War in Florida to an end. The war was caused by government attempts to carry out a removal treaty signed in 1832, which had been repudiated by the majority of the Seminoles. Although no pacifist, Ross certainly had recognized the folly of making war on the United States. Federal officials knew his views and hoped the chief could use his influence among the Seminoles as he had among his people in quelling armed disturbances.[1]

Ross had been approached confidentially on the Seminole affair as early as July 1837 by Colonel John H. Sherburne, a private emissary from Poinsett, who had led Ross to believe that if he could quiet the Seminole firebrand Osceola, the federal government would consider this a favor to repay. Sherburne also indicated that he and his superiors were so eager to see the Seminole disturbances quieted that "money will be no object to the Government." Ross was dubious of confidential and unofficial promises, and it was not until he arrived in Washington that he consented to help. Nevertheless, he promised Sherburne that if the Department of War requested his assistance, he would write a letter to the leading insurgents which could be delivered as an address by a special deputation of the Cherokees. Ross had carefully questioned Sherburne on his authority and intentions. One probing query stands out: "Are you authorized by the President of the U States to guarantee safety and protection to the lives of Oseola and such others of the Chiefs as may compose the Seminole delegation?"[2]

With assurances from Poinsett as to the authenticity of Sherburne's mission, four trusted Cherokees were commissioned to go to Florida, carrying with them Ross's address. He spoke to the Seminole chiefs as a stranger, but also as a brother and one who well understood the torment and anguish of division and removal. He wrote: "I know that a brave people when driven to a state of desperation, would sooner die under the strong arm of power, than to shrink and die the death of the coward. But I will speak to you as a friend, and with the voice of reason advise you, as a small but brave people, to act the part of a noble race, and at once throw yourselves upon the magnanimity and justice of the American people." Ross guaranteed the justice and sincerity of the United States and conveyed the assurances from Poinsett that a liberal treaty would be made.[3]

Ross's address and the mediation of the Cherokee delegation convinced some of the Seminole leaders to accompany their Indian brothers to Fort Mellon, headquarters of Major General Thomas S. Jesup, the area commander. The solemn entourage entered the fort "with the white scarf of peace rippling over our heads," but the wary Jesup gave the group a cool reception. A recalcitrant band of other Seminoles alarmed Jesup, who arrested the chiefs and warriors at Fort Mellon and shipped them to more secure quarters at Saint Augustine where Osceola was being held. Feeling that the Seminoles would hold them responsible for this unchivalrous act, the Cherokees pursued the captive band. At Saint Augustine they convinced the Seminole chiefs that the act was committed without their knowledge or sanction. Colonel Sherburne was present and suggested that the Cherokees accompany him to Washington where a settlement might be arranged to end the fighting. The swamps of the Florida Everglades would now be exchanged for the morass of Washington politics.[4]

They arrived in Washington on December 30, 1837, and within two days Ross sent off an angry letter to Poinsett vigorously protesting the arrest of the Seminole chiefs while they were negotiating for peace under a flag of truce. Further correspondence also revealed the unwillingness of the federal government to honor all the expenses of the Cherokee delegation to the Seminoles. In regard to Jesup's conduct, it might have been too much to expect a soldier to play the statesman, but certainly Poinsett should have fulfilled that role. With Sherburne's promises of federal obligations and limitless funds still fresh in his mind, Ross was disgusted that Poinsett would agree to pay less than a tenth of the amount requested by the travel-weary Cherokees; but eventually Ross had to settle for that amount.[5]

Other Washington negotiations proved equally frustrating. John Mason, Jr., had returned to Washington prior to Ross's arrival and was commissioned by Poinsett to carry on unofficial negotiations with the Cherokee delegation. The Cherokees agreed that Ross and Edward Gunter, a prominent Cherokee and a relative of Chief Ross, should participate in these private discussions. In conversations with Mason, Ross posed alternatives to the New Echota treaty similar to those that had been attempted with the Jackson administration. Hoping that the Van Buren regime might be more conciliatory, Ross suggested a large cession of Cherokee lands. Ross seemed confident from these early talks that Mason would prove more amenable to Cherokee demands than former government agents had been. In reporting prospects to friends in the Cherokee Nation, Ross may have been too optimistic, but he also wrote on several occasions of the serious and far-reaching adjustments the Cherokees faced. Ross realized that along with the forfeiture of Cherokee national lands the tribe would have to relinquish part of its national rights.[6]

Soon Ross and Gunter discovered that Mason was officially bound, if not personally disposed, to adhere to the Treaty of New Echota. Mason stated at one time "that if you [were] . . . to enter a compact precisely similar in every respect, your people would conform to its provisions without a murmur." Ross and Gunter explained that they held the confidence of the Cherokees because they had not abused it and, should they accede to United States demands, they would quickly lose that respect. They insisted that the Chero-

kees would no more readily accept the recommendation of the delegation to embrace the treaty, than Congress would follow "without
a murmur" a suggestion from President Van Buren to discard the
treaty. Nonetheless, Mason had the concurrence of the president,
and Poinsett maintained that removal would proceed as planned.[7]

Ross had hoped the western Cherokees would aid their eastern
brothers, and when his nephew William Shorey Coodey informed
him that the chiefs had not submitted a proposal to the tribe for
sending a delegation to Washington, Ross was surprised at their
apathy. Ross confided to Coodey that "the present administration is
doubtless afraid of the missiles from the Old Hickory stubble, and is
seeking a shelter behind the Senate." The congressional chambers
proved a suitable shelter. With little headway made in the executive
branch, the Cherokees turned to the legislative branch with a petition. The Senate printed the petition but took no action, while the
House of Representatives heard Georgia representatives give dire
warnings of a "Cherokee War" and eventually decided to table the
document by a decisive vote of 123 to 80. Nevertheless, Ross maintained his confidence that Congress eventually would advise the
president to negotiate a new arrangement with the tribe. Ross assured Assistant Principal Chief George Lowrey that the delegation
had "not yet abandoned our past," and he urged firmness and pacifism during the crisis.[8]

Ross's letters from Washington to his friends in the Cherokee Nation continued to have a marked effect on the program of emigration
and enrollment. Brigadier General Nathaniel Smith, the emigration
superintendent, noted that not one in five hundred was preparing to
move, and he wrote his superiors that one group of emigrants, after
traveling thirty miles along the removal route, stopped and returned
home upon hearing that Ross might gain a new treaty. The commissioner of Indian affairs was so upset at these reports that he sent
Smith a full report of negotiations between Mason and Ross, contending that it demonstrated that the Cherokees had been misled.
Actually, Ross was honest in his appraisals of Cherokee prospects;
his supporters in the Cherokee Nation probably were not. Smith
used the material in a widely publicized address to the Cherokees,
hoping to show them that they must now accept the inevitable and
begin removing. These maneuvers had little effect, for even several

weeks after Smith's address they showed little inclination to move. Indeed, the document had the reverse effect for, upon hearing of the address, Cherokee runners went throughout the country to get signatures on a petition protesting removal. Smith believed that no general enrollment would begin until Ross stated there was no other choice and, as long as he was absent, the Indians held out hope.[9]

On one occasion Ross wrote of his weariness of these constant accusations: "When obeying the will of my people, I have been grossly charged by others with controlling that will—When I advised the observance of patience and forbearance under the reliance of the faith of treaties, with the hope that the U. States would in the end be just—I have been unblushingly accused with holding out false hopes to the Cherokee people and a betrayal of their confidence!" Perhaps the reality of removal was finally becoming apparent to Ross. During the first months of 1838, Ross evolved another program for the Cherokees, a plan by which the Cherokees could direct and manage their own emigration. Ross wrote of his plan to John Howard Payne but, unsure of his own sentiments and fearing that the Cherokees were not yet ready to accept removal, asked that his thoughts be kept confidential.[10]

Perhaps Ross was able to forget his despair momentarily as he read lighthearted letters from his young relatives attending private academies at Lawrenceville, New Jersey. Araminta Ross, the daughter of Lewis Ross, wrote cheerful notes that were decidedly partisan. She protested the actions of President Van Buren, advised her uncle to "cut his head off," and wrote of her wish to be a man so she could better demonstrate Cherokee courage. Araminta's brothers, John McDonald Ross and Robert Daniel Ross, also wrote Ross of their studies at Lawrenceville Classical and Commercial High School. John in his senior year was valedictorian of the class of 1838. William Potter Ross, eldest son of Elizabeth Ross, received his uncle's financial support while in school, so he often forwarded information about various costs, which he considered much too high. Ambitious and politically astute, the young man asked for copies of Ross's political tracts and once told of a visit to Princeton College which he hoped to enter the next year. Ross answered this delightful correspondence as often as time would allow.[11]

In spite of their despondency, the Cherokees held firmly to their decision to remain on their ancestral lands. General Smith reported that the Cherokees had discovered that Ross and Gunter had instructed their overseers to begin planting crops, and this caused even greater reluctance to enroll for removal. Lewis Ross often served his brother as pulse to the Cherokee heartbeat when the chief was in Washington. At one point, "tired to death," he wrote Ross in Washington that it might be best, unless something could be accomplished soon, to tell the Cherokees that nothing else could be done and that they must accept removal.[12]

Governor George R. Gilmer of Georgia suggested to Poinsett that the only way to get the Cherokees on the move was to induce Ross to return and urge removal. Gilmer seemed more perceptive than many other officials, for he noted Cherokee suspicions and believed that even Ross might lose his power if he attempted to make a contract with the government. He thought personal persuasion might help and, in a complimentary letter to Ross, Gilmer emphasized the "law of necessity." He contrasted the dire prospect of using military force to remove the Cherokees, with the liberal compensation that could be furnished them to carry out their own removal. Gilmer believed that Ross could receive great personal satisfaction by saving his whole tribe with a peaceable removal. The governor's letter failed to change Ross's views.[13]

Early on the morning of March 10, 1838, Lewis Hildebrand, a Cherokee of the Ross persuasion, delivered to the chief a protest from the Cherokee Nation containing more than fifteen thousand signatures. Certainly a great many were invalid, for the total number of the tribe scarcely exceeded fifteen thousand persons; yet the document demonstrated again the Cherokees' firm commitment to remaining in their homelands and, no doubt, strengthened Ross in his position. He immediately presented the document with a short petition to Congress, but the Sub-Treasury Bill had so engrossed the two chambers that the petition lay unnoticed and later was simply tabled by the Senate. Ross was present when the vote was taken, and the Senate's action must have pushed the chief back into a state of despair, but still he refused to recognize federal intransigence. He wrote his brother, Lewis, that "the Delegation are now satisfied that the only alternative left us, in the last resort for an adjustment of the affairs is to negotiate a Treaty on the basis of removal." On April 5 Ross and Gunter met with Major Samuel Cooper, the acting secretary of war during Poinsett's illness, to open negotiations. Cooper insisted that Ross tell the Cherokees to quit planting crops and begin making preparation for removal before he would listen to any new proposals from the delegation.[14]

Thus stalemated, Ross addressed the president directly and declared that the delegation was ready to enter into a treaty for the cession of the entire Cherokee Nation. To this the delegation received a perfunctory reply from Cooper referring them to Mason's last communication stating President Van Buren would not alter the Treaty of New Echota. Ross made a final plea, hoping to gain the president's recognition of the new proposition, but he received merely another curt reply. In that communication Ross predicted with amazing accuracy the final reality of the removal cost. He surmised that the United States would need much less to form a new treaty and let the Cherokees remove themselves than to maintain an army and forcibly remove the tribe.[15]

The Cherokees had many supporters in the eastern United States, especially among the religious and philanthropic societies. During the months of April and May 1838 numerous petitions poured into the congressional chambers from citizens of the northeastern states protesting the execution of the New Echota treaty. The Quakers particularly had a long tradition of concern for Indians, and they asked Ross to speak before an assembly at the newly opened Philadelphia Hall in Pennsylvania. Curiously, they requested his appearance on May 23, 1838, the very day the Treaty of New Echota was to go into effect. Ross declined the invitation. Still hoping that some last-minute change might occur, he was reluctant to leave Washington. In place of a personal address to the Quakers, Ross forwarded a lengthy letter explaining Cherokee difficulties and the reasons for their resistance to the pact. Ross also was approached by O. S. Fowler of Philadelphia, who termed himself a "practical phrenologist." He seems to have made studies of Ross and other members of the delegation in 1836, and he now wished to make plaster casts of the present Cherokee delegates' heads to prove that the red man was neither intellectually nor morally inferior to the white man.[16]

In mid-May the Cherokee deputation sent Poinsett a projected treaty. It called for the relinquishment of all Cherokee lands east of the Mississippi River and a self-executed removal of the tribe within two years. The United States was to agree to "perfect the title of the Cherokee Nation" to the western lands and to allow the acknowledged chiefs to have complete control and distribution of the anticipated funds. The federal government also would pay arrears from former treaties and would make additional payments for claims and damages above those allocated in the 1835 treaty. The monetary increases were merely blank spaces in the proposed pact, since any such demands would necessitate considerable negotiations. Poinsett gave a point-by-point reply to this proposal, conceding that an additional two years for removal could be obtained. This assurance, however, was predicated on the approval of the states surrounding the Cherokees. Although Poinsett opposed any supplemental funds for removal, he promised that the government would be liberal in providing money owed the Cherokees, whether from past due or newly filed claims. In essence, he conceded modifications to the 1835 treaty but permitted no new pact.[17]

The Senate, upon hearing of these negotiations, demanded an account of any discussions which would modify the Treaty of New Echota. Since the delegation had left the monetary propositions blank, Poinsett reported the private interview of May 20 with Ross and Gunter but could furnish no specific amounts. In a detailed memorandum to the Senate Committee on Indian Affairs, Ross made rough estimates of the costs of public lands, private improvements, removal and subsistence for one year in the West which totaled altogether more than $13,000,000. The committee refused even to view these proposals, saying they were not presented by the executive branch or requested by order of the Senate. Poinsett responded with a statement of additional allowances for the Cherokee removal. This amounted to $1,047,067 plus an additional $100,000 for contingencies and $33,333 for annuities. These sums were appropriated in part by Congress in June, raising the total amount allowed for removal to $6,647,067. For some reason the delegation received only $32,000 of the amount appropriated to pay arrears on the annuities, and $7,000 of that amount was specified for expenses incurred by the delegation. The Senate rejected any extension of time. The delegates, feeling they had accomplished as much as possible in remodeling the Treaty of New Echota, prepared to leave Washington in mid-June. Furthermore, news of military movements in the Cherokee Nation heightened their desire to leave.[18]

Major General Winfield Scott was ordered to take charge of the United States troops in the Cherokee Nation in April 1838 and was supplied with additional forces. Ross had met Scott shortly before he received his new command, and they had had two long conversations concerning Cherokee removal, during which Scott assured the chief that more than anything else he hoped to prevent bloodshed. The general arrived in Athens, Tennessee, on May 8 and two days later issued a widely distributed address to the Cherokees in which he notified them that the two years to prepare for removal had elapsed and that emigration must now begin in haste. Scott in General Order Number 25 a week later admonished his troops to use kindness, indulgence, and civility toward the Cherokees. At first Scott felt his address had borne results, for soon sixty Indians presented themselves for emigration. But letters from some of the members of the delegation at Washington, assuring their friends that the prospects were good for a two-year extension, dried up further enrollment. Cherokee sluggishness could not daunt a soldier who knew his duty, however, and Scott emphatically declared: "My orders from Washington require that the collection of the Indians for emigration shall go on; and it shall."[19]

Poinsett forwarded a report of the proceedings at Washington between Ross and the executive department as a guideline for Scott's activities, but mail took nearly two weeks to reach the frontier, and by the time the general had received Poinsett's suggestions to turn removal over to the tribe, nearly all the Cherokees had been gathered at emigration depots about the Cherokee Nation and were preparing for transfer. The absence of so many of the Cherokee leaders made it difficult for the tribe to take over the arrangements. Misunderstandings were rife. Poinsett observed that it would be best to collect the Indians only shortly before their removal, and he projected the optimum time of arrival in the West as the month of October. The Cherokees had been rounded up well before Poinsett's recommendation was even written, and his ideas on the timing of removal necessitated a delay of sixty days before departure. Scott's frustration was readily apparent. Confused directives from

Washington in addition to white squatter zeal and Cherokee lethargy made removal an agonizing process. Furthermore the benevolent General Order Number 25 went awry. Participants in the
panoramic sweep, both Indian and white, recalled the summer a
half-century later to an attentive ethnologist:

Under Scott's orders the troops were disposed at various points throughout the Cherokee country, where stockade forts were erected for gathering
in and holding the Indians preparatory to removal. From these, squads of
troops were sent to search out with rifle and bayonet every small cabin
hidden away in the coves or by the sides of mountain streams, to seize and
bring in as prisoners all the occupants, however or wherever they might be
found. Families at dinners were startled by the sudden gleam of bayonets in
the doorway and rose up to be driven with blows and oaths along the weary
miles of trail that led to the stockade. Men were seized in their fields or
going along the road, women were taken from their wheels and children
from their play. In many cases, on turning for one last look as they crossed
the ridge, they saw their homes in flames, fired by the lawless rabble that
followed on the heels of the soldiers to loot and pillage. So keen were these
outlaws on the scent that in some instances they were driving off the cattle
and other stock of the Indians almost before the soldiers had fairly started
their owners in the other direction. Systematic hunts were made by the
same men for Indian graves, to rob them of the silver pendants and other
valuables deposited with the dead. A Georgia volunteer, afterward a colonel
in the Confederate service, said: "I fought through the civil war and have
seen men shot to pieces and slaughtered by thousands, but the Cherokee
removal was the cruelest work I ever knew."

To prevent escape the soldiers had been ordered to approach and surround
each house, so far as possible, so as to come upon the occupants without
warning. One old patriarch, when thus surprised, calmly called his children
and grandchildren around him, and, kneeling down, bid them pray with him
in their own language, while the astonished soldiers looked on in silence.
Then rising he led the way into exile. A woman, on finding the house surrounded, went to the door and called up the chickens to be fed for the last
time, after which, taking her infant on her back and her two other children
by the hand, she followed her husband with the soldiers.[20]

Scott sent off two parties in the first half of June 1838, but by the
middle of the month he had decided to suspend further emigration
until September. A third detachment had left Ross's Landing just
two days before Scott's announcement, but when members learned
of the temporary reprieve they began to desert the detachment in
droves. Nearly three hundred of the one thousand members of the

party escaped, and one reluctant traveler told General Smith, who had joined them at Waterloo, Alabama, that he "would go back Home the next morning and Shoot for [John] Ross that he had plenty of money and he would fight for him."[21]

Ross traveled to the Cherokee Nation by way of Salem to meet Jane who withdrew from school and returned home with her father. They stopped by the Cherokee Agency at Calhoun, Tennessee, on July 13, 1838, where one missionary noted "thousands pressed around him to greet him with a handshake." There also he delivered to Scott letters from Poinsett that he had carried from Washington. Ross visited with his family for the next few days, during which time he sent runners throughout the Cherokee Nation to convince uncaptured stragglers to come in for removal. Even the persuasive call of their revered chief left many of the North Carolina hill folk unswayed, and they remained as a small band who escaped the forced removal. Ross also called a meeting of the General Council at Red Clay, and on July 21 a resolution was passed asking "that the whole business of the emigration of our people shall be undertaken by the nation." The returned Washington delegation became an ad hoc committee to oversee emigration, and Ross took responsibility as superintendent. Scott was still committed to his September 1 deadline but finally permitted an extension with the provision that all removal would be completed by October 20.[22]

Ross, as superintendent, made his first estimate of expenses at the end of July. Measuring the distance of travel at eight hundred miles and contemplating eighty days for the journey, Ross asked $65.88 per person to cover the cost of teams, wagons, rations, conductors, physicians, and necessary purchases overland. Scott thought the estimate extravagant and asked that several of the expenses be reconsidered. Upon reconsideration Ross and the committee found that instead of lowering the sum, they actually needed to raise the amount, as they had neglected to add certain incidental costs. Scott reluctantly accepted these calculations. Before Ross took control of the general emigration of the Cherokees, the $600,000 set aside in the New Echota treaty had been exhausted. Now the monies used for the balance of the removal would be taken from the additional allowance of $1,047,067 made by Congress in June 1838.[23]

To manage the complex financial arrangements, the removal

committee appointed Lewis Ross and gave him specific instructions pertaining to prices for removal commodities. The whole arrangement infuriated General Smith whose office as superintendent had slipped into the hands of Lewis Ross. Even more upset was the swarm of officeholders and contract-seekers whose anticipated profits had vanished. Indeed, several disgruntled whites who had supplied the Cherokees up to that time offered Lewis Ross forty thousand dollars to let them have the contract to supply the Cherokee removal. The contract with the chief's brother was made without the knowledge of General Scott, but he quickly learned of the transaction from members of the treaty faction who still remained in the Cherokee Nation in the East. Declaring that Lewis Ross would make an enormous profit of nearly $180,000, they insisted that the contract be let to the lowest bidder among several available contractors stationed nearby. Scott hesitantly agreed, thinking earlier estimates only rough calculations and anticipating lower costs.[24]

Committee members replied vehemently to these charges that there was no advantage in such a method for the Cherokees. They considered the "health and comfort" of the tribe more important than saving a few dollars, and the committee stressed to Scott that the estimates had been made by experienced men from the best data available. Ross and other members of the committee felt that most of the protests came from disappointed white men who sought lucrative contracts or from Cherokees who were not concerned with saving money but were anxious to embarrass the antiremoval faction. The contract remained in the hands of Lewis Ross. The remaining treaty party members asked to leave independent of the mass migration under Ross and, numbering between six hundred fifty and seven hundred, they departed October 11, directed by John A. Bell.[25]

Scott's September 1 deadline passed. Not only was it hopelessly unrealistic but also it became apparent the Cherokees could not complete removal by the appointed October 20. Scott had suspended further emigration in June because of the drought that parched the region and continued well into October. There had been some talk of using the water routes for the remaining Cherokees, but the Tennessee River was so low as to be nearly impassable, and it was still falling in September. Reports that the Arkansas River was in nearly as unfavorable a condition convinced Scott that further parties must take the land routes. But even this was not feasible until cooler weather and rains appeared, for there was everywhere a scarcity of good drinking water. Not only was removal delayed, but the dragging days had a debilitating effect on the Cherokees interned in camps set up by General Scott. He called the camps "healthful and convenient," but the Cherokees must have seen them as strict stockades in light of their involuntary presence. Scott also felt that a daily march of twelve to fifteen miles would be beneficial exercise for many of the tribe.[26]

In the last days before departing, Ross organized the tribe into thirteen detachments of approximately one thousand persons each. A conductor and an assistant were over each group, which also included a physician, an interpreter, a wagon master, and a commissary agent. At least two parties started out in September but traveled only as far as Blythe's Ferry on the Tennessee River, where they waited for the rains to raise the river. Joined by another detachment, three parties were underway by the first week in October. The remainder of the month saw five more groups depart for the West from Ross's Landing, present-day Chattanooga. Four more groups left during the first week in November.[27]

Ross remained behind to direct the movements and to make final arrangements for each detachment. He took up residence at the Cherokee agency at Calhoun, Tennessee, where he received reports from the first detachments on what later groups could expect. One of the larger detachments had a number of the North Carolina Cherokees traveling with it. It seems that twenty-five to fifty of them led by some persuasive renegade escaped their party and began a trek back to their Smoky Mountain homes. When Scott learned of the escape, he must have regretted his decision not to send troops along. He reported that he "lectured Mr. Ross, rather sharply" and sent his troops in search of the deserters. Ross followed, hoping to reconvert the scattered fugitives.[28]

The route established for this phase of Cherokee removal, known as the "Trail of Tears," was faithfully followed by each successive wave as men, women, and children thrust their meager belongings aboard the wagons and lumbered laboriously off from Ross's Landing. They crossed the Tennessee River at Blythe's Ferry where the Hiwassee River flowed into that stream, then journeyed to Pikesville, McMinnville, and Nashville. At Nashville the parties were met by Lewis Ross who issued rations and supplies which—as the winter was quickly setting in—included cloaks, bearskins, blankets, overcoats, thick boots, and heavy socks. From Nashville the detachments crossed the Cumberland River and continued northwesterly toward Hopkinsville, Kentucky. The route pointed the Cherokees to Marion, Kentucky, where they turned sharply west to cross the Ohio River at Golconda, Illinois, and then across southern Illinois where they crossed the Mississippi River at Cape Girardeau, Missouri. At both the Ohio and Mississippi rivers the detachments were detained, as ice and insufficient supplies halted their progress. A northern sweep took the later parties through Farmington, Rolla, and Lebanon in Missouri, as earlier parties had cleared the direct route of game. When they entered Arkansas, they turned due west near Fayetteville, and journeyed on into their new country.[29]

No accurate figures exist for the number who died as a result of this tragic trek, and present generations have but a slight sense of the suffering involved. Some put the death toll at sixteen hundred. When added to the number who fell victim to the harsh encampments before removal and the many who succumbed to the debilitating circumstances after arrival, nearly four thousand Cherokees —or a quarter of the tribe—were lost in the process.[30]

Ross organized a special small party under John Drew numbering about two hundred thirty old, sick, and lame. This group got underway December 4, 1838, and chose the easier water route. Ross spent his last days at Red Hill helping his family prepare to move. Ross took great care in packing the precious Cherokee Nation papers which dated from the earliest contacts with the United States and which chronicled the unalterable course that had led to removal. All the while local white citizens milled about, prepared to bargain for his livestock or to take possession of his abandoned cabin. Half a century later an army private from North Carolina who had accompanied the removal remembered one act of unselfish heroism displayed by Quatie Ross: "This noble hearted woman died a martyr to childhood. Giving her only Blanket for the protection of a sick child she rode thinly clad through a blinding sleet and snow storm developed Pneumonia and died in the still Hours of a bleak winter night." This story, probably apocryphal, at least gives another glimpse at the largely unknown first wife of Chief Ross. She was buried at Little Rock, Arkansas, after the steamboat Victoria churned up to the landing about February 1, 1839. The remaining passengers completed the last part of the journey and arrived in Cherokee lands in mid-March.[31]

Disputes over the cost of removal elicited at least as much controversy as the heavily debated Treaty of New Echota. The fund of $1,047,067 established by Congress in June 1838 had been based on moving the tribe at $30 per head. This figure had proved entirely unrealistic, as those members of the treaty party who moved west shortly before the mass migration under Ross had required about $61.70 per individual. Furthermore, the actual cost under Ross was even greater than the $65.88 he had initially estimated, for rather than eighty days the trip took on the average of one hundred twenty-five days, and the cost was slightly over $103.25 per person.[32]

Ross initiated the controversy when he presented Washington officials his claims in May 1840, stating that expenses for the thirteen detachments were $1,263,338.48, to which he added two other claims, one for a requisition on Scott which had not been honored and the other an omitted item in that requisition which brought the total claim to $1,357,745.86. A portion of this amount had been received by Ross prior to his departure for the West, so that the balance due the Cherokee Nation came to $581,346.88.[33]

These claims were not readily accepted by the Van Buren administration. T. Hartley Crawford, the new commissioner of Indian affairs, presented Poinsett with an elaborate document that stripped the claims of alleged excesses. At the outset Crawford disallowed the unpaid requisition and the smaller omitted item which amounted to $94,407.38. Chief Ross contended that it was not the fault of the Cherokees that the long drought had caused delays of more than thirty days before the march began. The commissioner noted that of the sixteen cents per day allowed for rations, only seven to nine cents were actually used. Likewise, the horse ration of forty cents had cost only about twenty-five cents. In short, he rejected these claims. The controversy revolved around the remaining claim of $486,939.50.[34]

Crawford discovered a number of objectionable features in this application, the worst being discrepancies in the number of Cherokees in each party. There were three counts for each of the thirteen detachments. Ross submitted one count, the disbursing agent another, and the receiving agent in the West a third. In only one case was Ross's number lower than the disbursing agent's, and in every case his was higher than that of the receiving agent, which can only partly be accounted for by deaths and defections. Crawford discounted the minor variances due to death or desertion and merely recorded the differences between Ross's figures and the receiving agent's count, a difference which varied from 52 to 455 persons per detachment for a total difference of 1,633 persons. According to Crawford's estimate, this discrepancy in the number actually removed, converted into funds, amounted to $107,571.94 which the commissioner believed should not be paid. By using these same figures, Crawford also cut the number of wagons and the amount dispensed on horse rations; this overcharge he computed at $96,705.04. Since the wagons were never returned, he lopped off another $180,600 for a total reduction of $384,876.98. The commissioner surmised that given the time and necessary vouchers he could find additional reductions. He recommended rejection of the entire claim, $486,939.50.[35]

Ross appealed to Poinsett, who supported Crawford's decision. The case was then brought before President Van Buren. He was willing to have the lesser amount examined and, if General Scott would certify that the delays grew out of his orders, the president would consider payment. On the larger sum of nearly $500,000 the president felt differently. He considered the agreement between Scott and the Cherokees a contract for a specific sum, i.e. emigration at $65.88 per person and, since that sum had been paid, no further money should be allotted. At this point the Cherokee Nation employed Matthew St. Clair Clark, sometime clerk for the House of Representatives, as its legal counsel to adjudicate its claims against the United States. Taking Van Buren's suggestions, he gathered testimony from General Scott in reference to the lesser claim. The general conceded that several detachments were delayed with his approval, as it was impossible to find sufficient water on the road. Yet he also noted that after sufficient water was available, the parties were dilatory in their movements. In a self-justifying statement, Scott later declared "but for the drought, I would have quashed the contract with Lewis Ross as extravagant, and the renewed movement, beginning with September, would have escaped ice, snow, and bad roads, and been ended in eighty days, by each detachment." A further appeal to the president brought identical results: disapproval of the larger claim and indecision on the lesser.[36]

Martin Van Buren lost the bid for the presidency in 1840, and the new Whig administration which took office in 1841 was much more conciliatory to Cherokee demands. In the spring of 1841, shortly after his elevation to the presidency, John Tyler ordered Secretary of War John Bell to reexamine the Cherokee case. Further testimony was taken from General Scott, who felt that a portion of the lesser sum was justly due, but also believed that a number of issues were charged to "swell the profits" of Lewis Ross. "Indeed," the skeptical general stated, "the more I look back upon the correspondence, and all the circumstances of the time, the more suspicions gains [sic] upon me." Yet he felt the lesser sum valid since all the wagon teams and emigrants had to be fed for several weeks before the commencement of removal on October 1. As to the larger amount of money requested by Ross, Scott attributed the delays partially to the Cherokees who, he said, "are proverbially dilatory in their migrations, even when entirely voluntary." Nevertheless, he ascribed delays to the cold weather, snow, ice, and the resulting bad roads rather than to "any connivance on the part of John or Lewis Ross." Consequently, he suggested that the sums be paid in whole with the remainder being referred to a board of commissioners.[37]

Bell's reassessment virtually assured the Cherokees of their requests, and in August and September 1841 the entire claim of $581,346.88 was paid to Ross and the Cherokee delegates in Washington. Referring to the payment, two impartial federal investigators observed more than half a century later: "If the emigration had been undertaken under the conduct of the United States Army it would not only have involved a very great expense for military escort, but the emigrants would necessarily have to be kept under very strict guard to avoid desertion. Even under the voluntary emigration the desertions ranged from 1 to 18 per cent." After a lengthy investigation, they concluded, "It cannot reasonably be claimed that the expense of removal was seriously exaggerated. . . . Removal was accomplished with . . . much less expense to the United States than if it had been involuntary, under the direction of Gen. Scott."[38]

Ross, as superintendent for removal, used the $486,939.50 received from the Tyler administration to pay debts owed for emigration. Ross distributed the money during the period between his return from Washington December 1841 and his departure for the capital city again the following April, but it was not sufficient time to complete all the necessary transactions. The Cherokees began to grow apprehensive about the money promised them by the United States for a per capita distribution. Understanding that Ross had made this settlement, one group demanded an accounting of Cherokee funds that Ross possessed in December 1842. Ross had only just returned to the Cherokee Nation, and disbursements on the claims were still unfinished. The following year, in his annual message, Ross promised a full account of the money. In the extended National Council meeting of 1843, Ross turned over to the nation $125,000 saved from the employment of wagons and teams. These savings had grown out of provisions in the agreement between Scott and Ross which allowed sums to be paid for the return of wagons and teams. Since a good many of these items belonged to Cherokees or were bought outright, there was no need to return many of them, and the consequent savings Ross used to employ extra physicians and otherwise provide for Cherokee comforts. Purchased wagons had been sold to the highest bidder, and the proceeds Ross had placed in Cherokee funds, but it seems that this transaction counted for little or nothing, since the wagons brought a poor price in the West.[39]

A source of irritation among the Cherokees, particularly opponents of Ross, was the action of the federal government in subtracting the $581,346.88 payment from the "five million fund." The five million dollars originally had been established in the Treaty of New Echota to cover the cost of removal and subsistence of the tribe for one year thereafter; to pay for improvements, ferries, and damages; and to settle additional debts and claims upon the Cherokee Nation. But Congress appropriated additional sums to cover all these costs with the exception of removal and subsistence. The reason for Cherokee bitterness was the provision that all money left after those payments was to be distributed on a per capita basis. The tremendous cost of removal, greatly augmented by the settlement with Ross, had cut deeply into the five million fund.[40]

Certainly profit was made in the Cherokee removal, but by whom and how much is largely indeterminable. Ross and the committee who had charge of the entire removal process saw no reason for Cherokee money to pass into the hands of white contractors whose primary concern was making a profit. Turning to Lewis Ross, they felt his major consideration would be Cherokee health and comfort. From the outset Lewis Ross was accused of using his office for personal aggrandizement. Commissioner Crawford estimated that he realized a clear profit of from one hundred and five thousand to one hundred and fifty thousand dollars from the contract, and Lewis's brother-in-law Thomas C. Hindman who served as a quartermaster supposedly told one individual who was intimate with removal costs that he would receive forty-four thousand dollars for his interest in the contract. Yet a good deal of the alleged profit was literally eaten up by the emigrants as they crossed the drought-ridden Trail of Tears. Each detachment discovered scarcer provisions and higher prices, and delays drove the cost of removal higher. Nor were the provisions particularly palatable or healthful, which contributed to sickness and death.[41]

Greed was rampant throughout the trip. One quartermaster reported to Chief Ross that the merchants at Nashville were charging exorbitant prices for goods and that they set the exchange rate for federal currency far below its actual value. Ferry owners and toll road keepers frequently raised their prices. Evan Jones the Baptist missionary who helped lead one detachment complained: "On the Cumberland mountains they fleeced us, 73 cents a wagon and 12½ cents a horse without the least abatement or thanks." Thus a portion of the supposed profits vanished into the hands of whites along the way. Lewis Ross undoubtedly realized a substantial profit from the contract, but how much may never be known. Chief Ross may have shared in Lewis's gain, but he received no salary for his work as superintendent. Indeed Ross did not even accept his salary as chief throughout the 1830s, and if he profited from the removal contracts even the most vigorous detractors could never trace the funds to his pockets.[42]

Had Ross remained in the Cherokee Nation in 1838 and counseled voluntary removal, he doubtless would have been repudiated by a majority of the tribe, thus losing his effectiveness in easing military removal. As it was, even after he returned and acknowledged the inevitable, lethargy and desertion continued. Ross probably accepted the finality of the Cherokees' fate sometime in April or May 1838. Blocked by an uncompromising Congress and a vacillating secretary of war, Ross must have realized that all he could obtain was the additional sums appropriated. But Ross may have been led to believe that some new agreement could be attained. Friends from within and without the federal government prompted his confidence that the Cherokees would not have to abandon their homes. Here Ross's political skills failed him. He should have sensed that President Van Buren would carry out the removal and that prolonged negotiations would not yield significant changes. Nevertheless, as late as mid-May Poinsett held out hopes that a two-year extension could be arranged. Moreover, as news from the Cherokee Nation was delayed two weeks to a month after an event, Scott's actions in the Cherokee country were unknown to Ross until the eve of his departure from Washington. Dismal and deadly as removal became, it was certainly less harsh than it would have been had it been executed under the heavy hand of martial law.

Over the next decade and nearly into the next century, the question at issue between the United States and the Cherokee Nation was whether the expense of removal was properly chargeable to the five million fund. Moreover, the reduction of the per capita payment lay at the heart of the bitter Cherokee feuds that ensued in the coming years. The Cherokee Treaty of 1846 would settle this question only partially, and the final determination would not come until long after Ross's time.

7

INTERREGNUM

THE YEARS after removal to the west were both lonely and politically eventful for Ross. Doubtless the fervency with which he threw himself into Cherokee affairs was partially owing to decreasing demands from his family. He found some relief from loneliness and political strife in correspondence with his younger sons and his niece and nephews. His youngest sons, George and Silas, attended the Lawrenceville Classical and Commercial High School in New Jersey and wrote of their progress and their interests.[1]

Ross also continued to correspond with his two nephews, Daniel H. and William P. Ross. In fatherly tones, Ross was quick to admonish the boys on the importance of punctuality and perseverance: "Making up for lost lessons by over-studying will not remove the objectionable features in the irregularity of habit. . . . Economy & well spent *time* are the surest guarantees." These pieties did not turn the boys away; they continued to write of family and personal matters. Ross was concerned primarily that their conduct could reflect poorly on the character of the Indian race. He wished high honors for the boys "to show to the civilized world that the faculty of the North American Indian is not inferior to the white European." William proved particularly able, and besides supporting him at Lawrenceville, Ross paid his expenses at Princeton. Ross must have found it especially satisfying when in later years William aided him in political negotiations in Washington. William gained a great deal from these associations with his uncle, and when he succeeded Ross as chief, he drew widely on the knowledge gleaned in those early years.[2]

But this cheerful correspondence served only as a diversion from the somber aspects of the post-removal period. The devastating effects of the long march were not entirely relieved at the end of the journey. The firm of Glasgow and Harrison had been commissioned by the federal government to handle the portion of the Treaty of New Echota that provided for subsistence of the Cherokees for one year after their arrival in the West. From the first arrivals came complaints of the poor quality and scantiness of the rations. Only a few days after Ross reached the new homelands, he received a protest from two Cherokee friends who listed numerous grievances, among them that the Cherokees were offered grades of beef unfit for consumption, and that methods for weighing the corn given them were dishonest. Ross announced these inadequacies to Cherokee Agent Montfort Stokes on April 5, 1839, but Stokes's unresponsiveness elicited from Ross a documented complaint a couple of weeks later to the area army commander, Brigadier General Matthew Arbuckle. To ease their difficulties, the Cherokees requested that they be allowed to take over their own subsistence. Arbuckle merely packed Ross's papers off to the Indian superintendent for the western territory, William Armstrong, who forwarded them to Washington.[3]

The Cherokees were in a very difficult situation. If they would not accept the provisions, their only alternative was to accept money. As the money given the Cherokees for the beef ration amounted to only one dollar a month, they could hardly afford to buy food at the exorbitant frontier prices. Ross requested corrections for these injustices. The monetary exchange for the foodstuffs was supposed to be much higher than one dollar, but this unfairness was entirely overlooked at the time. Arbuckle had shown Ross's protest to the contractors, who forwarded their justification to the commissioner of Indian affairs. Glasgow and Harrison noted that other tribes they had supplied had given them no difficulty over the provisions, and they remarked that it was widely known "that the Cherokees are a complaining people." An independent investigator later disclosed that the Creeks also had suffered under the same contractors. Commissioner T. Hartley Crawford returned a lifeless letter in June 1839 to his agent in the West and called the provisions adequate in quantity, but cautioned that the quality at all times should be "good."[4]

On other issues, General Arbuckle was more responsive. An impressionable army lieutenant dashed off an anxious note to him, saying "this is no false alarm." He had just learned that Sitawakee was heading a band of Cherokees for an attack on the soldiers, and the lieutenant wanted two or three companies or "all the dragoons" at Fort Gibson by the next afternoon. Arbuckle, less excited yet partially taken in, asked Ross to put a check on his disorderly people. Ross found it somewhat comical when 200 dragoons were dispatched to an imaginary battlefield, while Sitawakee, "the dreaded chieftain, in the mean time was quietly engaged in business" at Ross's home. An infantry captain was detailed to investigate the rumors and discovered the Cherokees "generally employed in building houses, clearing and fencing land, and planting."[5]

Significant political problems faced the reunited Cherokees, for the government of the western Cherokees had not taken the direction of that of their eastern brothers and remained a loosely structured institution. Ross's old friend John Jolly, who had welcomed him when he visited the band in 1836, had died in December of that year. An interim government had then been established much like the one of Major Ridge and Ross after the death of Chiefs Charles Hicks and Pathkiller in 1827. John Brown was elected principal chief at a meeting of a small faction of the western Cherokee council, while John Rogers and John Looney served as assistants until a regular election was held in October 1839. Although the government of the Old Settlers (the western Cherokees) was not so intricate as the eastern model, the chiefs were hardly willing to yield their offices and power to the new arrivals. The treaty party that had removed in 1837 and 1838, separate from the general removal under Ross, had blended with the Old Settlers, and the principal protagonists, Major and John Ridge, Stand Watie, and Elias Boudinot, seemed uninterested in politics for a time. The Ross faction held the balance of power, for the thirteen thousand persons who had followed their chief outnumbered by more than two to one the remainder of the tribe.[6]

The initial confrontation occurred amiably enough on June 3, 1839, when the two groups called a meeting of the Cherokee Nation to meet at Takatoka (Double Springs) about four miles northwest of present-day Tahlequah, Oklahoma. By June 10 the assembly numbered between six thousand and seven thousand Cherokees, who listened to Ross recount the "mysterious dispensations of Providence" that had worked to bring the Cherokee Nation together again. Ross's ambition was to arrange a quick and permanent reunion for the welfare of the entire Cherokee Nation, and he ended his address on that note: "Let us never forget this self-evident truth —that a house divided against itself, cannot stand."[7]

The Old Settler leadership was somewhat leery of the platitude and wanted a fuller explanation, a clearer understanding of the Ross faction's intentions. Ross and Assistant Chief George Lowrey forwarded a resolution of the eastern Cherokees requesting that a select committee be formed to revise and draft a code of laws for the united Cherokee Nation. The projected committee would include Ross, Lowrey, and Edward Gunter of the eastern band, and Brown, Looney, and Rogers of the western group, with three others to be selected by the six. The three Old Settler chiefs would not so readily relinquish their power. Their answer was given the same day which had seen the arrival on the council ground of the Ridges, Boudinot, and Stand Watie. Several observers thought that Major Ridge and his friends had influenced the Old Settler chiefs not to come to any agreement with the Ross party.[8]

The western chiefs had been upset from the beginning, partially because the eastern Cherokee resolution stipulated that two sets of laws would remain in effect until a new constitution was adopted. Of course, they wanted their institution to dominate. At this apparent impasse, the Old Settlers closed their portion of the council meeting. Ross reminded the eastern Cherokees of their action before removal when the General Council had resolved that the constitution and laws of the Cherokee Nation would remain in full force subject only to needed modifications. The upshot of this situation was the meeting of an ad hoc group of eastern and western Cherokees led by Sequoyah and Jesse Bushyhead that called for an assembly of the Cherokee Nation at the Illinois Camp Ground on July 1, 1839.[9]

What broke up these rather humdrum debates was the news of the brutal murders of the principal signers of the 1835 Treaty of New Echota. On June 22, 1839, a party of about twenty or twenty-five men surrounded the home of John Ridge at Honey Springs and

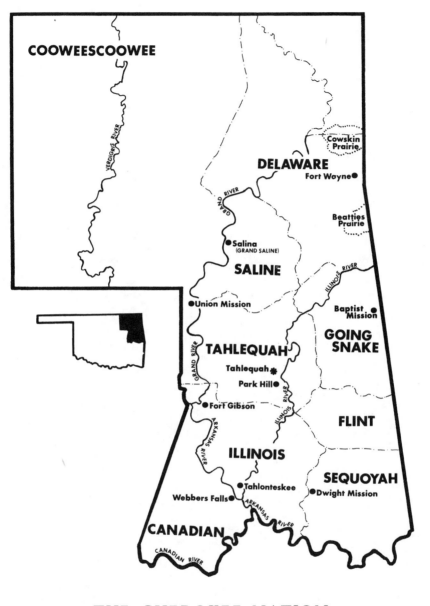

THE CHEROKEE NATION
1839–1866
WITH DISTRICT SUBDIVISIONS

dragged him from bed amid the screams of his wife and children, stabbing him repeatedly until he fell dead. Major Ridge had left his home to visit some of his Negro slaves in Arkansas and had spent the night at the home of a friend. The next morning, on June 22, as he was returning, a group of Cherokees ambushed him, putting five bullets through his head and body. Elias Boudinot, the same day, was working at his home when four Cherokees asked him for some medicine; as he turned to see to their request, they assailed him with knives and tomahawks and continued to beat him even after they had downed him, breaking his skull in several places and mutilating his body. Obviously, the whole operation had been carefully planned and coordinated. A group of antitreaty men had met secretly one night and drawn for X-marked slips of paper which designated the executioners. Ross's son Allen, one of the plotters, recalled the clandestine affair many years later; he was to stay with his father and keep any knowledge of the plot from him. Others of the treaty party escaped the well-laid plan, and Stand Watie, John A. Bell, and George W. Adair quickly turned to General Arbuckle at Fort Gibson for protection.[10]

As soon as Ross received news of the murders, he sent his brother-in-law John G. Ross and other friends to the Boudinot house to investigate. They soon returned with a note from Mrs. Boudinot that Ross should flee for safety, as Watie was raising a company of men to kill him. Ross then turned to a clerk and asked him to write out a report of the incident to General Arbuckle and to ask for protection. But the clerk was too shaken to write, and the chief composed the note himself and handed it to a young white soldier who had accompanied the removal expedition and had volunteered to deliver the message. The soldier wore out two mules that day in his fevered rush. Arbuckle's reply was to advise Ross to enter Fort Gibson for protection. The general also hoped to arrange a meeting of Ross and the Old Settlers at the post. Ross's friends advised him against any travel, and in a short time they had more than two hundred guards stationed around his home.[11]

The murders grew out of more than just disputes over the sale of the Cherokee lands and the removal; they had roots in older personal feuds and ancestral traditions. Many of the treaty party men had noticed the Ridges and Boudinot at the June meeting and proba-

bly suspected that they had something to do with the failure of reunification. But finally, the deaths had origins in the ancient "blood
law," which established the death penalty for any person who disposed of public lands without the consent of the Nation. Although
the law had been passed down from antiquity, it was not committed
to writing until 1829 when, ironically enough, it was drawn up by
John Ridge. The younger Ridge well knew the penalty for his action
and confided to Commissioner John F. Schermerhorn a few months
before his death: "I may yet some day die by the hand of some poor
infatuated Indian, deluded by the counsel of Ross and his minions."
Yet no conclusive evidence exists to tie Ross to the murders. The
agent to the Cherokees, Montfort Stokes, believed Ross innocent
and declared: "He is a man of too much good sense to embroil his
nation at this critical time; and, besides, his character, since I have
known him, which is now twenty-five years, has been pacific."
Ross's guilt lies more in his laxity in prosecuting those responsible,
but here again old Cherokee law gave approval to such acts, and
Ross may have feared the anger of his followers who considered such
murders just, if not heroic.[12]

The murders probably strengthened the resolve of the Old Settlers
not to integrate with their more numerous eastern brothers. Arbuckle, worried about further outbreaks of violence, hoped that in
the meeting called for July 1, 1839, a reunion could be worked out.
He invited western chiefs Brown, Looney, and Rogers to his headquarters, but they simply proposed to Ross that a convention be held
at Fort Gibson on July 25 and refused to attend the Illinois Camp
Ground meeting. General Arbuckle and Stokes both pressed Ross to
accept the Old Settlers' proposal. Ross refused and insisted that the
eastern faction had given the western group every chance for merger
on equal grounds, but the recent emigrants had received only con-
tempt. Ross by this time had enough of the Old Settlers on his side
to claim that his group actually better represented the entire nation.[13]

Ross invited not only the western chiefs to the Illinois Camp
Ground but also General Arbuckle, Stokes, and Armstrong. The
western leaders refused to attend, even after entreaties by several of
the respected Old Settlers who had gone over to Ross. Furthermore,

they called a meeting of their own for July 22, 1839. Arbuckle, impatient with the continued bickering and greatly upset by reports that citizens of Arkansas were abandoning their homes for fear of Indian uprisings, insisted that Ross restore quiet to the frontier. When Ross replied that frontier folk had no reason for alarm, Arbuckle, in his exasperation, washed his hands of the Cherokee mess and declared that he would not concern himself with Cherokee affairs. Subsequent actions of the general proved that declaration false.[14]

Anxious frontier citizens were not content to abandon their border homes. Believing the Cherokees were in a state of internal war and fearing violence in their own neighborhood, one Arkansas settlement organized a vigilance committee known as the Cane Hill Independent Regulators, who intended to mete out frontier justice from their base in Washington County. They had captured several suspects involved in a murder of a local resident and, after a quasi-legal hearing, had summarily executed three men. One of the accused had implicated a Cherokee, John R. Nicholson, and in the latter part of July the regulators demanded that Ross turn him over to them. Ross and the leading men of the Nation quickly apprised Stokes of this affair, asserting the innocence of Nicholson and protesting the illegal authority assumed by the regulators. Stokes, of course, would not sanction the conduct of the regulators and helped to gain testimony supporting Nicholson's innocence, but Nicholson was later arrested and held for one thousand dollars' bail. This heightened Cherokee unrest.[15]

Nearly two thousand Cherokees attended Ross's meeting at the Illinois Camp Ground on July 1, 1839, declaring themselves a general convention of the Cherokee Nation and drafting documents to establish a stable constitutional government. One of the first acts offered amnesty on humiliating terms to members of the treaty party who had exposed themselves to penalties "by their acts . . . of outlawry." Stripping them of eligibility for national office for five years, the convention further gave them only eight days to appear and retract their threats of revenge for the Ridge-Boudinot murders. The "eight-day" provision was extended indefinitely the next week, but not until the next year was it revoked entirely. Fewer than a dozen Cherokees came in under this decree, and militants like Stand

Watie declared that they would sooner "fall by the hand of the mid-night assassin" than sign that "infamous oath."[16]

In order to carry out the amnesty decree, the convention authorized the organization of eight "auxiliary police companies" to suppress disturbances. Watie stationed his own military force in Fort Wayne on Beattie's Prairie in the northeastern part of the Cherokee Nation, where he felt safe from aggressions of the eastern faction. Perhaps even more galling to treaty party members was the convention's absolving of everyone connected with the Ridge-Boudinot murders—and without the degrading terms set for Watie and his followers. All these developments reflected the tragedy of removal, even as had the bloody vendettas carried out a few weeks before. Ross set his hand to these decrees, but how energetically he had sought them is unclear. Certainly his influence was felt on every decision of the convention. Perhaps he later regretted these harsh terms as they had much to do with the civil strife that haunted the Cherokee Nation for the next half-dozen years.[17]

The Illinois Camp Ground convention also passed an Act of Union on July 12, 1839. Significantly, some important Old Settlers had linked themselves to this meeting, and John Looney attached his name to the act as "Acting Principal Chief Western Cherokees." During the convention, Ross kept General Arbuckle informed. What stirred Arbuckle's interest most was the amnesty decree, and he asked repeatedly for copies of the document. In an effort to create better understanding of their respective positions, Ross suggested a meeting between Arbuckle and convention leaders on July 16. At this meeting Arbuckle's expectation of conciliation was dashed when he found Ross and his deputation firmly attached to the amnesty decree; the general seriously believed civil war imminent. He also was disturbed by news that some of the Ross party intended to prevent an assembly of the Old Settlers on July 22. Ross seemed to have no apprehension of civil conflict; his intention, he informed Arbuckle, was to wage a "war of reason" on the unaffiliated western Cherokees. Actually, Ross proposed to send a delegation as observers to the western Cherokee meeting, and Arbuckle, still vacillating, seemed willing enough to acknowledge that both eastern and western Cherokees were represented at Ross's convention.[18]

Ross appointed eight men to attend the western meeting, which was held at Tahlonteskee near the mouth of the Illinois River. Strangely enough, John Looney rejoined that assembly and styled himself, along with Brown and Rogers, as one of the "Chiefs, Cherokee Nation." He even went so far as to appeal to Superintendent Armstrong and Arbuckle about Ross who, he declared, would not submit to "our [western] government and laws." Looney's trifling with the Old Settlers may have been a pretense; if not, he certainly redeemed himself later when he signed a paper to depose Brown and Rogers. The Ross delegates had little impact on the assembly. The Old Settler gathering must have caused a change of heart in Arbuckle, for shortly after it got underway he accused Ross of producing the difficulties in the Cherokee Nation and demanded that the government established by Ross be terminated. When Arbuckle offered the use of the facilities at Fort Gibson for a joint convention, the western Cherokees appointed fifteen men to meet a like number from the eastern band, but Ross refused. He felt the western Cherokees had given no consideration to his earlier proposals or to his committee of eight men who had visited them, and it seemed to him that any discussions could take place at the Illinois Camp Ground where the people were already assembled.[19]

There were other reasons for Ross's refusal. Many of the Ross faction were afraid to travel to Fort Gibson—they feared reprisals for the deaths of the Ridges and Boudinot. Further, Fort Gibson could not really be considered neutral ground as Ross surveyed "the great depth of *Policy* to which that distinguished Statesman and Scientific military chieftain in command has been winding his course, in reference to Cherokee matters." Nor was Ross willing to accept Arbuckle's censure for difficulties that Ross traced to the imprudence of the western chiefs at Takatoka in June.[20]

At this apparent impasse a group of Old Settlers, favorable to Ross's leadership, gathered as an ad hoc group at the Illinois Camp Ground on August 23, 1839. With the blessing of some of the leading Old Settlers—John Looney, Sequoyah, Tobacco Will, John Drew and William Shorey Coodey—this group reviewed the actions of the Old Settlers under Brown and Rogers who, they contended, had opposed reunion and had further alienated themselves by identifying with the treaty party. In consequence, they deposed Brown and Rogers and disqualified the two from future office. While these Ross adherents estimated their number at nearly two hundred, Arbuckle called them a small minority acting under Ross's directions, and the Old Settlers led by Brown and Rogers ignored the meeting and their ouster.[21]

The treaty party faction convened at Price's Prairie on August 20, 1839. Blaming Ross for the murders and believing themselves in danger, they decided to send Bell and Watie to Washington. A committee drafted a plea to Secretary of War Joel R. Poinsett which traced Cherokee political difficulties and blamed Ross for all the murder, violence, and hatred that had ensued. Declaring that they valued Cherokee lives too much to engage in the "horrors of civil war," they also stressed that they would never acknowledge the "mobocracy of John Ross." While still in session, the treaty adherents received word that the time for signing the amnesty pledge had been extended, which merely served to harden their resolve.[22]

The Illinois Camp Ground convention ended about September 4, and two days later a constitutional convention, appointed from among the convention body, met to draft a new governing ordinance. The constitution adopted was virtually a carbon of the 1827 model, with one exception which would touch Ross. The 1827 constitution provided that the chief executive be elected by the National Council and National Committee meeting in General Council, while under the new document the principal chief and other officers would be chosen by the people directly. Henceforth the combined National Council and National Committee would be termed the National Council. An assembly at Tahlequah where the constitution was formed elected the entire range of national officers who would serve as if chosen for a regular term beginning the first Monday in October. Ross became principal chief, answering at least partially the charge that no elections had been held since 1830 and that he was not a duly authorized spokesman. The other leading officers were all Old Settlers. Joseph Vann became second principal chief, while William Shorey Coodey and Young Wolf were placed as heads of the National Committee and National Council.[23]

Ross opened the Cherokee National Council session about September 12, 1839, with an address in which he suggested legislation for the coming term. When during the course of the session, several missionaries applied to continue or to resume work among the tribe,

Ross took the occasion to congratulate them and to recommend their applications. Before the session concluded on October 12, it declared the union of the Cherokees consummated and appointed a delegation of nine men, headed by Ross, to attend to important Cherokee affairs in Washington.[24]

Near the end of September General Arbuckle and Armstrong directed Ross to deliver those individuals responsible for the Ridge-Boudinot murders, threatening military force. Ross, of course, would not hand over anyone to federal authorities, for he knew that Indians were not answerable in United States courts. Ross pointed out that the Cherokees had already disposed of the matter. Lewis Ross delivered his brother's message and privately intimated to the general that federal troops would be opposed. The general also discovered that several of the implicated assassins had promised to resist with force any attempt to take them. Arbuckle and Armstrong faced ambivalence from Washington officials. Crawford, after instructing them to apprehend the accused murderers, observed that a minority "must eventually yield to the great mass, whether they arrange their difficulties in a pacific temper, or a resort be had to violence." The commissioner's directions were glaringly inconsistent for, indeed, a Cherokee majority did rule and had absolved the accused murderers. Poinsett sent Arbuckle a similar note but stressed that he should allow no tyranny by the majority.[25]

Arbuckle was ready to show force to quell any disturbances. He believed that border warfare was likely, and rumors had convinced him that Ross was making overtures to surrounding tribes. Ross and other leaders at the Illinois Camp Ground convention actually had got in touch with chiefs of several of the nearby tribes, but principally to apprise them of Cherokee work, to invite them to the convention, and to assure them of Cherokee good will and friendship. It also seems that Arbuckle intended to use some Cherokees to aid his troops in searching for the murderers but found few willing to face violence from fellow tribesmen. When he sent a curt note to Ross on his difficulties, Ross protested the general's interference and again pointed out that the federal government's jurisdiction did not extend to the Cherokee Nation.[26]

During early November 1839 the western Cherokees had met at Takatoka, regrouped, and organized under a newly elected leadership. John Rogers became the principal chief while John Smith and Dutch assisted him. Former Old Settler Chief John Looney was firmly in the Ross camp by this time, and Chief John Brown had taken refuge with a small band of devoted followers in the Mexican province of Texas. In light of the deposition of Brown and Rogers by Old Settlers affiliated with Ross, the western Cherokees declared the proceedings of the Tahlequah meeting unlawful and unworthy of their consideration. When they appealed to Arbuckle to help them in bringing about a union, he was only too ready to agree that Ross's government was unauthorized and to acknowledge the legitimacy of the Old Settler government. The general even declared himself prepared to arrest and confine Ross had the chief not been on his way to Washington. Anxious to maintain their government and knowing that Ross was out of the way, Old Settlers renewed their invitation to the emigrant band to meet and form one nation.[27]

Receiving belated instructions from Washington, Arbuckle asked Joseph Vann, assistant principal chief of the eastern Cherokees, to call a meeting of his group to gain the consent of the dissident Old Settlers for reunification. The general found Vann as skilled in stalling tactics as Ross and every bit as reluctant to take action regarding the Ridge-Boudinot murders. Vann did call a meeting, but much to Arbuckle's chagrin, the group only briefly considered his request and went on to other matters. Stokes attended the meeting to work out an agreement with Vann for a general assembly of the Cherokee Nation on January 15, 1840, at Tahlequah. Rogers and the western faction protested, but the meeting went ahead as scheduled, resulting in two significant acts. The nearly two thousand assembled Cherokees voted to revoke the earlier amnesty decree which the treaty party had found so odious, and they ratified the Act of Union and the Cherokee Constitution, both drawn up in 1839. Stokes certified that 115 Old Settlers were present, while the unaffiliated Old Settlers counted only thirty-five. Arbuckle felt that Stokes had been "overreached by Ross friends" and was ready to stop the meeting but reconsidered, thinking that he might put it to his own use by getting the Cherokees to depose Ross.[28]

William Shorey Coodey, who had remained behind when the Cherokee delegation left for Washington in November, kept Ross informed. He noted in one communication, "Stokes will carry out

our argument he told me." Such was the case, for as Arbuckle relayed dire warnings of civil disaster, Stokes calmly related to Poinsett: "I think that the present state of affairs is as favorable as could
be expected." Indian Superintendent Armstrong also had determined to recognize the new government, and irascible General
Arbuckle reluctantly informed the western Cherokees that their
government had ceased.[29]

Still not content, Arbuckle consented to a meeting of Old Settlers
at Fort Gibson the first week in February 1840. One Ross advocate
commented: "Those little damn'd Councils at the Fort will lead to
mischief." Not surprisingly, when the Old Settlers met, they called
Ross a usurper and claimed theirs the only legal government. Arbuckle insisted that if he had his own way, he would dissolve the
two governments and reorganize them, giving each party propor-
tional representation in a new establishment. Stirred by these reports, Poinsett suspended Stokes and gave Arbuckle sufficient power
to direct a reorganization of the Cherokee government. He instructed Arbuckle to call another meeting and frame a constitution
in harmony with the United States ideals.[30]

Arbuckle acted quickly. Ross was in Washington, and if anything
was to be accomplished it had to be done before his return. The
general requested Vann of the eastern band and Rogers of the Old
Settlers to appoint fifteen or twenty men each to meet with him at
Fort Gibson on April 20, 1840. Anticipating Arbuckle's actions, the
delegation at Washington sent Looney Price back to the Cherokee
Nation with news of its work. From Price the eastern Cherokees
learned that the federal government had been unwilling to recognize
the legitimacy of their union or to accept Ross as principal chief.
Arbuckle addressed the assembly on April 21 and, hoping to mollify
the eastern faction, he passed quickly over Poinsett's action toward
Ross and implied that it would not be permanent. The eastern faction responded to Arbuckle the next day, stating that all obstacles to
the recognition of the union had been taken care of in January and
that they would not accept Ross's deposition, even temporarily. The
western Cherokees left the post within a few days, so little came of
Arbuckle's work except a promise that Vann would call another assembly of the eastern Cherokees. The general found Vann as pro-
crastinating as ever, and the meeting at Fort Gibson, originally

scheduled for April 20, did not get underway until May 25, and the Cherokees were uncompromising when they learned that an essential element of Arbuckle's plan for a new government was that Ross should have no part in it.[31]

Again Arbuckle called a meeting of the two factions at Fort Gibson for June 10, 1840. After ten days of rigorous negotiations, Arbuckle realized that he could not get the eastern faction to compromise on the Cherokee Act of Union or the Constitution, so he turned his attention to the Old Settlers. Agreements eventually were worked out to accept the constitution in its original form and the Act of Union with only slight modifications. These additions to the Act of Union would entitle the Old Settlers to part of the per capita payments and to certain offices in the new government.[32]

Ross and the delegation had left the Cherokee Nation about November 15, 1839. Ross traveled to New Jersey to place his son Silas in the Lawrenceville Classical and Commercial High School there before proceeding to Washington, where he joined the other delegates at Fuller's Hotel. The group sent a note to Poinsett on December 31 requesting an interview. Poinsett replied that they were welcome as representatives of "their portion" of the Cherokees, but that no communication would be held with Ross until a full investigation of the murders of the Ridges and Boudinot was accomplished, as Ross was suspected of being the "instigator and abettor of the foul murders." The delegation declined any audience without their chief. To Ross's note asking for the names of those who implicated him in the murders, Poinsett replied that evidence would be supplied in the course of the investigation. Lewis Ross discovered that although Poinsett did not believe Ross had personally ordered the murders, he felt the chief's innocence was questionable because of his refusal to produce the accused assassins. The secretary concluded that the federal government would not acknowledge Ross as chief or deal with him as such.[33]

Two rival delegations were also present in the capital city: John Bell, Stand Watie, and William Rogers represented the treaty faction, and the Old Settlers had sent a group of eight men who agreed to pay their own expenses. The two groups worked in tandem in an effort to offset Ross's effectiveness. Considering themselves a "distinct community," they sought to alleviate "the late bloody proceedings of the Ross Party" by dividing the Cherokee Nation. They appealed to Poinsett to allow them to merge the treaty party and the Old Settlers independent of the Ross faction, with a division of the annuities proportionate to their numbers. Poinsett would not consent to this plan or accept the factions as a "separate independent community."[34]

Ross looked to his friends in the East for assistance. Several men loaned the delegation money to meet Washington expenses, and Ross garnered the talents of John Howard Payne for work on several Cherokee petitions. Payne possessed copies of many Cherokee documents which he planned to use in a projected history of the tribe. Ross asked that he bring his notes along and told him of his present status: "The bar of the Executive door which has been bolted against my admission into the presence of His transitory Highness of the White House, is still closed—but I do not despair of yet finding entrance thro the Legislative Hall." Directing their appeal to Congress after Poinsett had closed the executive entrance, the Ross delegation laid out a mass of correspondence. Only touching on the forced removal, they detailed the events which had left their country in a state of disunity and near anarchy. Deploring the stubbornness of the Old Settlers and the nonrecognition of their chief by Poinsett, they declared themselves the legitimate authority of the tribe. Even though the House Committee on Indian Affairs took up the petition and censured the Department of War, the House of Representatives refused to publish the committee's findings. The report became public only after a member, John Bell of Tennessee, leaked it to the press.[35]

William Shorey Coodey, an Old Settler who aligned with his uncle Chief Ross, arrived in Washington in March to join the delegation, bringing additional documents to lend support to the eastern Cherokee case. He also brought hope that difficulties may have been settled at the January meeting called by Stokes. Coodey met with Poinsett to discuss Ross's proscription and the Ridge-Boudinot murders. Somewhat overzealous, he made the statement that the Cherokees looked upon the Ridges and Boudinot as traitors and that tribal laws demanded that they be punished. Coodey's emphasis was a reaction to Poinsett's characterization of the dominant faction as a *"murderous majority."* Coodey's outburst, however, angered the secretary, and he refused to have any further dealing with the Cherokees.[36]

The Ross delegation applied for tribal annuities, but were unsuccessful; no money would be paid until internal difficulties ceased. Such a ruling appeared to the delegation as an attempt to starve the Cherokees into submission by forcing them to recognize the New Echota treaty. What particularly upset the Ross group was the knowledge that the western delegation had been paid over three thousand dollars in annuities. Actually, this payment came out of earlier money owed the western Cherokees, but the timing of the payment gave the appearance of favoritism. Ross also made a personal request for the money owed him for his improvements taken under the Treaty of New Echota. He was careful that his request not be construed as a final settlement for his claim or as an indemnity for removal damages and insisted that this payment should in no way be viewed as a recognition of the Treaty of New Echota. He was surprised to learn that the claim had been reduced by $342.56 by some debts of which he knew nothing. He was even more surprised to learn that Commissioner of Indian Affairs Crawford perceived his request "objectionable in tone" and had withdrawn the requisition. Ross had wanted to make certain that by accepting some payment at that time he would not damage his rights to a future claim, as he thought his property in the old Cherokee Nation worth more than double the award. Ross needed the money and withdrew the "protest." The money was paid, but the reduction remained, and he received $23,323.18, which he used in part to pay the expenses of the delegation in Washington.[37]

In the latter part of August 1840 Ross left Washington for Indian Territory. Accompanied by John Howard Payne, the delegation went overland by way of New Orleans, then up the Arkansas River to Van Buren. Bad roads and low water so slowed the trip that several Cherokees, apprehensive for their chief, sent a party after him and escorted the delegation into Tahlequah. Soon after Ross arrived, runners were sent throughout the Cherokee Nation to call the National Council into session. When Ross addressed the assembly on October 28, he regretfully announced the "entire failure to gain any of the objects of their mission." Ross laid before the legislature the petitions and papers presented at Washington and the reports of the

United States executive department on Cherokee questions. Ross explained that part of the delay by Congress was due to the approaching presidential election that had absorbed the Washington community's attention and then he turned the meeting to legislative action with the hope that their "labors for the public good merit the smile of Heaven." The National Council appointed Ross, David Vann, and John Benge as delegates to Washington, and they departed from the Cherokee Nation about February 1, 1841.[38]

General Arbuckle at Fort Gibson was still under orders not to recognize the validity of Ross's leadership, and his correspondence with the Cherokee National Council was in this vein. The orders fit nicely with his personal feelings, for he believed that Ross hampered a return to peace. The National Council took up the general's points regarding military activities but were adamant that "no external authority exists for displacing or appointing Chiefs or officers of any Indian Nation." They informed Arbuckle that they believed Poinsett would soon remove Ross's proscription and recognize him as chief. This actually happened in November 1840, when Poinsett lifted the ban on payments of money due the tribe. Armstrong thus considered all objections to the Cherokee government removed and, for his own part, wished to see the Cherokees under their own authority. Bell's so-called suppressed report made Arbuckle appear a principal cause of Cherokee problems, and his continued presence must have been an embarrassment to the Department of War, for he soon was transferred to a new command in New Orleans and replaced by General Zachary Taylor. Montfort Stokes, temporarily removed from office, also was returned to his position as Cherokee agent.[39]

In many ways the immediate postremoval era proved more disruptive than the tormented years preceding the forced migration. In the old Cherokee Nation, tribal divisions had centered largely on ideological differences, while the new factionalism grew out of struggles for power, both political and economic. Ross clearly had the numerical edge and the political adroitness to settle the struggle. Had the Cherokees been left to their own devices, they might well have decided the contest without any more bloodshed than actually occurred, and probably with much less. This, of course, does not excuse vendettas carried out by hot-headed Ross adherents against the treaty party, apparently without the sanction or knowledge of Chief Ross. But the repeated interference of Arbuckle only prolonged a natural political reordering. Indeed, his actions can be explained only by assuming that he had a personal dislike of Ross. Had federal officials listened to the steadier counsel of Armstrong or Stokes, reunion might have been achieved more quickly and under less anguished circumstances. Ross himself may have delayed the reordering process, for a vigorous attempt on his part to discover and prosecute the Ridges' assassins might have lessened suspicions that he had a part in the murders. Ross moreover might have bid for restraint in the terms offered Stand Watie and his cohorts, thus making himself appear less a vengeful dictator. But violence persisted over the next half-dozen years, and unity was only a facade for deep-seated hatreds.

8

SEMBLANCE OF UNITY

ROSS arrived in Washington in February 1841 with renewed hope that the Cherokees could obtain a final settlement of their differences with the federal government. With the accession of a Whig administration under President William Henry Harrison and Vice President John Tyler, and with a friend of the Cherokees, John Bell, as secretary of war, Ross's confidence must have swelled as he entered the capital city. Indeed, the financial arrangements worked out that year went a long way to revive the sagging trust of the Cherokees in the United States government.

The Cherokee delegation members met with Harrison and Bell on March 23 and were greatly encouraged by their reception. Cherokee claims for removal damages was one pressing matter, for a great many of the Ross adherents had not registered demands in 1838, thinking that their chief could stop removal. That week the delegates requested a clearer definition of the relationship between the United States and the Cherokee Nation and asked to begin negotiations for a new treaty. Ross's hopes faltered at this point, for the new administration was hesitating in its approach to the Indian problem. Then the death of President Harrison in April and the accession of John Tyler caused further apprehension among the Cherokees, and indeed the transition caused further delay in the settlement of Cherokee grievances.[1]

Several weeks elapsed before the delegation again approached Secretary of War Bell. They depicted the Treaty of New Echota as "one of the most monstrous political frauds which ever stained the page of history" and called for a clear title to their lands to guarantee they would never be driven from their homes again. While these matters were left unanswered for a time, the Tyler administration paid

David Vann, Cherokee national treasurer and a delegate at the time, over one hundred thousand dollars due the Cherokees from interest on investments by the federal government as stipulated in the New Echota pact.[2]

During the sweltering summer, many Washingtonians visited fashionable resorts on the Atlantic coast. Ross also frequented these spots when the press of Cherokee business was not too confining. At Cape May in New Jersey, Saratoga Springs in New York, and Brandywine Springs in Delaware, Ross relaxed and met friends. Ross also toured the great cities of that day—Boston, New York, and Philadelphia. At Philadelphia he had a brief romantic interlude with Elizabeth Milligan, a woman he had known as early as 1838, but their relationship did not warm until 1841 when her mother Anne asked that Ross find some clerical work to relieve the listless spirits of her daughter. Ross, the perfect suitor, was ready to cheer Elizabeth by occasional walks in the countryside, and in quaint nineteenth-century prose he confided that "nothing would afford me more pleasure than to wait upon her at any time."[3]

The relationship culminated in a long letter to Elizabeth in which Ross wrote fatalistically of the mysterious future laid before them. He recounted the tragedies of his life and pointed out that only the "interposition of an all wise Being" enabled him to surmount them. With justifiable pride, he recorded the advancement of the Cherokees in the arts of civilization and projected their eventual union with the United States. Ross candidly reminded Elizabeth of his responsibilities as chief and of his duties to his people. These words, no doubt, were to serve as a warning to accompany the proposal he made, for if Elizabeth were to accept, it must be with the full knowledge of his divided loyalties. Having given this caution, Ross continued: "To say, that my long cherished friendship for you, has so ardently seized the affections of my heart, as to make my silent thoughts doat upon you as a lover, would be nothing more than an avowal of the solemn truth."[4]

From these affectionate terms, Ross, the politician and diplomat, moved to expressions less romantic, "presenting a petition craving your reply on the subject of my fervent desire for negotiating a treaty with you for the purpose of uniting our hearts in the bonds of matrimony!" Fearful that she might consider him too old, Ross stressed the soundness of his health and promised frank replies to any inquiries about himself. Either Elizabeth declined or Ross reconsidered. One year later he wrote her in less affectionate tones as he departed for Indian Territory and left her as a token of their friendship the sculptured bust of Red Jacket, a Seneca Indian chief. Perhaps Ross realized that loneliness and mutual regard were insufficient ingredients for a successful marriage.[5]

William Shorey Coodey joined the delegation in July 1841 to replace John Benge whose health was failing. Coodey kept Ross informed of Washington developments while the chief toured the East during the summer. Viewing the debates on Cherokee finances with a fresh outlook, Coodey commented that he felt chances were good to collect the money, but that the Whig Party was about to *"mire down"* in the treasury. The Whig administration had not made a clean sweep of the executive offices and had retained Commissioner of Indian Affairs T. Hartley Crawford who had hampered the Cherokees' financial settlements. The Whigs may have offered the job to another man, but Coodey observed that "Crawford sticks like a counterfeit dollar." Other offices were filled by Cherokee friends. In fact, for the first time in several years, Ross felt no need to appeal to Congress over President Tyler, and he placed no memorial before the legislative branch.[6]

In the latter days of August 1841 Ross appealed to Bell again. He stressed that although the Cherokee delegates had been in Washington since February, they could report no definite results and, as the time for the annual National Council was approaching, they would have to leave no later than mid-September. "To say to them," Ross said, "after so long an absence, that nothing has been concluded upon, may induce a distrust of us, or a loss of that fraternal regard, for the government of the United States." Again Ross asked for a new treaty and requested that Bell himself negotiate it because of his intimate knowledge of the Cherokee situation. In those final days Bell acted decisively. The Cherokees secured payment of the claim of over $500,000 and a further payment of $18,000 on interest from the trust fund. Nor was President Tyler any less accommodating. Meeting the delegation the day before their departure, the president presented them with a letter that gave the first ray of hope for a new treaty. Tyler solemnly assured the three men, "So far as it may be in my power to prevent it, you may be assured that it shall not again be said that a Cherokee has petitioned for justice in vain." But the passage that surely shone most brilliantly was Tyler's promise to negotiate a new treaty

which shall give to the Cherokee nation full indemnity for all wrongs which they may have suffered, establish upon a permanent basis the political rela-tions between them and the people of the United States, guaranty their lands in absolute fee simple, and prescribe specific rules in reference to sub-jects of the most interesting character to them and their remotest posterity, a new sun will have dawned upon them, in whose brightness their perma-nent happiness and true glory may be read by the whole world.

Had Ross written the message himself, he could not have been more thorough in touching the points he had worked so ardently to set-tle.[7]

In contrast to the two years before 1841, the Cherokee Nation had remained relatively peaceful during Ross's absence. The elections of August 1841 had proceeded with no great difficulty, and the National Council met in October with the new assistant principal chief, A. M. Vann, an Old Settler, presiding. Perhaps Ross had not been as diligent as usual in keeping his constituents posted on his progress at the federal capital. As many of the tribe were clamoring for their per capita payments, Vann addressed Bell endeavoring to discover what progress the delegation had made, especially regard-ing the per capita funds. Learning that the chief had received a large payment, the Cherokee legislature passed an act in October ordering that the per capita money "shall be applied to no other purpose whatever, than an equal division among the citizens of the Chero-kee Nation." One observer noted that some of Ross's warmest friends had supported this move. It seems likely that the act was an outgrowth of the Old Settlers' disenchantment, which augmented a general fear that the Cherokees would receive no recompense for their losses in the East.[8]

Ross arrived only in time for the last day of the National Council meeting, but the importance of Tyler's letter persuaded him to call an extra session of the legislature. Ross rode from Park Hill to the

Tahlequah assembly area shortly after noon on November 29. Major Ethan Allen Hitchcock, a special agent of the federal government, was on hand and closely observed Ross.

[Ross] tied his horse to a tree. Great numbers of the people were standing around but Indian-like no one approached him. I was the first to go up and speak to him. We shook hands and several questions of civility passed and we separated. He walked a short distance and then began a general greeting. Very many went up and shook hands with their head chief. It was nearly an hour after his arrival before he took his place in a sort of pulpit under a large shed and the Committee and Council and people assembled.[9]

Major Hitchcock remained during the meeting, making careful observations and writing brief sketches of the principal men of the Cherokee Nation. He left this description of Ross:

Much is said of him in the States, and like other conspicuous men he has been variously spoken of, in terms of great praise and great censure. He resides five miles from this place on a beautiful prairie in sight of Park Hill—is of mixed blood between 45 and 50 years of age—is under size and his manners, unless excited, have a dash of diffidence in them—is not of ready speech—speaks English principally and will not trust himself to address his own people in Cherokee—is a man of strong passions and settled purposes which he pursues with untiring zeal; is of undoubted courage unless it be that he fears the defeat of his plans more than the loss of life and would preserve the latter to execute the former. After much attentive observation I am of opinion that John Ross is an honest man and a patriot laboring for the good of his people. In the recent trouble of his nation, including several years, with almost unlimited opportunities he has not enriched himself. It is unfortunate for his reputation that several of his relatives, particularly his brother Lewis, have realized fortunes through his instrumentality, though it is fair to consider that this may have resulted from contracts properly made. It would be stranger if there was not ambition with the patriotism of Jno. Ross, but he seeks the fame of establishing his nation and heaping benefits upon his people. Though not a fluent speaker, even in conversation, he is a clear-minded accurate thinker of very far-reaching views.[10]

Tahlequah was barely a town in 1841, hardly a capital for a proud people, and the National Council chambers consisted of no more than a roof on several poles, while long split logs served as seats for twelve to fifteen councilmen. The chief read his message to the crowd, and it was translated into Cherokee, sentence by sentence, by Jesse Bushyhead, the chief justice of the Cherokee Supreme Court. Ross related the cordiality of the new administration and his personal confidence in Tyler's promises. Great care was given to the reading of Tyler's message. Before the close of the council that day, it was read twice more, and each reading elicited close attention. All other correspondence was also presented to the National Council, and Ross told of the various payments. Ross felt that another delegation should go immediately to Washington to work toward the fulfillment of Tyler's promises.[11]

In the following days the National Council dealt with several issues introduced by Ross in his message. The legislature appointed Ross as head of a new delegation and suspended the act relating to per capita funds until a new treaty could be negotiated. The National Council also acted upon Ross's suggestion for establishing a system of public education. A special fund had been set aside for this purpose in the Treaty of New Echota in 1835, and it had been a dream for a number of years. The education act of 1841 passed by the National Council called for eleven public schools in the Cherokee Nation and the necessary governing apparatus to keep them functioning. This was the beginning of an educational system that would be the envy of surrounding tribes and neighboring white communities as well.[12]

President Tyler had removed the aging Cherokee Agent Stokes from office in 1841 and had appointed in his place the vigorous Pierce Mason Butler. Butler arrived in Indian Territory in early December 1841 and witnessed the last days of the Cherokee National Council. After several months at his new post, he addressed a "confidential" letter to Crawford summarizing his observations during the period. He wrote of Chief Ross in terms very similar to those of Major Hitchcock: "I think him privately, a retiring, modest, good man; as a public man he has dignity and intelligence. He is ambitious and stubborn, often tenacious of his own views to an extent that prejudices both himself and his cause; wanting in Wisdom and policy in selecting at all times his own friends and partisans for public Employment. He looks rather to what he thinks the rights of his people than to what is expedient or to what is to be obtained for them."[13]

Ross left for Washington the last week of March 1842 accom-

panied by Jesse Bushyhead and John Benge; Vann and Coodey were
to join them later. Making a leisurely trip of nearly six weeks, Ross
stopped off in New Jersey to enroll his son George in the Lawrenceville Classical and Commercial High School. Before leaving Ross
had learned of the appointment of John C. Spencer to the post of
secretary of war vacated by John Bell, but to the Cherokees' disap-
pointment, Crawford remained as commissioner of Indian affairs
throughout Tyler's tenure. Ross had hoped his friend Thomas L.
McKenney might be elevated to the office.[14]

Within a few months after they arrived, Spencer requested the
Cherokee delegates to put the objects of their mission in writing.
Three times in June 1842 the delegates laid out Cherokee grievances, but Spencer never seemed satisfied that he had a full understanding of their problems. Their correspondence centered on seven
points: that a new treaty be drafted with provisions for permanent
title to Cherokee lands; that liberal allowance be made for their
abandoned lands; that military posts be moved beyond the limits of
the Cherokee Nation; that licensed traders in their country be cur-
tailed; that the practice of trying Cherokee citizens in surrounding
state courts be ended; that administration of Cherokee public funds
be changed; and that removal and resettlement claims under the
Treaty of New Echota of 1835 be finally settled. On the last point
the delegation was explicit. Learning that a board of commissioners
was being organized to settle these claims, the delegates were ready
to present the mass of documents they had so carefully gathered
before leaving the Cherokee Nation. Most of that work proved useless, as the board was not organized until November 1842 and then
spent a good deal of its time registering North Carolina Cherokees.
This board also was reluctant to approve the claims of the Ross party
emigrants as they had not moved under the two-year stipulation of
the Treaty of New Echota.[15]

Meanwhile, it was well into August 1842 before Spencer presented
Ross and his colleagues with "Articles of a New Convention."
After several days of carefully examining the document, the delegates replied that it fell so far short of their expectations that they
could not accept it. The secretary in return implied that the Cherokees were not actually prepared to accept a new treaty until the
Treaty of New Echota was "annulled." Ross's reply was that treaties

with the tribe had been made time and again without first voiding earlier pacts. Ross recalled the bright hopes given the Cherokees by Tyler's letter of the preceding year, and he was bitterly disappointed in this turn in the negotiations. Ross reasoned that perhaps "we have unwittingly been induced to expect too much, to infer what was never intended." The delegation discontinued negotiations but left Butler, who was also in Washington, a memorandum of the provisions they hoped for in a new treaty. These Butler relayed to Spencer shortly before they left about September 1842.[16]

Like other tribes of Indian Territory, the Cherokees had adopted many of the institutions of the southern states, including slavery. In time, slavery became an intimate part of their lives, and they developed an elaborate system of laws to govern it and faced the normal problems associated with human bondage. In November 1842 some twenty blacks escaped from their owners Joseph Vann and other Cherokee citizens after some plundering. Ross and the National Council ordered Captain John Drew to gather a force of 100 armed men and follow this band into the Creek Nation; Drew's force would be held blameless if any resisting Negroes were killed. Within a month Drew had rounded up the blacks and delivered them to Fort Gibson for safekeeping, as the Cherokee Nation had no jails.[17]

Removal to Indian Territory had brought the Five Civilized Tribes, the Cherokees, Choctaws, Chickasaws, Creeks, and Seminoles, closer together and had activated common problems that had been dormant in their old homes. Realizing the need for a general Indian convention, the Cherokee legislature during the 1842 session acted to bring about a meeting of the surrounding tribes. Chief Ross and John Looney, a member of the Cherokee Executive Council, met the chiefs of the Creek Nation, Rolly McIntosh and Ufalar Harjo, at Fort Gibson in January 1843, where Cherokee Agent Butler helped to organize the proposed convention.[18]

The chiefs set the meeting of the general convention for mid-June 1843 at Tahlequah and invited numerous tribes from throughout the West. Delegates and onlookers from at least eighteen tribes began assembling two weeks before the convention got underway and were housed in log buildings on the Cherokee Council Grounds at Tahlequah. William H. Goode, an observer just arrived in Indian

Territory to set up a Methodist mission at the abandoned Fort Coffee, noted that Ross had only the faintest marking of an Indian and that he was similar in appearance and size to ex-President Martin Van Buren. As Goode walked about the council ground, he observed the "motley appearance" of the crowd: "The costume of the Indian tribes is greatly varied, from the richest and most genteel style of their white neighbors to the rudest and simplest form of savage dress . . . a singular and fantastic comingling of tastes . . . a great passion for gay colors." [19]

Meeting under a large shed on June 23, the delegations were seated on crude benches around a central table on which peace pipes had been placed. A blast of the horn signaled the opening of the meeting; then Ross expressed the purpose for the gathering. "Brothers," he began, "you have also smoked the pipe of peace, and taken the hand of friendship around the council-fire, newly rekindled here at Tahlequah in the West." Then Ross paused for interpreters to translate to their tribes, and Goode listened to the low murmurs of approval and understanding. Ross continued, "When we look back to the history of our race, we see some green spots that are pleasing to us. We also see many things to make our hearts sad. . . . We are grateful to our Creator for having united the hearts of the red men in peace. . . . We should, therefore, extend the hand of peace from tribe to tribe, till peace is established between every nation of red men within the reach of our voice." [20]

After four weeks the tribes worked out a compact promising perpetual peace and friendship. They also pledged never to "cede . . . to the United States, any part of their present Territory." This article came as something of a surprise to the federal agents present, and they likely were offended. Other articles were less startling. Although only three tribes—the Cherokees, Creeks, and Osages—signed the pact, copies were made generally available, and most delegates returned to their homes with good feeling. [21]

The convention ended a little over a month before the first general election in the Cherokee Nation. As in 1841, all members of the national legislature would stand election, but August 1843 marked the first occasion since the ratification of the Cherokee Constitution in 1840 for the election of the principal chief and the assistant principal chief. Ross had as his running mate George Lowrey, who had served as assistant principal chief for nearly a year after the death of A. M. Vann. Opposing them were two Old Settlers, Joseph Vann and W. S. Adair. In an overwhelming victory Ross polled nearly two-thirds of the ballots cast, winning by a majority of nearly nine hundred votes.[22]

Despite the general quietude, there remained groups in some election districts still vehemently opposed to the Ross government, particularly in the Saline District where serious trouble broke out. There David Vann and Isaac Bushyhead, both Ross supporters, served as election superintendents, and on August 8 were making out the election returns when one George West attacked Bushyhead and stabbed him to death. Vann, trying to mount his horse, was held by Jacob West, George's father, who yelled "kill him" while several men beat Vann nearly to death with clubs. When bystanders tried to intervene, their lives were likewise threatened, but they eventually saved Vann and Elijah Hicks, another Ross supporter who also was attacked.[23]

As news of this outrage spread, more than two hundred armed men met at Ross's house at Park Hill to protect the chief and to seek out the offenders. Ross sent out runners to investigate the incident and then turned the apprehension of the criminals over to Cherokee sheriffs in the appropriate districts. Jacob West and his son John were apprehended and taken into custody, but George seems to have escaped. Jacob West tried to claim immunity as a white man, since he had married into the tribe, but his petition was denied and he was subsequently tried and executed by Cherokee authorities. John West received 100 lashes and was deprived of Cherokee citizenship, and at least two others who were caught probably received similar treatment.[24]

The annual meeting of the Cherokee National Council convened in October 1843 at Tahlequah, and Ross addressed the assembly, recounting the events of the preceding year. He spoke of the violence in the August election and the actions taken toward the captured criminals. When the chief reviewed the general convention of neighboring tribes in June and presented the covenant adopted there, it was quickly ratified. Ross, mentioning the receipt from Boston through the American Board of Foreign Missions of a printing press and type in the Cherokee and English languages, suggested legislation to establish a national newspaper. Within a few days, the National Council established the *Cherokee Advocate*. William P. Ross, Ross's nephew who had just graduated from Princeton College, became editor and remained in that capacity for the greater part of the life of the newspaper. Funds were appropriated for a building to house the press in Tahlequah, and the National Council provided that the paper would serve as a training ground for Cherokee youths in the "art of printing."[25]

Because of the continuing excited conditions in the Cherokee Nation, the National Council also authorized the appointment of a guard of six men, at $1.50 per day, to be stationed at Park Hill for the safety of Ross and of the Cherokee national records. Ross also was authorized to hire a secretary to assist him with correspondence. The National Council further determined to send Ross and four others as a Washington delegation, which included, besides Ross, Elijah Hicks, John Benge, and David Vann, and William P. Ross as secretary.[26]

Ross reached Washington in mid-April 1844, settled at Fuller's Hotel, and presented the credentials of the delegation to the new secretary of war, William Wilkins of Pennsylvania, in a personal meeting on April 22. As was customary, the delegation wrote down the purposes of its mission, which were forwarded to Wilkins two weeks later. Enclosing a copy of President Tyler's letter of September 20, 1841, which had generated so much hope, the delegation expressed a desire to begin negotiations there. Wilkins's pleasant but noncommittal reply brought the first hint of problems Ross and his comrades were to face that year in Washington. Wilkins advised the delegates that President Tyler had received numerous complaints from two dissatisfied factions of the Cherokee Nation and presented Ross with a communication their representatives had placed before the president at Wilkins' request. The document called for a portion of the Cherokee lands to be set apart for the exclusive use of the Old Settler and treaty-party factions. The Old Settlers also desired their traditional one-third share of the annuities, while the treaty party demanded the payment of the per capita funds promised in the Treaty of New Echota of 1835.[27]

Representatives of both factions had arrived in Washington before the Ross delegation and had laid petitions before Congress. The treaty party, represented by John A. Bell and Ezekiel Starr, accused Ross of misappropriating the funds provided in the New Echota treaty; the Old Settler delegates John Rogers, Thomas L. Rogers, and James Carey denounced Ross as an unrelenting tyrant. The Cherokee National Council in 1842, learning that Rogers at that time intended to plead the dissatisfied Old Settlers' case in Washington, had protested his authority and his recognition by the federal government. Ross also had complained of Rogers's activities and emphasized to Pierce Mason Butler, "No good can grow out of the intermeddlings of private individuals in public affairs. . . . It is high time that the functionaries of the Govt. should check the evil growing out of this pernicious source." While the dissatisfied factions had no immediate success in their petitions, they effectively checked Ross's progress.[28]

Although Ross and his colleagues charged that the other parties in Washington were unauthorized and that the Old Settlers were well represented in the Cherokee government, their pleas for readjusting Cherokee–United States relations gained little sympathy from Wilkins. He found the tribe too divided to allow him to negotiate only with Ross. Not wishing to become entangled in the "intricate labyrinths of diplomacy," the delegation outlined its main negotiating points: a "just indemnity" for Cherokee lands in the East; permanent rights to the lands in the West; clearly defined political relations between the United States and the Cherokee Nation; guarantees that stocks purchased for the Cherokees by the United States would yield a specific sum; and provisions for the remainder of Cherokees in the East to emigrate West. In short, these were the provisions they had sought from Tyler in 1841 and largely the items he had promised. A personal interview made little headway, and negotiations were further stalled when Wilkins took a short vacation in June 1844.[29]

With Wilkins's return in early July came a lengthy letter which answered explicitly the delegation's five points. On every point he referred the delegates to the New Echota treaty, for in its terms he found adequate response to all their problems. Wilkins also acknowledged the complaints of the Old Settlers and the treaty party, and related to Ross that he had decided to send a commission into the Cherokee Nation to "ascertain the true and exact extent of the

discontent and spirit of hostility" among the Cherokees. The delegates, disheartened by the lack of any substantial agreements, force-
fully belittled the "supposed division and domestic strife" in the
Cherokee Nation. The Creek Nation, they indicated, had endured
more violence and discord than ever existed among the Cherokees,
but the federal government had never attempted to establish authority over them. Capricious gestures such as this were why Ross kept
pleading for an unambiguous definition of the relationship between
the two governments. Its work seemingly counterproductive, the
delegation decided to return home in late August 1844. Ross and his
nephew William spent some time in the East while the others
turned toward the Cherokee Nation.[30]

Ross's first destination was Wilmington, Delaware, and the home
of a young Quaker girl who had captured his attention as no one ever
had. In time she would fill an emotional void in his life that his
grown children and political friends could not, and she became the
companion that Quatie never was. Mary Bryan Stapler was the
youngest daughter of a Wilmington merchant, John Stapler. Mary's
mother had died in 1838 and left Mary in the care of the young girl's
older sister Sarah. Ann B. Stapler had raised her children—Sarah,
James, John W., and Mary—in strict Quaker conformity and enrolled
them at the Wilmington Meetinghouse in 1835. Mary converted
of her own accord in 1843. Raised in Quaker affluence, she had all
the advantages money could obtain, attending the best schools in
Pennsylvania, where her father had additional business interests,
and receiving part of her education at the Moravian Female Academy in Bethlehem, Pennsylvania. Only fifteen when she penned her
first coquettish letter to Ross in 1841, her maturity and refinement
grew steadily in the next three years of their courtship. Ross's de-
light in Mary came quickly and was eagerly shown, perhaps too eagerly. He was compelled to apologize to Sarah, the couple's mutual
confidant, for overlooking regulations of the Moravian school and
corresponding directly with Mary. Mary called it her "imprisonment," but Ross, a strict adherent to order, considered the discipline
proper.[31]

The steady flow of their secret correspondence did not begin until
the summer of 1844. The couple hid their growing affection from
Mary's father, knowing he would object to the 36-year difference in

their ages. In flirting tones to her "esteemed Uncle," Mary asked "has time and absence quite obliterated from thy memory one whom thee honored with the name of Niece," and requested his return to rekindle their acquaintance. Ross's quick reply caught the spirit of this young Quaker lass, "the same bewitching and playfull Molly who was wont to touch the heart for the sake of mirth." Duty in Washington had prevented an early rendezvous.[32]

Youthful uncertainty was apparent in Mary's correspondence. She needed reassurance that Ross's affection was sincere and often chided him for his delay in replying to her letters. In fact, she felt for a time that Ross actually loved a friend, Grave Levy, and that "little Cupid had sent forth his darts from her bright eyes into thy heart." She offered her services as a go-between and coyly advised Ross that "a faint heart never won a fair Lady." Ross thought it unlikely that a lady such as Miss Levy could be won by a "sachem of the Western wilds." He drew a picture of that elegant lady "seated in a circular wigwam, canopyed with the soft dressed buffalo skins, and there as mistress of the lodge receiving the salutations of the painted and plumed Chieftains and their dark-eyed Brunettes."[33]

Mary often feared she intruded into Ross's life. She hesitated even when scolding his tardiness, wondering if she had presumed too much. Mary reminded him that nearly two years had passed since they had last met, and she was concerned that during the interval they might have lost the bond that brought them together. Ross assured her that his delay was nothing more than unfamiliarity with "soft and bewitching subjects." Like a schoolboy on his first romance, he sent her lovers' verses, which she confessed not to understand. Ross also had his moments of uncertainty. Curious as to the "hearts that have been disposed of," he was particularly anxious to know "what has become of Molly's?"[34]

Their attraction for each other increased during the summer months of 1844, but Mary's doubts persisted. When she confided that she had pledged never to give her hand without first relinquishing her heart, Ross advised her to keep that pledge and to give her love only when it was fully reciprocated. Ross was so certain by midsummer of his affection that he revealed the purchase of a gem "to be a bosom companion for me all the days of my life!" Certainly he hoped soon to place the stone on Mary's hand.[35]

John Neagle, ca. 1848   *Oklahoma Historical Society*

MARY BRIAN STAPLER ROSS (1825–1865)

One meeting, much too brief, convinced them of their love. Ross reminisced of the delightful walks along the Brandywine and compared his heart to the palpitations of a "wounded fluttering bird." The restless nights convinced young Mary that she had given up her heart, and she thought constantly of Ross. "Why should we longer be separated," Ross questioned, "if our hearts do not deceive us, and our affections for each other be really formed? As to mine they are pure sincere and ardent. And once united with yours in the solemn ties of matrimony, I am sure that nothing but the cold hand of death could ever extinguish them from my bosom." He asked Mary to search her heart and to set an early date for the wedding. Mary consented to the marriage and suggested a spring ceremony. The date was altered because of tribal business, so Mary began making plans for a fall wedding.[36]

In August 1844 Ross wrote Mary's father and sister requesting her hand in marriage, declaring his love for Mary and promising to "confer upon her, the ordinary comforts and happiness of this life." In his letter to Sarah, he acknowledged the vast age difference but again declared his devotion and begged her blessing. It is not surprising that John Stapler, Mary's father, objected to his daughter's marriage, though he seems not to have objected to Ross personally. He was concerned that Mary would live so far away from her home, but Mary's happiness was his first consideration, and ultimately he and Sarah both gave their consent.[37]

The marriage took place on September 2, 1844, in Philadelphia with only a few friends and relatives present. Because Mary was dismissed from the Quaker Church when she decided to marry outside her faith, the ceremony was conducted by Reverend Orson Douglass of the Mariners' Church. Thomas L. McKenney, who most likely had introduced Ross to Mary, was present. In a circumspect letter Ross teased McKenney's curiosity as to the identity of his intended bride, but finally related that "it is the same identical little school girl, whom you once called Molly!" The local newspapers carried the story of the wedding and intimated that Ross was worth half a million dollars.[38]

After a short honeymoon in New York, Ross returned with Mary and his sister-in-law Sarah to the beautiful Rose Cottage at Park Hill just southeast of Tahlequah. When Ross first came to Park Hill, he had established his family in a crude log cabin quite unlike the home he and Mary now approached. John Howard Payne visited Ross in 1840 and described that first dwelling as lacking everything except dirt and space. Payne had noted the unfastened doors with the constant passage of Indians to and fro, dressed in "queer, wild, garb; and blanket coats of every hue." At meals there Ross had entertained as many as the table would accommodate, and Payne wondered how the housekeeper could prepare an evening meal, not knowing whether she would have to feed and lodge twenty-five, fifty, or double that number.[39]

Although the house to which Ross now took Mary was quite different, the spirit was unchanged. Few people who journeyed through the Cherokee Nation during the years before the Civil War could resist the hospitality of the Cherokee chief, and many described the comfortable surroundings of Rose Cottage so unfamiliar to the Indian wilds. The yellow house was situated on a hillside surrounded by abundant native oaks and elms for shade, while numerous fruit trees graced the grounds. Approached by a winding driveway bordered by a variety of roses, it was one of the most notable in all the Indian Territory. Two-storied, it faced north with a pillared porch extending the length of the front. At each end there were large chimneys of native stone. Across the road was a garden of nearly two acres filled with fruits, melons, and grapes. The ample interior included guest rooms, family rooms, a library, and a parlor, all exquisitely furnished with mahogany and rosewood furniture brought from the eastern United States. Delicate china and rich linen graced a table certain to be surrounded by a host of travelers and Indian friends. The noted artist John Mix Stanley visited the Ross mansion shortly after Mary's arrival and wrote glowingly of Ross's unbounded hospitality. Waddy Thompson, a personal friend of the Rosses and sometime counsel during Cherokee-Washington negotiations, left this description of Rose Cottage and its master: "He resides about four miles from Tahlequah, in a very spacious wooden house, furnished with great taste and elegance. I have seen few men who perform the office of host with such a combination of ease, dignity and cordiality. The whole establishment, house, furniture, host and hostess are a perfect pattern of the residence of the country gentleman."[40]

Ross and his bride arrived in Tahlequah in time for the last days of the National Council of 1844. Ross addressed the meeting and presented the correspondence of the delegation with Secretary of War Wilkins. Although his short message largely let the correspondence speak for itself, he did say that it appeared Wilkins's primary mission was to avoid fulfilling the pledge made by President Tyler in 1841. The *Cherokee Advocate* published all Ross's correspondence with Wilkins and also the measures adopted by the dissident factions in Washington. After the National Council had studied the events as reported, it passed an act declaring the "inalienable rights" of the Cherokees as a "separate and distinct Nation" which had formed into one nation under the Act of Union of 1840. The National Council protested the recognition of different elements within the tribe by the federal government and also objected to the commission to be appointed by Wilkins, feeling it would only fan factionalism and open the way to greater disturbances. In view of the disappointing results of previous years, the National Council appointed Ross and eight others to renew negotiations at Washington and gave them full powers to conclude a treaty.[41]

Secretary Wilkins appointed his promised committee consisting of Brigadier General Roger Jones, Lieutenant Colonel R. B. Mason, and Cherokee agent Pierce Mason Butler to investigate Cherokee factionalism and the "lengths of oppression, resistance, and violence, to which the excitement of each against the other has severally led the parties." The commissioners arrived on November 15, 1844, and, contrary to the wish of the National Council and over the protests of Chief Ross, met with a group of Old Settlers and treaty party members at Tahlonteskee some twenty-five miles south of Fort Gibson. There from December 17 to 24 both factions brought complaints before the commission. The complaints of the Old Settlers revolved around the legitimacy of the Act of Union of 1840, which they declared spurious. Adherents of the treaty party denounced the "mockery of a trial by jury" of Jacob and John West and the seizure and investigation of many of their people without explanation.[42]

Ross, anticipating that "no good could grow out of a meeting so convened," proposed several times that the commission meet at Tahlequah where the people could be assembled easily, including

John Rogers, the major complainant. Since the commissioners were set on meeting with the Old Settlers who would not agree to any coordinated conference with the Ross party, Ross delegated eleven men to attend the commission's inquiry and report the proceedings to the National Council. The delegation spent two days at Fort Gibson, December 17 and 18; they participated as the commissioners questioned the returned General Matthew Arbuckle and attempted to show that a union had been achieved in 1839. Finally they withdrew without questioning the Old Settler complainants.[43]

After the board had completed its examination of the Old Settlers and the treaty party, members went to Tahlequah to receive the testimony of the "Cherokee authorities." The commission presented accusations from the two dissident factions and invited Ross to respond. As to the lack of authenticity of the Act of Union, the Cherokee authorities replied that the complainants were not "legal representatives" of the Old Settlers and that legitimate agents for that group had signed the Act of Union. When presented with names of Old Settlers who had signed the Act of Union and who now denied their authority to have done so, the Ross adherents replied that by June 1840 the western Cherokees had largely joined the dominant faction. The Ross supporters easily documented the fact that the so-called acts of violence and oppression had been committed under legally constituted authority with the intention of lessening strife. As their final reply to these charges, the Ross group presented a breakdown showing a majority of the Cherokee government since 1839 to be made up of members of the treaty party and the Old Settler faction.[44]

Jones, Mason, and Butler gathered at Fort Gibson after hearing the testimonies of the contending parties. In their report, filed January 17, 1845, they took up the major complaints of the discontented parties, noting that of the 900 who assembled to complain of injustices, about 150 were not even Indians. The commissioners also discovered that many dissidents had come with the idea that their presence somehow might aid in the recovery of the per capita money. The commissioners believed the Act of Union to be legitimate, yet qualified this belief by noting many had signed it with assurances that they would later share in financial allotments. The three men also found the Old Settlers held many offices in the Cherokee government and that their allegation of oppression held little truth.[45]

The commissioners suggested that discord would continue among the Cherokees as long as the "discontented . . . find a ready audience at Washington." The three men advised against a division of the nation. Jones and Mason may have been persuaded on this point by Butler, who had become convinced earlier. They concluded that the "germ of discontent" lay in the nonpayment by the federal government of the per capita funds, and the commissioners favored expanding this fund, as they felt the United States should repay any money taken from the five million fund. In the interest of restoring harmony, they recommended that a new treaty be concluded on the basis of President Tyler's letter of September 1841.[46]

Ross and his colleagues left for Washington on April 2, 1845, feeling that the commission's report would greatly increase their chances of obtaining a new treaty and the alleviation of many outstanding Cherokee difficulties, but the delegation was disappointed by the new administration in Washington. James K. Polk, a protégé of Andrew Jackson, had acceded to the presidency in March 1845 and had named William L. Marcy as secretary of war, while Crawford remained as commissioner of Indian affairs until October. Ross found the Democratic administration little disposed to accept the report of Jones, Mason, and Butler, but quite willing to listen to a treaty party delegation. Throughout the sticky summer months of 1845, Ross received only a cool reception from Washington officials. The one measure of success was the partial payment of the Cherokee annuities, which came only after repeated requests. Because of Polk's growing sympathy for the minority parties, Ross felt it necessary to remain in Washington throughout 1845.[47]

With the general acceptance after 1840 of the Cherokee Constitution of 1839 and the Act of Union of 1840, Ross doubtless envisioned an era of peace. Factional wounds, however, were not so easily healed, and dissidents found a ready ear at Washington. Again federal inconsistencies thwarted the Cherokees' national harmony. In spite of promises by President Tyler that the Cherokees would see a new dawn, internal difficulties made the Whig administration wary of negotiating a new treaty. Dissatisfied Old Settlers like Rogers could easily have been brought into the Cherokee government as had others from their faction, but it seems these men were more intent on disrupting normal political processes than in settling actual grievances. The sometimes indiscriminate use of "police forces" by Ross and his adherents probably jeopardized easy acceptance of the chief's leadership. A careful check on zealous subordinates would have been prudent. When Ross finally appeared justified as the legitimate leader of the Cherokees by the report of Jones, Mason, and Butler, a new administration came into office at Washington and paid little attention to that report. Thus the Cherokees faced another period of bitter animosities before unity became more than merely a dream of their chief.

9

TRAVAIL AND TRANQUILITY

THE years 1845 and 1846 were the bloodiest and most divisive in the history of the Cherokee Nation. Each incident of bloodshed aggravated party vendettas as the treaty party and the Old Settlers aligned themselves against the real and imagined oppression of the Ross party. Violence emanated also from groups of desperadoes who clothed themselves in the sanctity of "party" as they plundered the countryside.

Intense tribal terrorism dated from 1839 when the Cherokee patriarch James Starr had been marked for death with the Ridges and Boudinot. Three of his sons, Tom, Bean, and Ellis, the notorious "Starr boys," in 1843 viciously murdered a Cherokee family near Fort Gibson, ravaged their home, and then set it afire. The Cherokee authorities quickly offered rewards and organized police companies against such outrages, but their hands were tied when the Starr brothers crossed the line into Arkansas. Nor was Ross able to negotiate for the return of such fugitives. Often police companies faced lethargy or open opposition from the minority factions who viewed the police as armed vigilance committees established solely to punish Ross opponents. Stand Watie kept his own armed men at old Fort Wayne prepared for an attack by administration forces, and the treaty party came to praise the Starrs as heroes in this drama, when in quieter times they would have been labeled the criminals they were. Violence finally reached such intensity that the Cherokee agent reported in one ten-month period in 1845–46, a total of thirty-four killings, mainly of a political nature. Certainly the situation was near anarchy.[1]

Unable to touch the carefully guarded chief at Rose Cottage, several bandits looted and burned to the ground the home of Ross's daughter Jane one quiet, cold Sunday evening in November 1845. A force of eight hundred men organized to find the criminals captured and summarily executed the elder Starr and wounded two of his sons in open battle. Watie mustered a force of sixty men and awaited siege by the Ross faction at old Fort Wayne; it never came, but skirmishes and killings remained frequent in the Cherokee Nation. The continued violence and threats of open warfare convinced the weaker factions that the only way to escape Ross's tyranny was to divide the nation politically before it split into two armed camps. Watie joined his comrades of the treaty party, and they set out for Washington to air their grievances, where they linked themselves to the embittered Old Settlers who already were working toward a political split.[2]

The western Cherokees had retained two able lawyers, Samuel C. Stambaugh and Amos Kendall, who began a series of appeals to Secretary of War William L. Marcy in October 1845. Stambaugh and Kendall vigorously pointed out injustices the Old Settlers had suffered at the hands of "Ross and his foreign horde." Characterizing the history of the Cherokees since 1839 as a period of political usurpation and domestic strife, they depicted Ross as an "extraordinary man" whose "ruling passion is avarice." They dredged up the recurring charge that Ross could not even claim to be a Cherokee because of his slight degree of Indian blood and because his land settlement outside the Cherokee Nation under the Treaty of 1819 had deprived him of Cherokee citizenship. They also reviewed the financial arrangements Ross had made for removal and, not surprisingly, declared he had profited enormously by plundering his people. The thrust of their indictment was to show the western Cherokees as independent, the Act of Union of 1840 as illegal, and Ross as dishonest and tyrannical. The solution, they contended, was to divide the Cherokee Nation.[3]

When members of the treaty party delegation reached Washington in March 1846, they presented federal officials a series of petitions outlining their grievances developed with the aid of their legal adviser George W. Paschal, an Arkansas lawyer and brother-in-law of the late Major Ridge. Complaining that no member of the treaty party could consider himself safe in the Cherokee Nation, they too emphasized that division was the only possible remedy for Cherokee strife. Beyond that, they exhibited an estimate of money due the Cherokees, a part of which they said had already been despotically squandered by Ross. The treaty party delegation determined that a balance of $2,475,734 was due the tribe on a per capita basis of $147.86 for each Cherokee. The settlement with Ross of over $500,000 in 1841 had eaten into the per capita fund considerably, and extensive payments by the government to Cherokee creditors (treaty party members were generally unaware of this reduction) had taken well over $1,000,000 from the per capita distribution money. The treaty faction delegates protested these large reductions in the fund and demanded the per capita money they felt justly due them.[4]

Ross and his colleagues had appealed to the federal government concerning the favorable report of Jones, Mason, and Butler the previous January. Of course they also referred again to the still unfulfilled promises of former President Tyler. These expressions gained little sympathy and less action. Understanding that the treaty party had met and appointed a delegation, the authorities of the Cherokee Nation circulated a petition among the tribe and forwarded it to Washington. This petition declared that the difficulties in the Cherokee Nation had arisen from the "stealthy incursions of a number of banditti" and not from party strife. The petition further stated that Ross and his colleagues were the only legitimate Cherokee delegates in Washington.[5]

By the latter part of March 1846, the Polk administration was moving toward a decision in accord with the views of the minority faction and refused even to accept a further appeal from Ross. After a brief meeting with Ross on March 25, Polk directed the commissioner of Indian affairs to complete his report. The chief and his comrades then turned to Congress with a memorial, the first since 1838. They declared the Act of Union of 1840 effectively represented the wishes of the majority of the Cherokees and that none of the measures proposed by the minority factions was desired by the great mass of the tribe. Because Congress at that time was embroiled in the Oregon question, the Cherokee petition gained slight attention.[6]

The new commissioner of Indian affairs, William Medill, submitted his conclusions to President Polk after examining the several petitions of the three factions. Medill recommended that Ross and his associates not be recognized as authorized delegates but only as representatives of their particular faction. On other points Medill also sided with the treaty party and the Old Settlers. Disregarding the report of Jones, Mason, and Butler, the commissioner embraced many arguments the three investigators had deemed untenable and concluded that a "separation, both of the old settlers and the treaty party, from the Ross party is imperatively required." Enclosing Medill's recommendation and the mass of documents and petitions to illustrate the government's case, President Polk submitted a message to Congress in April 1846, announcing his determination to divide the Cherokees politically and geographically. Congress seemed amenable and in June reported on its acceptance; all seemed in readiness for a political division of the Cherokee Nation.[7]

At this point Ross worked feverishly to forestall what appeared inevitable. Fortunately for the Ross faction, Indian Superintendent William Armstrong had arrived from the western frontier and suggested to Commissioner Medill that a committee be appointed to make a last attempt to mediate factional differences. President Polk then appointed Armstrong, Commissioner of the Patent Office Edmund Burke, and Second Comptroller of the Treasury Albion K. Parris for the task; during the month of July they hammered out an agreement suitable to all factions. The ominous threat of division doubtless made Ross more conciliatory, and measures were offered the dissatisfied groups to gain their support. President Polk presented the document to the Senate on August 7, the day after its completion, and it was approved by a majority of one vote with only minor changes. On August 13 when the three delegations gathered in Polk's office to sign the treaty as approved by Congress, twenty Cherokees affixed their names to the treaty, clasped hands, and renounced animosities. Undoubtedly, there was tension in the hands of those old foes as Ross and Watie pressed palms and pledged good faith. When Polk exhorted the men to forget the past, Ross replied that all were satisfied and could now live in harmony.[8]

The principal goals of the Treaty of 1846 were unity and the end of violence in the Cherokee Nation. It provided general amnesty for all offenses, the safe return of all fugitives, and an end to police or military organizations. The Old Settlers gave up claim to exclusive ownership of the Cherokee domain and received the right to share in the per capita payments. The treaty party received a special indemnity of $115,000; of this money $5,000 was to be paid to each set of heirs of the two Ridges and Boudinot. The remaining would pay the expenses of the delegation and settle claims of individual treaty party members. The Cherokees were assured title to the lands they occupied, hardly the unimpaired guarantee Ross desired but the only stipulation he could obtain. The Ross party received $2,000 for the old *Cherokee Phoenix* printing press, $5,000 for arms taken by Major General Winfield Scott prior to the Cherokee roundup in 1838, and $20,000 for other miscellaneous national claims. Finally, the United States agreed to reimburse the Cherokees for money "unjustly" deducted from the five million fund and to make a final settlement of all money due under the per capita stipulation.[9]

The Treaty of 1846 heralded a new and pacific era in Cherokee politics and more than a dozen years of uninterrupted tranquility. The settlement was not entirely smooth, however. The Cherokees were prepared to achieve not only peace but also financial stability, anticipating as they were a lucrative per capita payment.

But the federal government was slow to reimburse them for unjust deductions from the five million fund. Within a year of the signing of the Treaty of 1846, the Senate Committee on Indian Affairs reported on its understanding of the various moneys due the Cherokees. The committee determined that the cost of subsistence and removal should not have been charged to the five million fund, but, in spite of Ross's efforts, no action appears to have been taken on the report. After an extensive examination of accounts and vouchers, United States Treasury auditors determined that $627,603.95 was due the Cherokees for a per capita distribution. Congress made two additional appropriations in September 1850 and in February 1851, which brought the total amount for distribution to $914,026.13. As the Cherokees remaining in North Carolina also were included in the distribution, the sums finally allotted, which included another addition of nearly $600,000, amounted to $92.79 for each Cherokee, hardly the largess expected.[10]

The per capita payments were made in two allotments. The first was made to the Old Settlers by Southern Indian Superintendent John Drennen at Fort Gibson in September and October 1851. Drennen was so well satisfied with the Fort Gibson location that he suggested it as an appropriate spot to pay the emigrant Cherokees.

The eastern Cherokees disagreed, and the National Council in November 1851 directed Ross to ask that the payment be made at Tahlequah because of its central location. When Ross asked Drennen, the superintendent told him that he feared disorder at any other location and that he was determined to stay at Fort Gibson. Ross noted not only the inconvenience to the eastern Cherokees but also the health hazards of a convergence on Fort Gibson. More important, Fort Gibson was a place of corruption where card sharks and grog shops were sure to take the Indians' money or where ranging criminals might rob them as they returned to their homes. Drennen had considered Tahlequah but, finding a force of fifty soldiers unavailable, had decided on Fort Gibson, a decision "approved by a majority of the most intelligent men in the nation, the chief and a few others about Tahlequah excepted," he noted. The per capita money was paid out to the emigrant Cherokees in April and May 1852 and, contrary to Drennen's observations, the Cherokees suffered all the problems anticipated.[11]

In his annual address following the per capita allotments, Ross referred to the payment as "partial." Indeed, the National Council protested that the payments were not nearly as large as they should have been under the treaty provisions. As Congress had decided that the subsistence item was not properly charged to the five million fund, the Cherokees felt that the additional charges for removal under Ross were not proper either. Ross had questioned this apparent inconsistency a number of times, and it had been the basis for treaty party complaints in 1846, but the protest received little attention during Ross's lifetime. Nearly half a century later United States auditors concluded that the Cherokee claim was just and recommended a payment of over one million dollars due the tribe from the Treaty of 1835.[12]

During the postremoval period Ross had been so engrossed in Cherokee political affairs that his personal financial interests deteriorated. In the tranquil days after the Treaty of 1846 he could turn again to his own business affairs. Ross's wealth came partly from his extensive land improvements and partly from his business enterprises. His salary as chief was meager; it was hardly five hundred dollars a year at this time. In 1849 Ross took over the mercantile business of his son-in-law Return J. Meigs, who had caught the

California gold rush fever. Ross opened the store under the care of his favorite nephews William P. and Daniel H. Ross. The store opened in September on the northeast corner of the public square in Tahlequah, and the first advertisement appeared in the *Cherokee Advocate* on October 8, 1849, under the title, "John Ross & Co.," with the heading "Call at the Brick Store." The short-lived association was dissolved in November of 1850, but William and Daniel independently reopened the business a short time later. Ross soon entered business with Mary's elder brother John W. Stapler. Stapler opened a firm just across the street from the office of the *Cherokee Advocate* in July 1851. In time Ross was brought in as a partner, and the firm was named "Ross & Stapler." These enterprises seem to have been moderately successful. Ross had outstanding accounts of nearly three thousand dollars owed him from the first business. Whether he ever collected on these is uncertain, and some of the largest debts were made by relatives. He was able to draw nearly six hundred dollars from the Ross & Stapler store in one quarterly period. When the firm was dissolved in January 1860, Ross received over thirteen hundred dollars for his share, a large part of which was a mortgage on property in Wilmington, Delaware.[13]

As was typical of southern gentlemen of the antebellum period, Ross maintained a good share of his wealth in land improvements and in slaves. Cherokee lands, held in the same manner in the West as in the old Cherokee Nation, were common property, but improvements belonged to the individual. Besides the extensive farm lands and orchards surrounding Rose Cottage, Ross occasionally bought the improvements of nearby Park Hill neighbors, whether for personal use or for speculation is uncertain; nor is the amount of the lands he tended determinable. He also seemed to own considerable stock. One visitor counted 93 sheep "all very fine and large" and also noted other livestock. Before removal to the West, Ross had owned fewer than twenty blacks, but by the time of the Civil War he had over fifty. He seems to have been benevolent toward his slaves. When absent, he requested reports on their health with a concern more than an interest in costly property, and after the Civil War he wrote of visits with them, and they appeared pleased to see him.[14]

As one of the more substantial members of Cherokee society, Ross felt keenly his social obligation. The artist John Mix Stanley, who visited the Cherokees in 1844, described Ross's house as "the refuge of the poor, starved, and naked Indian." There a destitute guest would find food and lodging. Ross frequently offered his resources to those less fortunate than he, once allotting Evan Jones, the Baptist missionary, over two thousand dollars for the purchase of corn to feed the poor. He also belonged and contributed to several local aid societies.[15]

In spite of the monetary arrangements in the Treaty of 1846, the Cherokees continued to be plagued by financial difficulties. Ross at first proposed retrenchment, but the National Council pursued that course only halfheartedly. Whether from policy or scarcity of funds, the National Council moved in the direction of retrenchment in 1848 when the officers of the Cherokee Nation were paid only half-salaries for the year. Two years later the National Council moved more vigorously and reduced salaries for the nation's administrators. Ross's stipend was reduced from five hundred dollars per year to four hundred dollars. National Council debate was quite heated on this issue; Ross seemed to favor larger salaries for Cherokee Nation officials, and he generally had his way. These reductions, however, probably had little effect on easing the growing Cherokee deficit.[16]

In Ross's annual message of 1849 he suggested alleviating the public debt by taxing the more profitable occupations in the Cherokee Nation—such as stores, mills, and ferries—and by charging a small poll tax. He also suggested a small percentage of the money received by Cherokees for the sale of public lands in the East be taxed. The National Council, hesitant to act, sought advice from the people. A general meeting of all Cherokees in November 1849 accomplished little, and the question again was thrown back to the legislators. Ross pushed for some sort of individual tax, and William P. Ross in the columns of the *Cherokee Advocate* supported him, but the bulk of the tribe effectively blocked this action. Eventually a small tax on owners of ferries and on lawyers was passed. The only effective personal tax, levied in November 1851, provided that 5 percent of the emigrants' per capita payment be used to pay the legal counselors retained by the Ross faction at Washington in 1846.[17]

The Cherokee national debt had been growing steadily since 1839, as the annuities derived from investments made by the United

States were never adequate to meet Cherokee expenditures. By 1851 the debt had reached nearly two hundred thousand dollars. Warrants were issued by the National Council to pay expenses—usually bought by wealthy Cherokees hoping for brighter days, but many eventually reaching the hands of whites. Ross contended that the salary reductions had some stabilizing effect, and with the tax on ferry owners and lawyers and with other small sources of income, the debt was reduced gradually until in 1859 it amounted to about one hundred thousand dollars.[18]

Had Ross's other plan for raising money been effected, the debt might have been entirely erased. In the general meeting in 1849 the sale of the Neutral Lands was discussed. This area in the northeastern part of the Cherokee Nation, comprising eight hundred thousand acres, had been obtained for five hundred thousand dollars by the Cherokees under the Treaty of New Echota. Ross felt the area had been forced on the Cherokees as merely another means of cutting into Cherokee removal funds. The National Council in 1851 unanimously agreed on its sale to the United States and directed a delegation to Washington to negotiate it. Although Ross was appointed as a delegate, he declined, as the coming per capita payment demanded attention and the assistant principal chief was too ill to carry out the duties of the executive office. Ross reported the following year that the delegation had been unsuccessful.[19]

Throughout the 1850s repeated attempts were made to sell the Neutral Lands. The Cherokees hoped to sell it for the original five hundred thousand dollars plus 5 percent interest, or about eight hundred thousand dollars. The various Cherokee agents agreed with this plan, but it never engendered any enthusiasm at Washington. The federal government seemed willing to pay the original five hundred thousand dollars but would not agree to any interest. The Cherokee delegation in 1854 under instructions from Chief Ross proposed an exaggerated offer to sell the Neutral Lands to the United States for a high $1.25 per acre, which would have yielded the tribe one million dollars in revenue, and tempted the federal government by noting the excellent location of lands for railroads. This was something quite alien to the Cherokees' original intent that no one but Indians be settled in this area. Negotiations dragged on this price, however, and the delegation moved back to the earlier proposal of the original price plus 5 percent interest since 1835. Finally the Cherokees proposed their bottom price—the original cost plus 5 percent interest from 1846, or a total of about seven hundred thousand dollars. The commissioner of Indian affairs stuck to the five hundred thousand dollar amount, and no compromise could be worked out. The Nation reluctantly began to accept the reality of the lower figure. Ross had hoped the money could be used for improving social conditions but a vigorous group pushed for the money to be divided per capita. The tribe, however, did not have to face these questions because the United States did not repurchase the lands until 1866.[20]

In the late 1850s the question of the Neutral Lands was caught up in another vexing problem. The newly opened Kansas Territory attracted settlers who looked enviously beyond their southern border at Cherokee lands. As early as 1856 the Cherokee agent, George Butler, was reporting white intruders on the Neutral Lands. The regional Indian superintendent was authorized to use forces from Fort Gibson to remove these squatters but, as was the case in the old Cherokee Nation, the federal government had little persuasive power over land hunters. Burning their cabins seemed no more effective.[21]

In his annual message of 1857, Ross mentioned these abuses. Recalling perhaps the systematic incursions on the eastern Cherokee lands, Ross reminded the National Council that "quiet submission to such treatment in one case is but encouragement for its repetition in another." Ross felt Cherokee political rights ought to be "zealously maintained, and no violation of them be permitted to pass without invoking redress from the United States government." He quoted at length from the inaugural address of the territorial governor of Kansas, Robert J. Walker, who spoke generally of the "salubrious and fertile" Indian Territory and brazenly suggested that Indian treaties would be no obstacle to moving the Indians to the western portion and giving the eastern part to whites for eventual statehood. Whether or not they were caused by Walker's address, intrusions on Cherokee Neutral Lands steadily increased in the next few years and the federal government was not willing to use force to remove intruders. In 1859 the Kansas territorial legislature passed an act dividing the Neutral Lands into counties and generally treating the area as a part of the state's domain. Ross went to Washington as a Cherokee delegate in 1860, the first time since 1846, and called the government's attention to whites who "trespassed . . . with impunity." Again the Cherokees proposed retrocession but found Washington opinions on the matter unchanged, while white settlers continued to invade.[22]

An inadequately financed government also hindered the Cherokees' social progress. Ross frequently used his annual messages to stress needed social reforms and, had the necessary money been available, the tribe might have moved even further in that direction. In his annual message of 1851 Ross endorsed more moderate punishments for crimes. Corporal punishment should be done away with, he argued, and existing laws needed better enforcement. Ross felt particularly that an adequate jail would both relieve the pressure to prescribe corporal punishment and also allow criminals to do useful labor. Upon Ross's suggestion the National Council allocated nearly nineteen hundred dollars for building a jail, with construction to be completed in September 1852. The practice up to that time had been to employ a Cherokee guard and detain the criminal at some Indian's house; both the guard and the housekeeper were paid out of the Cherokee Nation's funds. There seems to have been just enough chance for personal gain in this method for voters to turn down repeatedly any allocation of funds for building a jail, and it did not become a reality until after Ross's time.[23]

Financial distress also hampered the Cherokee Nation's educational system, and Ross's dream for Cherokee progress was not realized. In 1852 Chief Ross even suggested building a national library, but his vision far exceeded the realities of the era. In one instance Ross saw his hopes at least partially fulfilled. He had urged in his annual message of 1846 that the Cherokees establish two seminaries, both high schools, one for males and one for females. The National Council readily passed legislation for the two buildings, which together were estimated to cost about thirty-five thousand dollars. A board of directors, with Ross as ex officio president, oversaw maintenance and instruction. Every year the high schools were to have two sessions of twenty weeks each, with allowances for short vacations. Meeting five days a week, six hours each day, the students were taught geography, history, arithmetic,

English elocution, and the classical languages. Twenty-five pupils were to be enrolled the first year and a like number each successive year in February until the schools met their prescribed limit of one hundred students.[24]

The seminaries opened in May 1851 with all the pomp and finery that the Cherokees could display. Chief Ross made the opening remarks, contrasting education of the day with that of his boyhood. The military band from Fort Gibson was on hand to honor the teachers, recently arrived from Mount Holyoke, and the pupils—"the Flower of the Cherokee Nation." A May queen was crowned that day, and for years afterward the schools celebrated the anniversary of the opening. The seminaries played an important role in the Cherokee Nation, for they became the principal source of instructors for the Cherokee public schools. The seminaries were situated at Park Hill just north of Ross's home, and the chief could easily point them out to guests who called at Rose Cottage.[25]

George Butler, federal agent to the Cherokees, noted in his report for 1856 that the seminaries appeared to be in jeopardy due to the depleted finances, and that fall the institutions were closed. Ross was bitterly disappointed and felt that if the federal government had purchased the Neutral Lands, the Cherokees could have maintained the seminaries. Ross sadly observed: "It has checked the course of education, meted out a stinted pittance to every person engaged in public service, defrauded the honest holders of public scrip, and disgraced the fair fame of the nation by an act of substantial repudiation. . . . It disturbs the harmony of the people, excites disagreements and divisions, and is insidiously sapping the foundations of the government by withholding means really necessary for its successful administration." Ross had hoped that the schools would be closed for a short time only and in 1859 urged the National Council to reopen them on some economical plan. But the school doors remained shut, not to be reopened until after the Civil War and, sadly enough, after the passing of the man who had given them life.[26]

Cherokee-white encounters were more frequent around the settled regions in the eastern part of the Cherokee Nation than in the Neutral Lands. These encounters were not appreciated by Ross or many of the leading Cherokees, for the whites were largely card sharks and whiskey peddlers from the small settlement that had grown up around Fort Gibson. Butler queried Ross on Cherokee opinion about the United States' abandoning the fort and found Ross in complete agreement with the idea. Of course Ross knew that the Treaty of New Echota of 1835 provided that on its abandonment the site would revert to the Cherokees. He also knew that the fort was the only adequate spot in the Cherokee Nation for steamboat docking, an added commercial advantage, and he hoped that in time a respectable town might grow up there. For some years he had been disturbed by the "pernicious practice of trafficing and using intoxicating liquors about Fort Gibson," and he thought its reversion to the tribe might end such annoyances. Although he was not the sort of activist who joined the local temperance societies that flourished under the guidance of the missionaries, he had strong feelings about alcoholic beverages and on one occasion said: "Were it possible, to drive this monstrous hydra entirely away from out of this land so that its pestiferous fumes may never again be inhaled by inhabitants, no one would rejoice more in the happy result than . . . John Ross."[27]

By 1857 the federal government decided to remove the post's last military forces and prepared to sell the buildings at public auction. When Ross learned of this and quickly reminded the commissioner of Indian affairs of treaty provisions, the error was corrected, and in September 1857 the fort reverted to the Cherokees. At the next annual National Council session, the site was christened Ketoowha and laid out into lots for public sale, which brought in about twenty thousand dollars to the national treasury the first year. Ross had hoped to use some of the buildings for the planned jail but found them in such dilapidated condition that the idea was impractical. There was a movement at one time to have the capital moved to Ketoowha, and the idea even passed the National Council but was vetoed by Ross.[28]

The political atmosphere of the Cherokee Nation during the 1850s was calm, and major disruptions were virtually unknown. The elections of the post-1846 era were tranquil though actively contested. In 1847 Ross stood for reelection against his friend and relative William Shorey Coodey. Ross won handily, 1,898 to 877. His next stand at the polls elicited only slightly more opposition;

indeed, David Vann and Lewis Ross declined nominations before Joseph Vann opposed the chief. One disturbance occurred in the off-year election of 1853, when George W. and Andrew Adair were killed. Ross viewed it as a "neighborhood feud" growing out of the murder of Isaac Proctor some years before, to which the Adairs had been a party. The remaining elections throughout the decade passed without incident, and the Cherokees showed their confidence in Ross by returning him to executive office in 1855 and again in 1859.[29]

Members of the Stapler family frequently visited the Ross home during the peaceful years after 1846. Sarah, Ross's sister-in-law, remained at Park Hill and taught for a time in the Cherokee schools. As Ross returned home from business trips to the East, he occasionally brought with him members of the Stapler household. Perhaps they came to visit Annie, born in 1845, and John, Jr., who was born two years later. Mary's father died on his visit in 1858, and the pleasant atmosphere of Rose Cottage was darkened for a time. Death again invaded the Ross home in 1860 when a cousin, Mary F. Stapler, came to visit and to tutor Annie and John, Jr. As Miss Stapler sat next to the blaze in an open fireplace, her dress caught fire and in spite of Ross's efforts to rescue her, the burns proved fatal. In a poignant letter to her mother, Ross told of the deep sorrow in their household. He suggested that perhaps a trip to the Cherokee Nation would help to relieve her grief, and he forwarded the money for her to make the journey.[30]

Questions over slavery in the Cherokee Nation came up more frequently during the decade of the 1850s than in any other period. This was a reflection both of problems in the United States, particularly nearby Kansas Territory, and of internal differences between the mixed-blood slaveholders and the more numerous full-bloods. Ross had long ago tied his fortunes and ideals to the full-bloods and, in spite of his mixed-blood ancestry and his possession of slaves, the chief clearly had the support of the full-blood majority.

The National Council took up antislavery activities in the annual meeting of 1855. Declaring that the Cherokees were a slaveholding people "in a Christian like spirit," the National Council passed a bill directing Ross to correspond with the various missionary societies on the subject of slavery "as a Church principle." Further, the National Council made it unlawful for any missionary to advise a slave "to the detriment of his owner . . . under the penalty of being removed," or for teachers to be hired in the Cherokee public grade schools who were known to have abolitionist views. Ross vetoed this bill, probably more because of his friendships with the missionaries, particularly Evan Jones and his son John, than for any antislavery views. Although it gained the necessary two-thirds majority in the National Committee to override his veto, the bill failed in the National Council, the lower house. The closeness of the vote seemed not to disturb the Joneses, for in 1858 Agent Butler reported the dismissal of slaveholding members from their congregations.[31]

By 1859 the slavery question had grown to such a degree that the Cherokees were forming opposing camps, split generally between mixed-bloods and full-bloods. A secret organization had been formed among the full-bloods known as the Keetoowah Society or the Pins, whose members wore crossed pins on their shirts. Beyond the desire to maintain old Cherokee codes (probably the primary function), the society also may have been led by the Joneses to favor antislavery positions. Some of the mixed-bloods organized into a proslavery faction called the Knights of the Golden Circle, but the group became active only after 1861. It is doubtful that Ross used the Pins for any political purpose, for by 1860 he looked not to renewing factional fights but to peace and contentment for his last years.[32]

During the late 1840s and throughout the 1850s Ross had passed the function of yearly trips to Washington to rising politicians in the Cherokee community. In 1860 Ross returned to Washington as a Cherokee delegate and took the occasion to travel with Mary and the children to visit her relatives in Pennsylvania and New Jersey. The family made a stop at Chattanooga on the way east and spent a few days there while Ross visited his father's grave and his old home place. They reached their destination in late February, and Ross left Mary and their children at Wilmington, Delaware while he went on to Washington alone. Ross's primary object was to gain permission from the federal government to tax white traders within the Cherokee Nation as a means of reducing the public debt. He hoped also to work out arrangements for the retrocession of the Neutral Lands, or at least to gain a clearer definition of their boundaries, and he intended to demand some sort of payment for damages caused by white intruders. He was no more successful on these points than were the Cherokee delegations that had preceded him throughout the 1850s.[33]

While Ross was in Washington in April and May 1860, the capital was filled with talk of the national nominating convention of the Democratic party at Charleston, South Carolina. In answer to one letter from her husband, Mary asked who might be selected at Charleston, and Ross predicted the convention would not be able to settle on one candidate, and that the party would split and nominate two candidates. If this occurred, Ross thought the Democrats would be defeated at the next election and this perhaps would signal the "knell of a closing scene in the political drama of the Democratic party!" Americans should choose "some great & good conservative Patriotic Man, as a Washington, and elect him President . . . under the Banner of the union and *Constitution*," Ross believed. He predicted that Stephen A. Douglas would be one of the Democratic candidates, but the senator certainly would not have received the chief's support, for Ross had an Indian's view of "popular sovereignty": "As to the Political dogmas of the day, that Power under 'Squatter Sovereignty' recognize the Principle that '*might gives right*' and may be exercised under the Policy of expediency and necessity, by filibusterism. There can be no safety or security for the person or property of the weaker party. And having experienced great injustice from this Policy, I cannot but abhor and detest it. It is only a flimsy pretext for the Tyrants plea—and the robber's justification."[34]

The Treaty of 1846 had seemed to prepare the way for a tranquil era unknown to the Cherokees since the peaceful days of Chief Ross's youth. He championed several social advances that he had planned for years. The seminaries, a national library, and the national press were the substance of his dreams, but Ross was more than just an idle dreamer and saw at the least the inception of a few of his projects. Financial problems dashed these hopes, and in his old age Chief Ross watched his dreams turn to dust as the seminaries closed, the *Cherokee Advocate* shut down, and the national library became only words on a tattered fragment of paper. With internal peace and unity achieved, Ross also looked forward to the final settlement of nagging problems between the Cherokee Nation and the United States. However, the paltry per capita payment and the continued haggling over the retrocession of the Neutral Lands frustrated Ross's ambitions, for they also increased Cherokee financial distress. By 1860 these problems appeared soluble, for the Cherokee debt was being paid and a Republican administration might be more amenable to Cherokee goals. Yet external disunity reawakened internal factionalism, and Chief Ross and the Cherokees again were thrust into an era of violence and disruption.

10

THE CIVIL WAR

THAT Ross had reached his seventieth year in 1860 was clearly evidenced by his whitened head and wrinkled brow. These years, however, had not reduced his able and energetic leadership, and he was little troubled by physical infirmities. At beautiful Rose Cottage he still lived comfortably with Mary and their two children. Frequent trips about the Cherokee Nation assured him of the presence of the peace and unity he cherished for his people. Yet the half-dozen years after 1860 proved the most trying of his career as factional fires were rekindled in the Cherokee Nation. During this divisive era the great theme of his life, unity within the Cherokee Nation, met its severest test, and only with his death in 1866 did it become a momentary reality.

The differences which spawned divisions in the Union at large were reenacted on the Indian Territory frontier in microcosm. The drift of secession sentiment reached the Cherokee Nation and widened the existing rift between the party of Ross and the reinvigorated Ridge party. As in the past, the Ross party was composed chiefly of full-bloods and nonslaveholders, while the opposition led by Stand Watie included mainly mixed-bloods and southern sympathizers.

An act of the Chickasaw legislature forwarded to Ross by Cyrus Harris, Chickasaw governor, signaled the first of a long series of communications between Ross and southern-minded individuals. The act called for a meeting of the Five Civilized Tribes to discuss forming a compact because of impending change in the United States. Ross's answer was cautionary and guarded, and he appointed a delegation of men loyal to him and his policies. The chief's careful

instructions advised the delegates against any "premature movement, on our part, which might produce excitement or be liable to
misrepresentation. . . . We have only to adhere firmly to our respective Treaties."[1]

In the first weeks of 1861 Ross was apparently trying to shape a
policy for the Cherokees that would not offend their southern-
minded neighbors in Arkansas but would keep the tribe true to their
treaty obligations with the federal government. He explained to the
readers of the Van Buren *Press* that the Cherokees would "go where
their institutions and their geographical position place them—with
Arkansas and Missouri." At the same time he answered Governor
Henry M. Rector of Arkansas with moderation and ambivalence,
when Rector sought Ross's cooperation in the defense of southern
institutions. Again Ross stressed friendship and likemindedness
with Arkansas but reminded the governor of the Cherokees' alliance
with the Union. The chief's attention was also called to the activities of Indian agents purportedly advocating secession. Principal
among these was Elias Rector, the federal superintendent of Indian
affairs, and R. J. Cowart, the Cherokee agent, both ardent supporters
of the southern cause. This correspondence indicated a problem
Ross would face often in the coming year as agents partisan to the
Confederate cause proselyted among his people.[2]

During the next two months Ross returned to the normal affairs of
the Cherokee Nation and, except for a visit in March by a Texas
commission which noted the chief's neutrality, the coming conflict
may have seemed remote. Arkansas seceded shortly after the capitu-
lation of Fort Sumter, and soon Ross received a letter from a number
of citizens of Boonsborough, Arkansas, insisting on knowing Ross's
intentions, saying they preferred "an open enemy to a doubtful
friend." That same week in May Colonel J. R. Kannady, the Confederate commander at Fort Smith, informed Ross that in his position
as defender of the western frontier he must know if the chief intended to support the South. Ross's replies to the Boonsborough residents and Kannady illustrate the dilemma he faced. He stressed his
great desire for peace and the hope that his people would be beyond
the southern appeal. Therefore, on May 17, 1861, he issued a proclamation reminding his tribe of its obligations to the United States,

advising the people not to be alarmed by false reports of scheming men, and advocating prudence and noninterference.[3]

Ross was only partially deluded into believing that the Cherokees could remain aloof as the hostilities spread to the borders of Indian Territory. Nor was the newly formed southern government willing to let the trans-Mississippi tribes remain federal by default. By May 1861 the Confederates had appointed two men destined to have a tremendous impact on Ross—an impact that would return to haunt him in the final months of his life.

Albert Pike, an attorney of Little Rock, Arkansas, was commissioned as special agent for the Confederacy to negotiate treaties with Indian tribes west of Arkansas. Before his departure for Ross's home at Park Hill, Pike gave first evidence of the wedge he would use to drive the chief from his avowed position. Pike revealed that he intended to treat with the leaders of the mixed-bloods if Ross refused to negotiate. Pike had long experience with Indians and appreciated Ross's abilities. He observed on one occasion: "He is very shrewd. If I fail with him it will not be my fault." Pike was in touch with Ross on June 6 as he departed from the Cherokee Nation, proposing a treaty of alliance between the Cherokee Nation and the Confederacy. He offered ample protection by Confederate troops; unrestricted Cherokee title and perpetual possession of their country; payment of $500,000 for the Neutral Lands with interest from the date of the Treaty of New Echota in 1835; assumption of the payment of all annuities; a delegate seat in the Confederate House of Representatives; and a Confederate court for the Cherokee Nation. These were the objects Cherokees had sought since 1846, but Ross still felt compelled to follow the treaties with the United States.[4]

Ross already had been informed of the appointment of the other Confederate commissioner to Indian Territory who was also its commanding general, Benjamin McCulloch. McCulloch was aware of the disunity among the Cherokees, but was determined to enlist Ross on the Confederate side to prevent Unionists from gaining a foothold in Indian Territory. McCulloch and Pike had arrived at Park Hill about the same time, and on June 5 they had an amiable audience with Ross at Rose Cottage. Although Ross had objected to McCulloch's desire to establish a military position in the Cherokee Nation, the general felt he had assurances from the chief that if an invasion came, Ross would lead a force to repel it. McCulloch did not press for the Cherokee base, fearing that a movement of his forces at that time might unite the Cherokees and damage any chance of negotiations, even with the mixed-bloods. That same week McCulloch told Ross: "Those of your people who are in favor of joining the Confederacy must be allowed to organize into military companies as home guards for the purpose of defending themselves in case of invasion from the North."[5]

These two emissaries were not the only Confederates who approached Ross. David Hubbard, the newly appointed commissioner of Indian affairs of the Confederacy, wrote Ross in June asking the chief to consider the debts, annuities, and other funds due the tribe by the northern government which Hubbard reasoned were lost but which, he explained, the Confederacy would redeem.[6]

Ross replied to both McCulloch and Hubbard on June 17 in the strongest and most definite terms he had used to date. The elderly chief suggested that McCulloch had misinterpreted his remarks about leading a force since he had no notion of any invasion and anticipated none. McCulloch, however, viewed the chief's neutrality as a pretext to await the outcome of events but because he had the Cherokees surrounded by Confederate forces, he was not overly concerned. In a long letter to Commissioner Hubbard, Ross recounted the treaty obligations of the Cherokees with the United States. Ross, confident that the federal government would not repudiate its debts, considered the Cherokees' annuities safe in either case, and he avoided Hubbard's trap. To Hubbard's assertions that the South had a more distinguished history of dealing with the Indians than the North, Ross added "but few Indians now press their feet upon the banks of either the Ohio or Tennessee."[7]

Pike was not so easily deterred from his mission to the Indian tribes west of Arkansas, and even the adroit Ross could not long divert this Confederate emissary. After Pike left Park Hill, he secured treaties with the Creeks, Chickasaws, Choctaws, and eventually the Seminoles. Pike then turned west and in the early part of August signed treaties with the plains tribes at the Wichita agency. In dealing with some tribes, Pike negotiated with the mixed-blood faction when he was unable to treat with the full-blood majority. As news of these treaties reached Park Hill, Ross felt compelled to con-

vene a Cherokee national conference to discuss the great issues his
people faced. Also, Ross was receiving reports of dissension among
the tribe in the Canadian District of the Cherokee Nation.[8]

Ross convened the Cherokee Executive Council from June 27 to
July 2 at Park Hill before the general assembly session and obtained
firm support for his policy. At a subsequent meeting they called a
Cherokee national conference for August 21 to determine a course
of action. Despite the hot August weather, the crowd of nearly four
thousand male Cherokees pressed close to hear the chief speak
eloquently of the problems which confronted them and the course
they must follow. As Ross recounted the events of the preceding few
months and the position he had taken, his words seemed almost
Lincolnian: "The great object with me has been to have the Cherokee people harmonious and united in the full and free exercise and
enjoyment of all their rights of person and property. Union is
strength; dissension is weakness, misery, ruin." The major part of
his speech justified his position of neutrality, and so it must have
come as something of a surprise when he uttered these final words:
"The time has now come . . . to adopt preliminary steps for an alliance with the Confederate States." After dinner the crowd reas-
sembled and, with Joseph Vann, assistant principal chief, acting as
president, accepted without dissent Ross's recommendations.[9]

Ross informed McCulloch by letter three days after the conference of the Cherokees' intention to ally with the Confederacy. Pike
was notified and was requested to return to Cherokee Nation to
work out terms of a treaty. At Pike's request Ross invited chiefs of
the Osages, Shawnees, and Senecas to Park Hill, and these three
tribes allied with the Confederacy during the first week of October.[10]

Over the camp which Pike had set up near Rose Cottage, he
proudly flew a flag carrying a red star for each treaty concluded with
Indian nations. The Cherokee star had been not so readily added.
Ross's delaying tactics made the Cherokees the last significant tribe
to align with the South, and the treaty included advantages sought
since 1846. Provisions included were: the lands of the Cherokees
could be dealt with as the tribe pleased; the Cherokee Nation could
incorporate Indians of other nations into the tribe; the Cherokees

were guaranteed the right of self-government and jurisdiction over persons and property within their territorial limits; agents of the Confederacy were appointed only with the consent of the Cherokee Nation and could be removed by its request; the Cherokee Nation was entitled to a delegate in the Confederate House of Representatives; and the Neutral Lands were to be sold to the United States if possible and, if not, the Confederates were to pay five hundred thousand dollars for them plus interest since 1835. After appropriate ceremonies Pike presented a Confederate flag to the Cherokee regiment, newly formed under Colonel John Drew. When Watie, present with a band of followers, stepped up to take the chief's hand, old animosities relaxed as the men again pledged harmony and unity.[11]

The reasons for Ross's change from Unionist to neutralist to Confederate ally are numerous and complex. Ross's first loyalty was to the Cherokees. All other considerations, whether Union or Confederate, were secondary. By April 1861 federal troops had withdrawn from Indian Territory, and the surrounding areas came under the control of Confederate forces. Although McCulloch kept his promise not to interfere with Cherokee neutrality, he had authorized Watie to raise a force over a month before the treaty was signed in October. The few Unionist Indian agents had left Indian Territory, and the remainder aligned with the South. Missionaries who were northern adherents with abolitionist tendencies departed as soon as clear prosouthern sentiment emerged. The abolitionist missionary Evan Jones was astounded at Ross's defection and felt his decision was made under duress. Jones's correspondence, however, reveals the deterioration of Unionism in the area.[12]

Not only were Confederate troops ominously near the Cherokee Nation, but also Pike had secured treaties with all the neighboring tribes. This had great impact on Ross, since many of the treaties were made with dissident factions. Watie and his southern followers were anxious to use this or any other means to gain the dominant hand in Cherokee affairs, and Pike was only too happy to negotiate with them. Several years later he recalled those eventful months: "I did not expect to effect any arrangement with Mr. Ross and my intention was to treat with the heads of the southern party—Stand

Watie and others." The security of the Cherokees must have weighed heavily on Ross and was perhaps a dominant factor in his decision to align with the Confederacy.[13]

Certainly Ross was influenced by Pike's promises for a liberal treaty to include provisions the Cherokees had sought for years but had been unable to obtain from the federal government. Financial advantages likewise could not be ignored by Ross, especially since the federal government had defaulted on the annuities and for some years had been unwilling to purchase the Neutral Lands. Pike was not content with only one attempt to entice Ross with promises of money for this area. In August 1861, before the general Cherokee meeting, Pike wrote Ross from the Seminole agency that he had decided to withdraw the proposition. This was surely another attempt at pressuring Ross into negotiating, for he quickly renewed the proposal and included the promises in the final treaty. Although Ross may have been swayed by this letter, money does not seem to have been a major factor in his decision. Pike himself considered Ross influenced by the battle of Wilson's Creek near Springfield, Missouri, on August 10, 1861, a decisive Confederate victory.[14]

Perhaps the most plausible reason for his decision was the pervasive theme of unity that dominated Ross's entire career. On public occasions when Ross spoke of the Confederate compact, he emphasized his desire for cohesion. One has but to recall his speech: "Union is strength; dissension is weakness, misery, ruin." Again he spoke of unity to the National Council on October 9, only two days after the signatures were laid on the treaty, and he called for "unanimity of sentiment" among the Cherokee people. Privately Ross admitted his fears that the Cherokees would be plunged into the conflict regardless of their allegiance. On the evening preceding the convention which would authorize the Confederate treaty he confided to some friends:

We are in the situation of a man standing alone upon a low, naked spot of ground, with the water rising rapidly all around him. He sees the danger but does not know what to do. If he remains where he is, his only alternative is to be swept away and perish. The tide carries by him, in its mad course, a drifting log. It, perchance, comes within reach of him. By refusing it, he is a doomed man. By seizing hold of it he has a chance for his life. He can but perish in the effort, and may be able to keep his head above water until rescued, or drift to where he can help himself.[15]

Not only did Ross urge unity among his tribe, but he also pressed for harmony among all Indians. During July he had communicated with Opothleyahola, leader of the loyal Creeks, urging solidarity in resisting Pike's entreaties. Chief Ross had even sent a delegation to Antelope Hills in the far western portion of Indian Territory to meet with Opothleyahola's followers and other tribes to promote the neutral position, so it was with some surprise that Opothleyahola received a note from Ross in late August telling of the Cherokee decision to go with the Confederacy. So incredulous was Opothleyahola, in fact, that he returned the message to Ross to assure its validity. Again Ross pleaded for unity and now advised the loyal Creek to join the Confederacy in order to maintain the "common rights and interest" of the Indians. To Motey Kennard, the leader of the Confederate Creeks who asserted that it would be necessary to put down Opothleyahola "at any cost," Ross urged restraint. Ross was heartbroken when the Creeks could not adjust their differences and civil conflict ensued.[16]

Although Ross had signed the Confederate treaty, speculation about his true allegiance continued. Evan Jones steadfastly insisted that only imminent peril and necessity had forced Ross into Confederate hands. On the other hand, Colonel James McIntosh of the Confederate army, visiting in early 1862, found him firm in his commitment to the South, although he did note that a sufficient force was in the vicinity to assure continued Cherokee allegiance.[17]

That the Cherokee Nation had signed a favorable treaty with the Confederacy was unquestionable, but what soon became apparent was the inability of the southern government to fulfill its promises. The Confederate Indian agents assigned to the Cherokee Nation served only part-time and increasingly found their primary military duty time consuming. Promised annuities were infrequent and inadequate, and the Cherokee regiment of Colonel John Drew was undermanned and not sufficiently supplied to guard the frontier. Quarrels and bickering among the Confederate commanders had brought government leadership in Indian Territory to a deplorable state, culminating in the arrest of the Indians' principal sponsor Albert Pike on charges of incompetence and suspected treason. Also, in direct contradiction to treaty stipulations, Cherokee forces had been used beyond their nation's border, most notably in the Confederate victory at Pea Ridge, Arkansas, in March 1862.[18]

Conditions had reached such a dismal state by May 1862 that Ross reminded Jefferson Davis of the treaty guarantees, pointing out the imminent threat posed by Union troops which were massing in the southwest corner of Missouri and requesting "means to defend ourselves as far as may be in our humble power." Ross waited for six weeks and then appealed to Major General Thomas C. Hindman, Confederate commander of the Trans-Mississippi District, concerning the lack of arms and clothing for Cherokee troops and deploring the "virtual abandonment of this nation" so that it was defended only by Cherokee troops, unprepared and unequipped.[19]

In June 1862 federal troops, under the command of Colonel William Weer, met little resistance as they moved south from Kansas toward Cherokee Nation. Included in this expedition was Ross's old friend Evan Jones, who carried a message from William G. Coffin, superintendent of Indian affairs, assuring the chief that the United States government would not overlook its obligations to the loyal Indian tribes. Doubtless Coffin was under the influence of Jones and did not consider Ross disloyal, but rather as one forced into an uncomfortable position. Coffin's trust in Ross was matched by Weer's, who predicted: "John Ross is undoubtedly with us, and will come out openly when we reach there."[20]

As Weer neared Tahlequah his confidence was somewhat shaken when Ross, believing that he must obtain faithful observance of Cherokee treaty obligations, refused the colonel an official interview. Yet the chief forwarded documents which would put him in good stead with the Unionists. These papers were sent to Brigadier General James G. Blunt, who discounted Ross's note to Weer by concluding that the chief "is evidently very cautious in committing himself on paper until he is assured of our ability to hold that country." Weer dispatched Captain Harris S. Greeno with a small party to Park Hill where Ross and several Confederate Cherokee officers as much as welcomed the federals on July 15. Weer likely regained his confidence in Ross when Greeno reported that the chief had ignored an order by Confederate Colonel Douglas H. Cooper to enlist all Cherokees between the ages of eighteen and thirty-five to repel the invasion. During the next two weeks Ross was guarded by a strong force from Colonel John Drew's Cherokee regiment. This band would soon give allegiance to the federals and add nearly fifteen hundred men to the Northern cause. Early on the morning of August 3, Ross, his family, and a number of refugee Cherokees set out for Fort Leavenworth, Kansas, the headquarters of General Blunt.[21]

After Ross arrived in Kansas, Blunt advised him to go to Washington to gain President Lincoln's sympathies for the tribe. Blunt wrote ahead to assure Lincoln of the chief's loyalty and recommended him "as a man of candor and frankness, upon whose representations you may rely." With family and refugee friends Ross made his way to the Stapler homes in Philadelphia and Wilmington, which Ross and Mary had apparently inherited. Ross carried with him the hurriedly packed Cherokee national papers and what few personal belongings the family could load. For the next three years Ross remained a refugee in the East. During these years, Mary and the family lived in Philadelphia, while Ross took the Cherokee case before the federal government in Washington. Ross lamented the separation from his family, fearing he had become an "old crusty, homeless Bachelor!" John, Jr., attended a boys' academy in Nazareth, Pennsylvania, and the Lawrenceville Classical and Commercial High School, while Annie remained with her mother. John queried his father about returning to the West, and he was particularly concerned about his horses left behind. He seems to have been a bright and dedicated student who promised to "put his shoulder to the wheel," but Ross admonished that "it is the 'long pull and the steady pull,' after all that achieves in life, the most." Although Annie was the same age her mother had been at her marriage to Ross, he continued to think of her as "Papa's baby." Nor did he forget Annie's birthday, and even in the difficult Civil War years found means to send her gifts.[22]

While in the East, Ross had two major political concerns. He had to convince the United States government that he had joined the Confederate side under duress. He also had to impress upon the government the beleaguered state of his tribe and to urge the reestablishment of federal troops to protect his people from marauding guerilla forces. During his first interview with President Lincoln on September 12, 1862, Ross outlined Cherokee needs, which he later detailed in writing. Ross stressed that the Cherokees had placed themselves under the protection of the United States, and that after the withdrawal of the promised protection, the Cherokees had been forced into a treaty with the Confederate States. They were unable to "assume their true position" until summer 1862, Ross contended, at which time "the great mass of the Cherokee people rallied spontaneously around the Authorities of the United States." He further pointed out that a loyal majority of Cherokee warriors was engaged in fighting on the Union side and that the reabandonment of the Cherokee Nation by federal troops that same summer had left the Cherokees in a distressing condition. Ross concluded by saying that the Cherokee people begged the government's recognition of existing treaties and ample military protection.[23]

Lincoln's careful response was less than reassuring. He was not prepared to admit to any governmental failure in protecting the Cherokees and was not convinced there was just cause for the Cherokee Nation's treaty with the Confederate government. However, Commissioner of Indian Affairs William P. Dole later recalled that the president had on one occasion appeared satisfied with Ross's explanations. Lincoln's note was only a tentative reply, and he promised a careful investigation of all the questions. Ross had more success with the president on getting forces sent back into the Cherokee Nation. At Ross's urging, Lincoln asked Major General Samuel R. Curtis of St. Louis, Missouri, to use the federal forces stationed at Fort Scott to occupy the Cherokee country. Curtis promised action, but it was slow to come. The reoccupation of Indian Territory was hampered by the political and military ambitions of Kansas citizens and by conflicts of interest between the Department of War and the Department of the Interior. Other attempts to return the Cherokees in March and July 1863 turned into utter routs; when they finally departed Kansas in spring 1864, it was too late to raise crops and proved a homecoming to further sickness and starvation.[24]

Ross continued to receive reports from the Cherokee Nation on the deplorable conditions of his people. The Cherokees, numbering perhaps six thousand old men, women, and children, were literally starving to death in Kansas. These unfortunate people became the pawns in the power struggle between the Departments of War and Interior as they were shuffled from place to place in Kansas and Missouri and up and down the weary war trail into Indian Territory. In the early part of 1863 the chief directed Lewis Ross, the Cherokee national treasurer, to purchase blankets, shoes, and other supplies to distribute among the Cherokees. Frequently, because of poor wartime communication, the only news Ross had of his countrymen came from newspapers. At one point Ross considered returning to the Cherokee Nation, but his family persuaded him not to go, knowing the dangers that awaited him there. In letters to the Cherokee Nation he repeatedly sought the information he needed to represent accurately the needs of his people to the federal government.[25]

The waste and destruction of the war fell on the Ross household when in 1863 Colonel Stand Watie's Confederate Cherokee forces burned Rose Cottage and its contents. Some of Ross's relatives remained in Indian Territory during the war, and his older sons, James, Allen, Silas, and George, served in the Third Regiment of the Federal Indian Home Guards organized from the ranks of former Confederate forces who joined the Union side when Weer reached the Cherokee Nation in 1862. James was captured by Confederate forces while returning to Park Hill to bring his family desperately needed supplies. He was subsequently transferred to several prison compounds in the South; the effects of long confinement caused his death in 1864. Ross's daughter Jane and some of her children had remained at Park Hill, and in 1863 their home was attacked by Confederate marauders. In the excesses so common to war, Jane's second husband Andrew Ross Nave was shot and killed trying to flee. To Jane's daughter, Ross sent words of encouragement and consolation and pointed out that her mother's courage at that hour could serve as an example to them to rise above adversity.[26]

These personal tragedies did not keep Ross from negotiating long-standing Cherokee national problems, among them clarification of the status of the Neutral Lands. Dole seemed anxious during the first year after Ross arrived to negotiate for the retrocession of these lands. Dole's interest soon waned because of other pressing duties and because he hoped that Cherokee lands in Indian Territory might be secured for the removal of additional tribes.[27]

Another major concern for Ross was the recognition of his right to speak for the Cherokee Nation. In August 1862 a mass meeting of the southern Cherokees was held and, in the absence of Ross, Colonel Stand Watie was elected chief. This posed some difficulty for Ross, especially because the Cherokee treaty with the Confederacy was still in force. It was not until February 1863 that the Union Cherokees were able to convene and pass bills recognizing Ross as the principal chief and empowering him and the delegation in Washington with full authority. This meeting also abrogated the treaty made with the Confederate states and abolished slavery, the first of the slaveholding Indian nations to do so. Ross quickly forwarded this document to Dole and again urged that military forces be moved into the Cherokee country to protect the refugees in Kansas who wished to return home. Ross also sent Dole a notarized copy of his oath of office, taken before a Washington justice of the peace on April 5, 1863.[28]

While in Washington and Philadelphia, Ross and his family and the delegation representing the Cherokees were dependent on the federal government for subsistence. The number of persons in the Cherokee retinue varied from thirty-three to thirty-six persons, of which Ross claimed from ten to twelve dependent on him. Ross's first claim for family subsistence was made in November 1862 to cover the period from the arrival in August of that year to January 31, 1863. In this claim he set the amount of subsistence money he would require throughout his stay, which amounted to $2,500 per year. Ross made a similar request for the next quarterly period. Frequently there was confusion as to what period of time the subsistence requests covered. In April 1863 Ross attempted to claim his quarterly subsistence, but Commissioner Dole adamantly replied that the money already paid covered up to April 30, 1863. After clarification by both parties, Ross was remitted $1,375 for the period ending July 31, 1863. Nevertheless, it was necessary during this quarter to draw $4,000 out of Chickasaw funds to pay the Cherokee delegation. The annuity monies of the Five Civilized Tribes had been placed in a common fund by order of Congress in July 1862 in order to meet such emergencies. In September 1863 Ross requested his regular quarterly family subsistence allowance and, after some delay, received it. After this date the records are scanty, but it may be assumed that Ross received his allowance without difficulty, at least until January 31, 1864.[29]

Nevertheless, difficulty arose in obtaining the quarterly allowance for subsequent periods. In July 1864 Ross's request for subsistence was opposed by John P. Usher, the secretary of the interior. Usher felt that drawing funds which belonged to other tribes could be done only by a very liberal interpretation of the law. Ross received the allowance but at a much reduced rate for a much longer period of time. The money was not granted until October 1864 and covered the period from January 31 of that year. In all it amounted to less than one hundred dollars per person for a period of eight and one-half months. Finding Dole engaged in other business and unwilling to attend to Cherokee finances, Ross wearily wrote Mary, "That old familiar tone, which have so often greeted my ear (when the purse string is about to be untied for *means* to relieve the wants of the Indian) crying there is no money—the appropriation is exhausted—its sound is, apparently, ready to vibrate in the distance."[30]

Ross occasionally needed money beyond what he received from the quarterly subsistence allowance. Under arrangements previously made with Dole, he received a draft of $500 in July 1863. That same month the Cherokee delegation claimed $4,000, part of which was to pay the group's room and board bill at Willard's Hotel in Washington. Ross's share of this sum was probably about $840. Ross also claimed another $4,000 in December 1863 to defray the Washington expenses of the delegation. In June of the next year the Cherokee delegation petitioned for $5,000, a part of which was to be used to pay travel expenses for two members of the group returning to the Cherokee Nation.[31]

During the summer of 1864 the Cherokee delegation, consisting of Ross, Evan Jones, James McDaniel, Lewis Ross, and Lewis Downing, attempted a plan which, had it succeeded, would have placed the northern Cherokees in a most advantageous position at the war's end. They proposed a treaty which included provisions for the sale of the Neutral Lands for $500,000 at 5 percent interest since the Treaty of New Echota in 1835; the admittance of the Delawares into the Cherokee Nation with a permanent home; a call for a fixed and permanently marked boundary of the Cherokee Nation; the "unrestricted right of self-government"; the privilege of consultation on choice of Indian agents; and payment by the United States for all losses and injuries "since the commencement of the present rebellion." The United States government never acted upon this proposal.[32]

The Cherokee delegation again was in Washington in February 1865 and sought $10,000 to meet expenses. Ross justified this amount by the expected arrival of three additional delegates. Dole was not willing to meet the delegation's demand because he was not aware of any business requiring the group's presence. He further asserted that what little money the Cherokees had could be better used for clothing and subsistence for "loyal Cherokees" in the West. The delegates refused to yield, declaring that their credentials were valid and that the Cherokee Nation always had maintained full control over its own monetary matters. Dole's use of the term "loyal Cherokees" must have troubled them, since they declared that "we represent the Cherokee Nation, who are now, and have been decidedly loyal." Dole forwarded the delegation's plea to Secretary of the Interior Usher who affirmed the decision not to honor it. The reason for this decision is unclear and appears especially surprising since a similar plea for $7,300 was accepted within a week after the $10,000 was denied. In addition, the various Cherokee Nation funds which derived from the federal government's sale of former Cherokee lands were held in trust by the United States and amounted to approximately $150,000 as of July 1, 1864. Ross appealed to Usher and the delegation received the money in the latter part of March 1865.[33]

Ross did not escape criticism for the money he received. William G. Coffin of the southern Indian superintendency accused Ross and his family and friends of living "in the most expensive manner." Coffin was probably disturbed because he daily viewed the appalling conditions of the refugee Cherokees on the frontier. He also may have been angered by the high prices these destitute people had to pay for the barest of commodities. He felt Ross indirectly responsible, since the store at Fort Gibson which supplied the Indians seemed to charge exorbitant prices and was owned, at least in part, by members of the Ross family. Ross replied to Coffin's charges in a point-by-point rebuttal. He asserted that Coffin's accusations were false and that the money he had received was due him as the appointed representative of the Cherokee Nation caring for its interests and welfare. Goods often had been shipped from the East to his people, but "through negligence or foul play," Ross surmised, they "have never reached their destination," and Ross implied that Coffin might be partly to blame. That some of these charges were made public record infuriated Ross. He demanded a retraction of the false accusations, declaring: *"I am not, was not . . . and never have been*, directly or indirectly, associated with the Mercantile firm of Fort Gibson."[34]

The passage of years and the agony of the Civil War did not diminish the affection of Ross and Mary. In Ross's absence Mary was besieged with loneliness and tears, and she turned often to Sarah for companionship. Frequent letters from Ross also helped cure what he called "that unhappy disease—'the Blues.'" Yet Ross regarded her as one in whom he could confide, and his letters were not confined to prattle of family matters. He related political news, and she showed a good understanding of his personal problems and of Cherokee Nation affairs. These lonely moments of separation were cheered by correspondence which Mary related "cast sunshine around my heart & dispelled the clouds that had gathered there." And she fell to reminiscing of "the land over which my dear Husband ruled & . . . the warm welcome I the lonely *white stranger* received far from my childhood's home." Ross also felt the pangs of loneliness during his frequent Washington trips and wrote "the little wife," as he affectionately called her, "altho I am in person still sitting in this wearisome city; yet my thoughts wander away off to thee and our loved ones."[35]

Mary's strict Quaker background influenced her greatly, and as her health declined in the 1860s her religious sentiments grew even stronger. Mary's health was a constant source of concern to Ross, and references to her illness were common. She had been deeply hurt when in 1846 the Friends dismissed her for marrying Ross, a non-Quaker. Ross consoled her and reminded her that those acquainted with her dismissal knew that it was not because of any offenses against the laws of God. He assured her that "thee [has] *one* friend on earth, for whose sake thou art dismissed; who will with all his heart and strength cling to thee, so long as life shall last." At Park Hill she became a mainstay to the missionary effort and in later years joined the Methodist Church and was content that she had influenced her husband and children to receive baptism also.[36]

Ross attended church infrequently, and his religion seems to have been superficial. Like other orators of his day, his speeches were clothed in Christian allusion, but there is little evidence of a real personal commitment. His association with Mary made him more sensitive and awakened a religious compassion, and early in their courtship he promised "hence forward to be a more regular attendant at the House of Worship, not merely as a looker-on upon the pretty faces of the fair Daughters of Adam but that with the hope that my own immortal spirit may be benefited." He carried out his promise, and most of his letters to Mary included some reference to church services, often with a note on the minister's text and sermon. He liked particularly a sermon in the "old style."[37]

Mary wrote with sadness of the fate of their beautiful Rose Cottage, but death took her before it was possible for her to return. After a long illness Mary died of lung congestion at Philadelphia on July 20, 1865, and was buried at Wilmington, Delaware, in the Stapler family plot. One obituary illustrates that in spite of her frailness she maintained a strength of spirit and a dauntless Quaker courage: "At one time a rebel mob had possession of their place [Rose Cottage?] and threatened to raise their flag on the premises. She publicly proclaimed if no one else took the step, she with her son a lad of fourteen years old, would cut it down." Ross's final year without Mary by his side made his homecoming less rewarding, and the war's desolation of the Cherokee Nation and its people touched him deeply. In his final days he turned more and more to Sarah, his sister-in-law, for consolation. Over the years he had developed a close relationship with her.[38]

The failure to obtain a new treaty was an omen of the problems that arose after the war when the northern faction struggled for its political future. The Civil War had caused the Cherokee factional quarrels again to erupt in bloodshed. During the war Ross was forced to be an opportunist, for first he sought neutrality, then he sided with the South, then finally with the North. To understand these apparent contradictions, it is necessary only to recall that a tribal split was a real threat and totally unacceptable to Ross. He apparently compromised when it was expedient, but in truth he disregarded his personal preferences to work for tribal unity. Perhaps Ross's years in Washington would have received less censure had he refrained from the high living to which he was accustomed. A trip to his beleaguered people, in spite of the dangers, also would have increased the creditability of his leadership and brought hope to the tribe.

With the war's end, smoldering factionalism would reignite as the two Cherokee parties grappled for power. The final year for Ross, as his health ebbed, would require his most forceful determination to recreate the fleeting unity he had so long sought. From September 1865 to August 1866 at Fort Smith and at Washington the very honor and station of Ross would be questioned and defamed as land-hungry whites and power-seeking Cherokees strove to split the Cherokee Nation and thwart his one great aim.

11

RECONSTRUCTION

WITH the end of the Civil War, Ross returned to the Cherokee Nation to find his once prosperous people huddled in the midst of vast physical destruction. Blackened chimneys marked the former sites of beautiful houses, while charred fences and desolate farmlands marred the once beautiful landscape. What Union and Confederate troops had not destroyed had been carried to Kansas or Missouri by the Cherokees in their repeated hasty retreats. Cherokee Agent Justin Harlan estimated that property losses might be as high as two million dollars. The extent of human suffering was inestimable, for hardly a Cherokee family had escaped the war's toll. Amid such devastation, bitter hatred and factional quarrels would not soon be forgotten, and now the groups would align with names that suited their Civil War sympathies, real or purported. Ross led the northern faction, while Stand Watie and Elias Cornelius Boudinot (son of the murdered Elias Boudinot) championed the southern cause.[1]

Arriving at Van Buren, Arkansas, late in August 1865, Ross wrote Sarah Stapler:

I know that I am fast approaching my country & my people, and that I shall soon meet with my dear children relatives & friends who will greet me with joyful hearts—but, where is that delightful House & the matron of the once happy family who so kindly & hospitably entertained our guests. Alas, I shall see them no more on earth. The loved wife and mother is at last in the Heavenly mansions prepared for the redeemed—And the family Homestead ruthlessly reduced to ashes by the hand of rebel incendiaries. And whilst the surviving members of our family circle are scattered abroad as refugees—I am here journeying as it were, alone to find myself, a stranger & Homeless, in my own country. . . . The picture is painful to my feeling.

He also depicted scenes of home and reunion to his daughter Annie. All were "overwhelmed with Joy & Sorrow at our meeting, joy for seeing me & grief for the death of your Dear Mother. I then hastened to our once lovely Home and witnessed the ruins and desolation of the premises. . . . I cannot express the sadness of my feelings in my ramblings over the place."²

As so many of the Indian tribes had signed treaties with the Confederacy during the war, the United States called for tribal representatives to meet peace commissioners at Fort Smith, Arkansas, in September 1865 to work out new treaty arrangements. The five United States commissioners were Dennis N. Cooley, commissioner of Indian affairs, as president; Elijah Sells, superintendent for southern Indians; Thomas Wistar of Pennsylvania; Major General W. S. Harney; Colonel Ely S. Parker; and Charles Mix as secretary. The Cherokee delegation at Fort Smith included some of the tribe's ablest men—Smith Christie, Thomas Pegg, White Catcher, H. D. Reese, and Lewis Downing of the northern faction; and Elias Cornelius Boudinot, Stand Watie, Richard Fields, William Penn Adair, and James M. Bell of the southern faction. Indeed, some of the keenest minds and most skilled negotiators attending the conference were from the Cherokee Nation.³

The deliberations at Fort Smith began on September 8, 1865, and on the second day Commissioner Cooley outlined basic stipulations which the new treaties must contain. The point on which the Cherokees were to focus involved the so-called Harlan Bill, a controversial provision which called for the consolidation of all tribes in Indian Territory into one government. Cooley, in his statement concerning the necessity for a treaty, began from the premise that all the Cherokees had been, as he termed them, "bona fide rebels." The next day, partly to get a denial of this charge into the commission's minutes and partly to gain more time to plan strategy, Reese of the northern faction offered a "not guilty" plea to Cooley's charges.⁴

On September 12 Cooley, in answer to Reese's statement of loyalty, disrupted and shocked the northern Cherokee delegation by attacking Ross's integrity and accusing him of plotting to align the Cherokees with the Confederacy. By an unfair and distorted use of documents, the commissioner traced the purported treachery of the chief, declaring that because of Ross's influence in carrying other tribes into the rebellion, the Cherokees were legally and morally subject to the will of the president.[5]

This was a total reversal from the accord which Ross had established with Commissioner of Indian Affairs William P. Dole during his refugee stay in Washington. Dole had accepted the coercive nature of their defection, and he recognized the legitimacy of Ross's leadership and his personal loyalty. Dole noted that Ross appeared "to have resisted the movements of the rebels so long as was in his power" and believed, therefore, that Lincoln should show "generous lenity and forbearance" to the Cherokees as they returned to their first alliance. The understanding that Ross and Dole had developed augured well for the difficult reconstruction period which lay ahead, but it did not carry over into the new administration. Cooley, President Andrew Johnson's new commissioner of Indian affairs, was prepared to question not only the loyalty of all the Cherokees—Union and Confederate—but also the integrity of Ross.[6]

The commission finally approved Cooley's position and presented a statement to the northern delegation declining to recognize Ross as principal chief. Not only did this paper declare Ross an emissary of the rebellious states but also reported him "still at heart an enemy of the United States, and disposed to breed discord among his people . . . and . . . not the choice of any considerable portion of the Cherokee nation for the office which he claims." At this point a conversation took place among Cooley, Ross, and Boudinot, the principal delegate of the southern faction. Doubtless under emotional stress, the old chief did not exhibit his usual clarity and eloquence as he professed his consistent loyalty to the laws of the United States and denied the charges against him. Ross recalled for the commissioners that during his three years in Washington he had never been charged with being an enemy of the United States, confessed to signing the treaty with the South, but insisted that "I did not do it within myself." Ross pointed out that he always had counseled the Cherokees, as a weak people, not to antagonize the United States but to remain obedient, but when the whole voice of the Cherokee Nation called for a treaty with the Confederacy, he believed that he could only follow that will. Rhetorically, he asked Cooley, "Could I do more than that?"[7]

In response, Boudinot charged Ross with instigating the dissensions that had divided the Cherokee Nation for years. "I will show," Boudinot continued, "the deep duplicity & falsity that have followed him from his childhood to the present day, when the winters of 65 or 70 years have silvered his head with sin, what can you expect of him now." Cooley did not intend for old feuds to be stirred up again, and he interrupted Boudinot's harangue. The next day, September 16, Boudinot showed how far the southern faction was willing to go to ensure Ross's continued disfavor, when he related that the southern Cherokees were "cheerfully" disposed to accept Cooley's treaty provisions with only two minor exceptions. What Boudinot demanded in return was nothing less than the division of the Cherokee Nation. The commission had no such authority, however, so the southern faction signed the treaty on September 18.[8]

The northern delegates had signed the treaty two days before their southern counterparts, but it was merely a treaty of peace and actually settled none of the major problems. In the hope that the rival parties could work out some agreement, Cooley instructed a joint committee of the two delegations to meet with his associate Wistar, but no reconciliation was obtained. Arrangements were made, therefore, to reconvene in Washington at the call of the secretary of the interior in order to negotiate a reconstruction treaty.[9]

During the course of the controversy over Ross's position and allegiance, Cooley rushed a telegram to Secretary of the Interior James Harlan informing him of his refusal to recognize Ross. The month-long communications lag no longer existed, and the message reached Harlan the next day. The secretary presented the document to President Johnson, who approved Cooley's course. Indeed, Harlan authorized the commissioner to recognize other parties from the tribe and permitted Cooley to treat with one or several factional representatives. Cooley must have considered it more politic to obtain the sanction of his superiors in these complications; thus his recommendations to move the negotiations to Washington.[10]

Why the abrupt shift in attitudes toward Ross among federal Indian officials? Harlan, Cooley, and Elijah Sells were close friends, all from Iowa, and all, especially Harlan, were interested in land and railroads. While senator from Iowa, Harlan was instrumental in promoting a transcontinental railroad. Kansas lobbyists were certainly influential in federal councils about Indian affairs, and they looked longingly at the lush Indian lands ripe for farming and eminently suitable for railroads. Ross's feelings concerning these designs were no secret. As early as 1848 and 1854 similar plans for consolidating the Indian tribes and incorporating their lands into adjoining states had been introduced in Congress, and in 1860 Ross was approached on the matter of allotting the Cherokee lands for private ownership. He found such ideas inconsistent with Cherokee treaties, unconstitutional under Cherokee laws, and in no way beneficial to his people. Perhaps federal officials thought they could work out reciprocal agreements with the southern faction: railway rights in exchange for a division of the tribe.[11]

The Cherokee National Council met on November 7, 1865, and appointed Ross to head a delegation to Washington. Ross led an array of capable Cherokees including Lewis Downing, Smith Christie, Daniel H. Ross, S. H. Benge, James McDaniel, and Thomas Pegg, while the Baptist missionary John B. Jones went along as adviser. One of the purposes of this group was to obtain an impartial investigation of the charges brought against Ross at Fort Smith. During the interim before the National Council met in November, Ross fell so ill with "ague & fever" that he discontinued his usual flow of letters to friends and relatives and was under the care of a doctor for over a week. It was the latter part of October before Ross regained his health and even then his weakness persisted. He spoke to Sarah of the Fort Smith conference and of the "groundless stigma . . . fabricated" there. Ross felt mortified and was anxious to go to Washington to defend himself against "the foul aspersions that have been published by designing men." Before leaving the Cherokee Nation he cut a sprout from Sarah's favorite tree on the Rose Cottage grounds and carried it to her as a gift. This would be Ross's last look at his Cherokee homeland, his final chance to redeem his character, and his closing effort to unify his people.[12]

The Washington conference was in many ways a repetition of the Fort Smith meeting. Indeed, it echoed the chorus of conferences through the years where repeated attempts had been made to dislodge Ross and to sever the Cherokee Nation. The great issue would be restatements of one theme—should the Cherokee Nation be divided? The southern delegation continued to insist that division was the only means of ending the internecine conflict that had characterized Cherokee political factionalism, while the northern faction maintained that only as a unified people could the Cherokees retain their national rights and become the prosperous race they once had been.

The fullest and most forceful argument of the loyalty of the northern delegates was issued on January 24, 1866, in a pamphlet to President Johnson. Here they reiterated their earlier position that only constant pressure and fear of invasion had forced them into the Confederacy, they noted their wholehearted and unreserved welcome of Colonel William Weer as he had brought federal forces back into the Cherokee Nation, and they pointed to the Cherokee National Council meeting on Cowskin Prairie in February 1863 at which the northern element of the tribe had abrogated the Confederate treaty, expelled from office disloyal persons, and abolished slavery. Before members of the Ross faction could hope to secure their aims, they had to be assured of their recognition as the Cherokee Nation's legitimate spokesmen. To have this assurance, their loyalty had to be above question.[13]

Not only the loyalty of the great mass of Cherokees had to be above suspicion if an adequate treaty was to be realized, but Ross's credentials had to be irrefutable. To secure his recognition and disprove the charges against him, another pamphlet was published in which the delegation charged that an element led by Watie and Boudinot had attempted to mislead the federal government into believing that Ross had been disloyal. The northern Cherokees recreated the situation as it had existed in 1861 and 1862 to show that Ross had had no other choice, and they produced a document which revealed that Albert Pike had been prepared to treat with the Watie faction if Ross had not come over to the southern side. They stressed that neither Ross nor the Cherokee National Council felt morally bound to the Confederate treaty any longer than the security of the Cherokee Nation demanded. They concluded that if Ross were counted an enemy, then the United States had no friend. "If he is a rebel," they declared, "then there are none loyal."[14]

Elias C. Boudinot and William Penn Adair had arrived in January 1866 ahead of the rest of the southern delegation and had petitioned Cooley in regard to certain alleged misuses of Cherokee funds by

Chief Ross. Adair and Boudinot said that Ross had received large sums for signing the Confederate treaty and requested information on the two hundred fifty thousand dollars which they said had been paid to the Cherokee "constituted authorities." Actually Ross had received about sixty or seventy thousand dollars in gold coin and about a hundred and fifty thousand dollars in Confederate currency from Albert Pike, the Confederate treaty commissioner, in early March 1862. Pike in 1866 admitted it was understood that the currency was to be used to redeem warrants of the Cherokees issued during the financial depression of the late 1840s and went on to say that the warrants were in the hands of Ross and his relatives. Pike's statement was patently untrue; had he had any knowledge of Cherokee financial matters, he would have known that these warrants had passed into the hands of white speculators long before the Confederate alliance. John W. Stapler, Ross's brother-in-law, maintained the Cherokee national safe in his store and informed Harlan that the gold had not been used for Ross's personal benefit. After the summer of 1862 Confederate currency was of little use to Ross as a refugee in Washington, if he even dared to carry it with him. In fact, he may have used it to pay on the Cherokee national debt which he had estimated at nearly one hundred thousand dollars in 1859.[15]

Evidence of Ross's financial situation during the Civil War years further belies the southern assertion that he used the money personally. The allowances of the federal government could not sustain the refugees who flocked to his Philadelphia home, and by the end of the war he was deep in debt, having mortgaged both his house and furniture far beyond their actual value. His only hope of recompense was in a final settlement for the destruction of his home and property in the Cherokee Nation.[16]

By January 30 Boudinot and Adair received a copy of the Union faction's pamphlet and busily set to work on their own apologia, refuting point by point the arguments of the opposing party. Boudinot and Adair used this opportunity to malign Ross and, more important, at least for their purposes, to push for the division of the Cherokee Nation. "We are already divided by political barriers," they insisted, "by mementoes of blood stronger than death. Let us be sundered by territorial boundaries." In a later presentation the southern faction pointed to the separation of the Choctaws and the Chickasaws in 1855 and the Creeks and the Seminoles in 1856. More important, the southern Cherokees insisted that the United States had recognized two separate Cherokee Nations in earlier treaties. They spoke highly of Commissioner of Indian Affairs Cooley who at Fort Smith and now in Washington had succumbed to their persuasion and frequently used his messages to support their own contentions. The northern faction insisted that the southern group wanted division for other reasons: "But it is not peace, security, and fraternity, these lately disloyal leaders want—it is political power. . . . Their distress arises not from fear for safety, but from hunger for power; which they cannot soon get but by a disruption of the nation."[17]

In the first months of 1866 Cooley came out against Ross even more strongly than he had at Fort Smith; his efforts would culminate that summer in a lengthy pamphlet entitled "The Cherokee Question." Even as early as February 1866 Cooley sent President Johnson a rough draft of his arguments concerning Ross's loyalty. In both of these papers Cooley challenged Ross's loyalty through the distorted use of letters, messages, and proposals. The northern Cherokees did not idly accept such denunciations of their chief. Calling the rejection of Ross at Fort Smith an "act of tyranny," they displayed a letter from Colonel William A. Phillips, one of the first federal officers to enter the Cherokee Nation in 1862 and commander of Union Indian troops during the war, in which Phillips insisted that Cooley's charges were "base calumnies" against Ross. Expressing the hope that these charges would not end the chief's brilliant career, he concluded by saying "I know he aided our cause; God forgive me if I forget it."[18]

The Ross delegation met with President Johnson, Secretary Harlan, and Commissioner Cooley on February 15, 1866 at the White House. When Harlan presented Ross to the president, Johnson spoke of his earlier acquaintance with the chief, and they shook hands warmly. Ross then introduced other members of the delegation, and Pegg presented the documents relating to their business in Washington, particularly the proceedings of the Fort Smith council. McDaniel asked to speak a few words to the president and then went into some detail explaining the cause of the Cherokee alliance with the Confederacy, making special reference to Ross's loyalty and sincerity. Ross and Cooley clashed at one point in discussion over whether Cooley had simply refused to recognize Ross as chief or, as Ross insisted, had attempted to remove him. Ross used the occasion to inform President Johnson of occurrences at the Fort Smith council which did not appear in Cooley's reports.[19]

The next week Ross attempted to bypass Cooley, believing him completely committed to the "rebel Cherokees," as Ross termed them, and met privately with Harlan where he gained assurances that negotiations would not be solely in Cooley's hands. Ross was elated after this meeting, and he wrote Sarah: "I feel myself as standing upon as firm ground, if not more so, with my own people, as Mr. Cooley does with his people—time will soon indicate whose official authority is resting upon a sandy foundation." Within a few days Harlan laid out to both Cherokee delegations suggestions for a treaty, and they busily set to work to outline their divergent schemes.[20]

Members of the northern faction presented their projected treaty to Harlan on March 15, 1866, laying out in sixteen articles terms which Ross declared based on "Humanity, equity & justice" and intended to "thwart the expectations of those mercenary cormorants who, *leach like*, have so long been sucking the vital resources of the Cherokees." The initial article affirmed all previous treaties with the United States, a slap at Cooley who at Fort Smith had announced the Cherokees had forfeited all former rights by their associations with the Confederacy. The remainder of the proposed pact provided rights to freedmen without citizenship; offered amnesty and pardon to southern Cherokees after taking a required loyalty oath; restricted settlement of other Indian tribes on Cherokee lands; listed judicial rights in Cherokee cases; included severe restrictions on railroads, white traders, and military posts in the Cherokee Nation; and provided for sale of the Neutral Lands to the United States at $1.25 per acre and the surveying of all Cherokee lands. Although the treaty was not a humble petition but a document designed by men who regarded themselves as unquestionably loyal to the United States, the northern Cherokees received little attention for their efforts, for Cooley was convinced by the southern delegates that a division of the tribe was imperative.[21]

At this point Ross nearly collapsed physically. He had been suffering during January and March from severe colds, but each time he seemed to recover. During the last week in March he complained of pains in his chest. The application of mustard plasters brought temporary relief, but intense pain soon settled in his stomach and was diagnosed as a "billious condition." The condition persisted through the first two weeks in April, and although Ross told friends that he hoped to be up and in his usual health soon, he called Sarah and his daughter Annie from Philadelphia to be at his side.[22]

While Ross was confined to his boarding house, he was visited by Cooley, Elijah Sells, and Justin Harlan. After the usual amenities, Cooley said: "I pray you Govr. not to allow business to trouble your mind. Keep quiet & get well & we will make every thing right." Cooley spoke these solicitous words less than two weeks after he sent President Johnson the memorandum maligning Ross. What Cooley wished to "make right" was the southern delegation's demands.[23]

The rival delegations met on April 7, 1866, by direction of Harlan and, although both spoke of peace, they were diametrically opposed. Several conferences were held in May with each of the delegations represented by legal counsel: Thomas Ewing for the Ross group and D. W. Voorhees for the southern Cherokees. Further meetings were held throughout May but with no results. Throughout these negotiations Ross was confined to bed but, living in the same boarding house with his colleagues, he received daily news of the proceedings and doubtless directed many of the northern faction's efforts.[24]

During June the southern delegates seemed to have everything in their favor. Ross was bedridden, and Cooley was on their side; one southern delegate informed a friend: "Ross will be beaten. . . . His day is done. Ours is rising fast and bright. We will get all we asked for, with perhaps, not so much money." Indeed, the situation seemed to justify his elation, for on June 13 Cooley actually concluded negotiations with the southern faction and sent the proposed treaty to President Johnson. To justify the act Cooley published in the same week "The Cherokee Question," designed to destroy

Ross's major argument that the Cherokees were decidedly loyal and that the Confederate treaty had been only a temporary aberration.[25]

The elation of the southern Cherokees turned to despair when Johnson refused to sign their document. No doubt the barrage of correspondence of the northern delegates and the unrelenting spirit of Ross did much to persuade the president. Ross and his friends appealed to Johnson's close advisers and also competed with the southern faction for public sentiment through the pages of the *New York Tribune*. Perhaps Johnson realized the inconsistency in dealing with a minor tribal faction which had supported the Confederacy both before and throughout the Civil War. Cooley returned to his bargaining, now with the northern Cherokees, and effected a treaty on July 19, 1866; it was quickly approved by the Senate and proclaimed on August 11, just ten days after Ross's death. But Ross lived to see himself vindicated, for early in July, during the northern faction's negotiations with Cooley, the delegates had insisted that any treaty carry Ross's signature as "Principal Chief of the Cherokees." Harlan concurred, noting that Ross's ouster at Fort Smith had been intended only to be temporary.[26]

A month before his death Ross made out a final will. He left to his two children by Mary, Annie and John, all his real estate in Wilmington. To each of his older children he bequeathed five thousand dollars and to the children of his late son James he left two thousand five hundred each. Many of Mary's personal effects were willed to Sarah and John W. Stapler. All the monetary provisions were to be paid out of money received from Ross's claims against the United States, for by the time of his death his wealth was nearly exhausted. In fact, Ross's oldest daughter Jane, twice widowed and now caring for the children of her deceased brother James, had to appeal for financial assistance from the federal government. She wrote, "While my father lived he provided for me and mine—he stood for all my liabilities and now he is gone." In June 1866 Ross also made out an account of his property lost during the conflict, for which he claimed over fifty-three thousand dollars. The question of Ross's loyalty to the United States during the Civil War did not end with his death. In 1870 Annie and William P. Ross as executors of Ross's estate, filed for payment with the Senate Committee on Claims.

After a careful examination of Ross's life and of his service to the Cherokees, and despite the testimony of Evan Jones and William A. Phillips, the committee concluded that the claim should not be honored as Ross's loyalty still remained questionable.[27]

Ross died in Washington about 7:00 on the evening of Wednesday, August 1, 1866. Funeral services were held at Jay's Hotel in Washington and also in Wilmington, Delaware, where his remains lay in state at the home of his brother-in-law, John W. Stapler. Services were conducted on Sunday afternoon at the Grace Methodist Episcopal Church, where Reverend Aaron Rittenhouse of St. Paul's Methodist Episcopal Church in Wilmington, read a beautiful eulogy. The cortege moved from Grace Church to the Brandywine Cemetery with the loyal Cherokee delegates serving as pall bearers. Ross's body was laid in the Stapler family plot near Mary's. The Reverend Rittenhouse spoke a final benediction, and the solemn entourage of family and friends departed.[28]

At its next regular session, the Cherokee National Council decreed that Ross's remains should be returned to Park Hill. On that occasion the chief's beloved nephew William P. Ross spoke these words: "We claim not for John Ross exemption from error and imperfection, but believe that he enjoyed in an eminent degree a power of intellect and endurance, a tenacity of purpose and an earnestness of soul which belong only to great men, qualities which impress themselves upon the character of the day, in which their possessors live, and send an influence far down the stream of time."[29]

The National Council directed William P. Ross, Jesse Bushyhead, and Riley Keys to return the chief's coffin to the Cherokee Nation. The three men returned in early May 1867 and placed the coffin at the male seminary where it lay in state until June 1, when the whole Cherokee Nation gathered to pay final tribute to the revered chief. The Moravian minister E. J. Mock conducted the final services, and William also spoke before the casket of his uncle:

It is proper, that here, should his dust mingle with kindred dust, and that a suitable memorial should arise, to mark the spot where repose the bones of our greatest chieftain. It will keep alive within our bosoms a spirit of patriotism. It will impart strength and hope in the hour of adversity. It will teach us to beware of domestic strife and division. It will serve to unite us more closely in peace, in concord and in devotion to the common welfare. It will soften our asperities and excite the thoughtful youth of our land to patience, to perseverance, to success and to renown.[30]

Ross was laid to rest at the Ross Cemetery near the ruins of Rose Cottage and among the people he had served so faithfully and so long.

12

IN RETROSPECT

THE career of Chief John Ross spanned nearly half a century of the most dynamic era in Cherokee history. Entering public service at the very time the Cherokees were undergoing significant political and social changes, he led them as the destiny of the Cherokee Nation intertwined with evolution of the United States. His ascendancy reflected these changes. With only a slight amount of Cherokee blood and few physical characteristics to reveal his kinship, Ross won the full-bloods' trust as his more likely looking opponents never did. He was selected for leadership because he displayed the requisite qualities for that epoch of change: an unfailing devotion to the sacred homelands and a facility for articulating the Cherokee cause. Beyond simply mirroring the full-bloods' attachment to their ancient lands, he led the Cherokees into new realms by adapting a subtle blend of tribal folkways and white techniques. Ross's genius lay in his ability to recognize boundaries, geographic and psychological, and to guide the cautious Cherokees within them.

Ross overcame his initial liabilities by assiduously cultivating Cherokee support through integrity, hard work, and constant association with them. At his father's business and in later years at his own warehouse and mercantile store, he gained the trust and respect of his Cherokee kinsmen. He also acquired a reputation for honesty by his candid exposure of an attempted bribe early in his public career. Ross linked himself to the beloved leader of the Cherokees Charles Hicks and from him learned the intricacies of tribal politics and gained a deeper respect for old Cherokee traditions. His superior abilities caught the attention of the Cherokee leadership, so that

Hicks and Major Ridge began early to groom young Ross for a career of responsibility.

Ross never developed the mercantile knack that his relatives exhibited; rather he discovered a skill in the measured art of political diplomacy. Weaned on Cherokee internal politics, Ross was hardly awed at Washington negotiations. From his first venture at the capital city in 1816 until the reconstruction negotiations of 1866, Ross displayed a prowess at the bargaining table that surprised each new set of Washington luminaries throughout his half-century of service. He became such a figure at the federal capital that mail addressed simply "John Ross, Washington" would reach him. The opening of each congressional term would find Ross and a delegation of Cherokees busily defending Cherokee interests. When not in attendance himself, he carefully tutored a young retinue of devoted followers to carry on and to be mindful of Cherokee inflexibility on certain basic issues.

Ross had two general goals in his negotiations with the federal government over the years. He worked to prod the United States to fulfill its treaty obligations and to guard the Cherokees against any further loss of land after the tribe had determined its narrowest boundary. Until the 1830s Ross was moderately successful in these goals, but with the accession of Andrew Jackson to the presidency and the spread of the states' rights doctrine, Ross was plagued by repeated bitter defeats. Although the Cherokee position was upheld in the decisions of the United States Supreme Court and several Georgia courts, these judgments had little effect in an era of executive and congressional dominance. Court decrees had even less influence among the restless frontier settlers who coveted the Cherokee farmlands and gold. Moreover, Ross faced a three-pronged assault. Not only were Georgia and the federal government unrelenting, but internal erosion also weakened the Cherokee foundation.

Ross's opposition in the Cherokee Nation constantly accused him of deluding the Cherokees into believing that they would not have to remove. Ross himself may have been deceived. Some of the best legal thinkers in the United States assured Ross that the Cherokees had an excellent case against Georgia, but they neglected to tell him that court decisions could be circumvented by a determined executive. Friends within Congress led Ross to think that the Cherokees could avoid removal by appeals to the Senate and the House of Representatives, and knowledgeable white men assured Ross that Congress would not ignore the mass of petitions that poured into Washington in support of the Cherokee cause. However, assurances proved empty when Congress accepted Jackson's position—though by the narrowest of margins. Ross also was misled by members of President Van Buren's administration. At the very time the Cherokees should have been removed under treaty provisions, Secretary of War Joel R. Poinsett was holding out hope of a two-year extension. Special agent John Mason indicated by his presence in the Cherokee Nation in 1837 and by his attitude that new negotiations were in the offing, but in Washington he pursued the same relentless course followed by his predecessors.

Perhaps Ross was politically naive or allowed himself to be deceived at this point. Certainly he must have known, through firsthand acquaintance and the general's reputation, Jackson's attitudes toward Indians. He also must have realized that Jackson had the political power and unbending personality to carry out his aims. Moreover, reliable friends told Ross that Van Buren was Jackson's man; thus the chief should not have been taken in by the delaying tactics so common to Washington officials.

Even if Ross had not met vacillating and contradictory positions by Washington officials, he probably would have been in Washington until the last minute trying to prevent Cherokee removal. Ross's opponents insisted that he should have been in the Cherokee Nation working with his people to convince them of the folly of refusing removal and of the certainty of greater harm if they did not go voluntarily. This, of course, presumes that Ross was deceitful, that he knew removal was inevitable, and that he believed life in the West would be more hospitable in the long run. Actually, Ross did not accept any of these positions until well into 1838, and some he may never have accepted. In all probability Ross would have been rejected by the majority of Cherokees had he gone to them, even as late as the early months of 1838, and pled the wisdom of removal. Certainly Ross would have lost his position as chief, and perhaps in one sense this is why he worked so diligently against removal. Ross relished his position as chief and all the prestige and power that were a part of the office, but he was not using the office for his own malevolent purposes. He knew that without his leadership, removal would become a nightmare and a disaster even beyond the actual dismal event. Removal became a reality to the Cherokees only when they were rounded up at gunpoint, herded into stockades, and transported under armed guard. Only after such stark reality could Ross publicly but reluctantly support removal, and ably but sadly guide his people westward.

The Cherokee treaty party charged that Ross had merely delayed removal to obtain a better monetary bargain and to fill his own pockets. These opponents and some Washington officials also speculated that he resisted the Treaty of New Echota of 1835 simply because he did not have a hand in it. Although he did oppose the treaty partially on these grounds, his reasoning was more complex. Certainly the worth of the Cherokee lands far exceeded the initial price offered by the federal government, nor did subsequent increases meet its actual value. Furthermore, from long experience Ross had learned that the federal government felt no great urgency to make payments under treaties with the Cherokees. That the treaty was made with a small clique of unauthorized individuals was a legitimate reason for Ross to oppose it. The Cherokee constitution clearly spelled out the treaty-making process, and the Cherokees voiced their disapproval of any of the proposed pacts over a number of years. It must have been especially galling to Ross that at the very time the Treaty of New Echota was being formed, he was enroute to Washington to work out some removal agreement. Ross seemed unable or unwilling to yield positions once they were taken, at least until some critical point demanded change. Such was the case in 1846 and in 1866 when the federal government seemed ready to settle treaty arrangements with his foes. Had Ross been willing to come to face reality earlier, all parties might have avoided unnecessary delays in settling their problems.

Ross had an unflagging confidence in the legitimacy of his authority. As early as 1826 his right to speak for the Cherokees was challenged by federal officials, and in succeeding years his capacity as chief was questioned repeatedly. Ross knew he spoke for a large majority of the Cherokees and realized that to allow doubts of his authority was to lessen the credibility of the independence of the

Cherokee Nation. In 1832 and 1839 discordant elements within the tribe were ready to question his command, but here again Ross knew that he expressed the sentiments of a large majority of the Cherokees. In every election from 1828 to 1866, he was the overwhelming choice for the highest office. This remarkable achievement indicates a trust by his people that few other men in substantial elective positions can match.

Nevertheless, Ross frequently dealt with his people in a paternalistic manner, telling them only what he believed they could understand. Sometimes, therefore, he left them without an adequate knowledge of their position before the federal government and with little chance to make intelligent decisions. He could even go so far as to misrepresent matters. He described, for instance, the western country as lacking sufficient wood and water. This was untrue, and Ross must have known better. His visits to the region in 1813 and 1836 should have convinced him that the Cherokees could easily live there in their customary manner.

The majority of Cherokees demonstrated their faith in Ross by an unquestioning trust in his use of national funds. During Ross's lifetime the Cherokees, through the sale of lands, acquired thousands of dollars turned over to the tribe in yearly allotments or annuities. Ross as chief and as head of numerous delegations receiving these payments never once was found to be careless with the money. Nor were the Cherokees so backward that they did not understand the financial arrangements made. Certainly for many years Ross faced a ready opposition anxious to prove his misapplication of Cherokee funds. Indeed, he had to answer recurring charges that he used the privileges of his office for personal aggrandizement. Although charges were made particularly in regard to removal money, no conclusive evidence exists to tie Ross to any personal plundering of Cherokee funds. Moreover, the accusations of his detractors came at periods when new arrangements were in progress for the Cherokee Nation, times when it could be expected that opponents would take extreme positions to further their own cause. The charge of extravagance seems more easily verified. The six-month sojourns in Washington were often made in lavish and leisurely fashion. Ross lived well in private and probably did not curtail his habits when engaged in Cherokee business.

Ross was a shrewd manager of his personal finances, as well as of Cherokee public funds. He was never content in the mercantile business which other members of his family found so profitable. Rather he discovered his competence as a planter. Careful direction of his extensive land improvements, both before removal and in the new lands in the West, built for him a fortune already well established from his family inheritance and a successful merchandising operation. Ross also prospered as an entrepreneurial collaborator. His associations with his nephews, Daniel H. and William P. Ross, and his brother-in-law John Stapler afforded extra areas for financial advancement. He was similar in many ways to the politico-entrepreneur-businessmen with whom he came in contact in Washington. Connected enterprises were typical of Jackson, Webster, or Clay as well as of several prominent Cherokees. As to his agrarian operations, Ross was also something of a land speculator and doubtless profited well from his land transactions in the easily marketable acres of east Tennessee. Perhaps he had become accustomed to the financial security he had acquired over the years, for during the Civil War years he did not know how to retrench, and in the end left his surviving family only a meager inheritance.

Ross knew war—its brief moment of glory and its costly destruction of human life and personal property. He had served with distinction in the War of 1812 and always pointed with pride to the Cherokees' service to the United States in that conflict. But it was the waste of war that he remembered best, from the internal conflicts in the Cherokee community to the vast desolation of the Civil War. Ross consistently worked to neutralize and arbitrate conflicts. He willingly served as a mediator in the Seminole War and constantly counseled surrounding tribes on the importance of maintaining peace. During periods of the greatest anguish when force seemed the only recourse to repeated invasions of the Cherokee homelands, he urged his people to lay down their arms and to submit peacefully to removal. Even when his own life was threatened and friends rushed to stop would-be assassins, he advised against violence and exhorted rash supporters to wait for legal action. The murders of 1839 are an instance of his inability to deter the violent actions of some of his hotheaded followers.

The personal life of Ross reveals more than a calculating politician and a crafty negotiator. The wholehearted, straitlaced gentility of Whiggish conservatism is readily evident in his letters to his nieces, nephews, and children. Yet he loved them sincerely and supported them, not only financially but with sympathetic paternal regard. Even during the most pressing political negotiations, he took time to write them or to attend their school ceremonies. They must have considered him more than a stodgy old man, for they often looked to him for advice. Ross always pointed these young people to greater accomplishments. If his ambitions seem somewhat antique to later generations, the ideas at least were those upon which his own life and career were built—hard work and personal integrity.

Ross's life with Quatie is a shadowy story. She was the quiet partner to a rising Cherokee political star and perhaps found her fulfillment in her home and children. By the time Ross met Mary, his emotions had long since been covered with Victorian piety. The gilded prose of his labored love letters hides as much as it reveals. Mary was a young, beautiful coquette with a dash of romantic idealism to flavor her Quaker sobriety. She added new dimensions to Ross's life as she brought a splash of gaiety to an otherwise somber figure. Mary also taught her husband the deeper meanings of religious commitment beyond the mere quoting of Biblical passages for rhetorical effect. She awakened in Ross a sense of the everlasting, and his later letters to her reveal a concern not only for sermons and scriptural passages but also for personal commitment to Christian beliefs.

Ross was a humanitarian, but in the fashion of his era he worked in an indirect and impersonal manner—through the missionary efforts which he sponsored and supported throughout his life, but also in the way he opened his heart and his home to less prosperous Cherokees. His table often was crowded with both Indian guests and itinerant white men. Moreover, Ross's social awareness spilled into other areas of his life, and he used his office as chief to encourage the cultural development of his people. His dreams of a national press, schools, libraries, and corrective institutions were aspects of his plans for the social, intellectual, and moral development of the Cherokees. The tragic events of removal and the Civil War frustrated Ross's dreams, while financial distress and lethargy slowed the progress of Cherokee advancement.

Ross's able leadership, often autocratic and rarely passive, spanned nearly fifty years by the time of his death on August 1, 1866. During this period the Cherokees endured a series of bitter factional quarrels. The opposition faction contended that Ross used his position to further personal and party goals. Indeed, he frequently felt his policies so obviously correct that he disregarded justified criticism. His overwhelming desire for Cherokee unity led him at times to accept positions that he did not personally support, but on other occasions he would practice personal chicanery to get his way. His methods, sometimes aimed arbitrarily at a desired end, often alienated those whose assistance he needed most. Yet one thing could not be denied: his first and ultimate loyalty was to the Cherokees. Facing, as he did, the superior and relentlessly advancing United States, he had to make firm and frequently brutal decisions. Moreover, he feared that factionalism would lead to the division of the Cherokees and make the great plan of his life, Cherokee unity, unattainable.

NOTES

CHAPTER 1

1. Daniel H. Ross to William P. Ross, April 3, 1866, John Ross Papers, Thomas Gilcrease Institute of American History and Art, Tulsa, Oklahoma.

2. Henry Timberlake, *Memoirs, 1756–1765*, ed. Samuel Cole Williams (Marietta, Ga.: Continental Book Co., 1948), pp. 128–32, 164; Emmet Starr, *History of the Cherokee Indians* (Oklahoma City: Warden, 1921), p. 410.

3. Starr, *History*, pp. 410, 367, 309; statements of Elizabeth Lowrey, September 22, 1837, January 22, 1841, and March 14, 1845, Ross Papers, Gilcrease Institute; U.S. Congress, *American State Papers*, Indian Affairs, 2 vols. (1832–61), 1: 434; John McDonald to Alexander McKee, April 10, 1794, in Philip M. Hamer, "The British in Canada and the Southern Indians, 1790–1794," *East Tennessee Historical Society's Publications*, no. 2 (1930), p. 127; Charles J. Kappler, comp. and ed., *Indian Affairs: Laws and Treaties*, 5 vols. (Washington, D.C.: Government Printing Office, 1904–41), 2: 82–83, 90–91.

4. Last will of William Shorey, April 1809, Records of the Cherokee Indian Agency in Tennessee, Office of Indian Affairs, National Archives, Washington, D.C.; Starr, *History*, pp. 367, 309; Carolyn Thomas Foreman, "A Cherokee Pioneer: Ella Flora Coodey Robinson," *Chronicles of Oklahoma*, 7, no. 4 (December 1929), pp. 364–65. Anne followed her brother's wishes to care for the girls and that same year enrolled Alcy at the Springplace Mission School (Adelaide L. Fries and Douglas LeTell Rights, eds., *Records of the Moravians in North Carolina*, 8 vols. [Raleigh, N.C.: State Department of Archives and History, 1922–54], 8: 3791).

5. McDonald to Return J. Meigs, April 20, 1809, Elizabeth Lowrey to Meigs, April 26 and October 2, 1809, Pathkiller to Meigs, May 27, 1809, Anne McDonald to Timothy Meigs, June 9, 1809, Records of the Cherokee Indian Agency in Tennessee.

6. Emmet Starr, notes for *History of the Cherokee Indians*, Oklahoma Historical Society, Oklahoma City, Gilbert Eaton Govan and James W. Livingood, *The Chattanooga Country, 1540–1951* (New York: E. P. Dutton, 1952), pp. 26–27.

7. John P. Brown, *Old Frontiers: The Story of the Cherokees from Earliest Times to the Date of Their Removal to the West, 1838* (Kingsport, Tenn.: Southern Publishers, 1938), pp. 122–23; John P. Brown, "Eastern Cherokee Chiefs," *Chronicles of Oklahoma*, 16, no. 1 (March 1938), p. 19.

8. Philip M. Hamer, *Tennessee: A History, 1673–1932*, 4 vols. (New York: American Historical Society, 1933), 1: 93; Brown, "Eastern Cherokee Chiefs," p. 32; Brown, *Old Frontiers*, p. 247. In regard to McDonald's skill with the Cherokee language, one traveler noted: "Not more than 2 or 3 white men ever learned the Cherokee so as to speak it correctly; one of these was John MacDonald" (Grant Foreman Collection of Notes, Typescripts, Photostats, and United States Government Publications, Gilcrease Institute).

9. Brown, "Eastern Cherokee Chiefs," p. 32; A. P. Whitaker, "Spain and the Cherokee Indians, 1783–1798," *North Carolina Historical Review*, 4, no. 3 (July 1927), pp. 257–59, 264–65, 268–69; John McDonald to Joseph Martain, September 6, 1785, Cherokee Collection, Tennessee State Library and Archives, Nashville, Tenn.; U.S. Congress, *American State papers*, Indian Affairs, 1: 327–28, 434, 532; McDonald to Alexander McKee, April 10, 1794, in Hamer, "The British in Canada and the Southern Indians," p. 128. McDonald was slow to relinquish his British sympathies, for he wrote McKee that "in case of a secont quarell between Great Britain & America . . . the Cherokees, would readly espouse the cause of their ancient Fathers" (McDonald to McKee, December 26, 1794, Hamer, "The British in Canada and the Southern Indians," p. 134).

10. Thomas L. McKenney, *History of the Indian Tribes of North America with Biographical Sketches and Anecdotes of the Principal Chiefs*, 3 vols. (Philadelphia: Rice, Rutler, 1870), 2: 292; Govan and Livingood, *The Chattanooga Country, 1540–1951*, p. 39, 39 n. 4; statement of Daniel Ross, December 10 and 21, 1829, Cherokee Agency East Letters Received, Office of Indian Affairs, National Archives.

11. Statement of Daniel Ross, December 10 and 21, 1829, Cherokee Agency East Letters Received; Starr, *History*, pp. 410, 582; McKenney, *History of the Indian Tribes of North America*, 2: 292; Penelope Johnson Allen, "John Ross' Log Mansion," *Chattanooga Sunday Times*, February 2, 1936.

12. Penelope Johnson Allen, "John Ross' Log Mansion," pp. 7, 11; Samuel A. Worcester to William Shorey Coodey, March 15, 1830, in *Missionary Herald*, May 1830, p. 154. For Ross's adult Cherokee name his own adaptation has been used, although other sources give it as Coowescoowe or Kooweskowe (Robert Sparks Walker, *Lookout: The Story of a Mountain* [Kingsport, Tenn.: Southern Publishers, 1941], pp. 226–29; Moses Fisk to John Wheelock, April 14, 1800, Moses Fisk Papers, Dartmouth College Library, Hanover, N.H.; Samuel Cole Williams, "Christian Missions to the Overhill Cherokees," *Chronicles of Oklahoma*, 12, no. 1 (March 1934), p. 68. Evidence on Ross's education is inconclusive. He may also have studied

with Daniel Sullivan and the Reverend Isaac Anderson (See Robert Sparks Walker, *Torchlights to the Cherokees: The Brainerd Mission* [New York: Macmillan Co., 1931], pp. 21, 177, and Mrs. William P. Ross, ed., *The Life and Times of Honorable William P. Ross of the Cherokee Nation* [Fort Smith, Ark.: Weldon and Williams, 1893], pp. 187–88).

13. Linton M. Collins, "The Activities of Missionaries Among the Cherokees," *Georgia Historical Quarterly*, 6, no. 4 (December 1922), pp. 296–99; Walker, *Torchlights*, pp. 23–28; Fries, ed., *Records of the Moravians in North Carolina*, 7: 3118–19; Gilbert E. Govan, "Some Sidelights on the History of Chattanooga," *Tennessee Historical Quarterly*, 6, no. 2 (June 1947), p. 149; Kingsbury to John C. Calhoun, May 15, 1818, Letters Received by the Secretary of War, Indian Affairs, National Archives.

14. Henry Thompson Malone, *Cherokees of the Old South: A People in Transition* (Athens: University of Georgia Press, 1956), p. 103; Marion L. Starkey, *The Cherokee Nation* (New York: Alfred A. Knopf, 1946), pp. 52–53, 221. For the missionaries' attitudes toward Ross, see Starkey, *Cherokee Nation*, pp. 224–25. O. P. Fitzgerald, *John B. McFerrin: A Biography* (Nashville, Tenn.: Southern Methodist Publishing House, 1889), pp. 69–70, 442–43; Robert Paine, *Life and Times of Bishop McKendree*, 2 vols. (Nashville, Tenn.: Southern Methodist Publishing House, 1869), 2: 119–20; *Christian Advocate*, November 13, 1829; Elizur Butler to David Greene, February 27, 1830, Cherokee Mission Papers, Houghton Library, Harvard University, Cambridge, Mass.; certificate of Ross's initiation as a Master Mason, April 5, 1827, Ross Papers, Gilcrease Institute.

15. Samuel Cole Williams, ed., *Early Travels in Tennessee Country, 1540–1800* (Johnson City, Tenn.: Watauga Press, 1928), p. 312; Samuel Cole Williams, ed., "The Executive Journal of Governor John Sevier," *East Tennessee Historical Society's Publications*, no. 4 (1932), p. 109; account of Ross, May 3, 1807, Penelope Johnson Allen Collection, Chattanooga, Tenn.; account of Ross, June 27, 1808, Cherokee Collection, Tennessee State Library and Archives; Meigs to Cherokees, February 1, 1801, Records of the Cherokee Indian Agency in Tennessee; entries, April 1804, Return J. Meigs, "Memorandum Book of Occurrences in the Cherokee . . . Country, 1796–1807," Indian Collection, Manuscript Division, Library of Congress, Washington, D.C.; John Ross, *Letter from John Ross . . . in Answer to Inquiries from a Friend regarding the Cherokee Affairs with the United States* (n.p., 1836), p. 10.

16. Account of Meigs and Ross, November 6 and December 8, 1815, Penelope Johnson Allen Collection; Abstract of Disbursements, October 21, 1813, and Daniel Ross to Meigs, November 10, 1808, Records of the Cherokee Indian Agency in Tennessee.

17. Meigs to General Armstrong, June 4, 1814, Ross to Meigs, April 11, 1817, and Big Half Breede et al. to Meigs, April 29, 1817, Records of the Cherokee Indian Agency in Tennessee.

18. Account of John and Lewis Ross, March 11, 1818, and Meigs to Calhoun, August 10, 1818, ibid.; Govan, "Some Sidelights," pp. 150–51; "Journal of the Mission at Brainerd," *Panoplist (Missionary Herald)*, March 1820, p. 123; Hugh Montgomery to James Barbour, July 15, 1825, Cherokee Agency East Letters Received.

19. McKenney, *History of the Indian Tribes of North America*, 2: 294.

20. Ross to Meigs, September 1, 1812, Records of the Cherokee Indian Agency in Tennessee; William Eustis to Meigs, September 4, 1812, Letters Sent by the Secretary of War, Office of Indian Affairs, National Archives.

21. Ross's invoice, November 30, 1812, and Ross to Meigs, December 15 and 31, 1812, Penelope Johnson Allen Collection; Cherokee Day Book, 1810–1817, Records of the Cherokee Indian Agency in Tennessee.

22. Ross to Meigs, December 31, 1812, and January 3, 1813, and Riley's invoices, December, 1811, Records of Cherokee Indian Agency in Tennessee; McKenney, *History of the Indian Tribes of North America*, 2: 294–95.

23. Ross to Meigs, July 30, 1813, Penelope Johnson Allen Collection; James Mooney, "Myths of the Cherokees," Bureau of American Ethnology, *Nineteenth Annual Report*, 2 parts (Washington, D.C.: Government Printing Office, 1900), part 2, pp. 87–89.

24. Muster rolls and pay rolls of Colonel Morgan's regiment of Cherokee Indians, October 7, 1813, to April 11, 1814, Adjutant General's Office, National Archives; Mooney, "Myths of the Cherokees," part 2, pp. 90–91.

25. Mooney, "Myths of the Cherokees," part 2, pp. 92–96.

26. Ross to Meigs, March 2, 1814, Records of the Cherokee Indian Agency in Tennessee.

27. Mooney, "Myths of the Cherokees," part 2, pp. 92–96; *Niles' Register*, April 30, 1814, pp. 148–49, and April 19, 1817, pp. 121–22; statement of The Whale, February 18, 1843, Cherokee Agency Letters Received, Office of Indian Affairs, National Archives.

28. Statement of The Whale, February 18, 1843, Cherokee Agency Letters Received; Ross's report of killed and wounded in Morgan's regiment, John Ross Papers, Ayer Collection, Newberry Library, Chicago, Ill.; John Rogers to Andrew Jackson, August 7, 1820, and Cyrus Kingsbury to John Calhoun, May 15, 1818, Letters Received by the Secretary of War, Office of Indian Affairs, National Archives. In September 1856 Ross received a grant of 160 acres of federal public lands on a military bounty land warrant for his service in the War of 1812. Ross placed his claim for public sale; it was taken for $132.80 by Lyman B. Holman who located on public lands in Minnesota (Ross's bounty land claim and bounty land warrant, Records of the General Land Office, National Archives).

29. McKenney, *History of the Indian Tribes of North America*, 2: 304; John P. Brown, "Chronological History of Chief John Ross," in *Chief John Ross: His Life with Historic Notes on the State of Georgia, Walker County* (Rossville, Ga.: North Georgia Publishing Company, 1937), p. 11; Penelope

J. Allen, "Leaves from the Family Tree," *Chattanooga Sunday Times*, February 9, 1936; Starr, notes for *History of the Cherokee Indians*; John W. H. Underwood, "Reminiscences of the Cherokees," *Cartersville* (Georgia) *Courant*, March 19, 1885; Diary of S. A. Worcester, 1824–30, Alice Robertson Collection, University of Tulsa Library, Tulsa, Okla.

30. In a petition of Congress in 1836 after his home had been taken from him by the Georgian state military guard, Ross wrote of the "remains of his dear babe" buried on those grounds, U.S., House, "Memorial and Protest of the Cherokee Nation," 24th Cong., 1st sess., *Document 286* (serial 292), p. 6; Starr, notes for the *History of the Cherokee Indians*; Edmund Schwarze, *History of the Moravian Missions among Southern Indian Tribes of the United States* (Bethlehem, Pa.: Times Publishing Company, 1923), p. 293.

31. Last will of John Ross, July 11, 1866, Ross Papers, Gilcrease Institute; *Arkansas Gazette*, February 6, 1839; Obituary of James McDonald Ross, in Grant Foreman, comp., "Copies of Letters . . . and Miscellaneous Documents Relative to the Cherokee and Creek Indians, 1836–1933," typescripts, Oklahoma Historical Society.

CHAPTER 2

1. Meigs to Charles Hicks, December 19, 1815, and Pathkiller to the Cherokee Delegation, January 10, 1816, Ross Papers, Gilcrease Institute; Meigs to William H. Crawford, January 10, 1816, Letters Received by the Secretary of War.

2. Thurman Wilkins, *Cherokee Tragedy: The Story of the Ridge Family and of the Decimation of a People* (New York: Macmillan Co., 1970), p. 88; *Niles' Register*, March 2, 1816, p. 16; Crawford to Meigs, March 2, 1816, and substance of a conversation between Lowrey and Madison, February 22, 1816, Ross Papers, Gilcrease Institute.

3. Meigs to Lowrey et al., February 28, 1816, Division of Manuscripts, Western History Collections, University of Oklahoma, Norman; Lowrey et al. to George Graham, March 4 and 23, 1816, Ross Papers, Gilcrease Institute; Lowrey et al. to Crawford, March 12, 1816, Letters Received by the Secretary of War.

4. Charles C. Royce, "The Cherokee Nation of Indians," Bureau of American Ethnology, *Fifth Annual Report*, 2 parts (Washington, D.C.: Government Printing Office, 1887), part 2, pp. 197–209.

5. Ibid., pp. 209–11; *Niles' Register*, July 20, 1816, p. 352; R. S. Cotterill, *The Southern Indians: The Story of the Civilized Tribes before Removal* (Norman: University of Oklahoma Press, 1954), pp. 200–201.

6. Ross to Meigs, April 11, 1817 [two letters], Records of the Cherokee Indian Agency in Tennessee.

7. *Niles' Register*, June 21, 1817, p. 272, and August 2, 1817, p. 368;

Royce, "The Cherokee Nation of Indians," pp. 212–19. For the official correspondence of the commission see *American State Papers*, Indian Affairs, 2: 140–43.

8. *Laws of the Cherokee Nation Adopted by the Council at Various Periods* (Tahlequah, Cherokee Nation: Cherokee Advocate Office, 1852), pp. 4–5; Resolution of the Cherokee Committee, September 3, 1817, John Howard Payne Papers, Ayer Collection, Newberry Library; Royce, "The Cherokee Nation of Indians," part 2, p. 219.

9. Royce, "The Cherokee Nation of Indians," part 2, p. 218 n.2; George Graham to McMinn, December 2, 1817, McMinn to the king, chiefs, headmen, and warriors of the Cherokee Nation, November 24, 1818, and Cherokee chiefs to McMinn, November 21, 1818, *American State Papers*, Indian Affairs, 2: 478, 486–88; McKenney, *History of the Indian Tribes of North America*, 2: 297; Ross to Calvin Jones, December 8, 1818, Miscellaneous File, Tennessee Historical Society Collection, Tennessee State Library and Archives.

10. Pathkiller to Meigs, December 12, 1818, and Pathkiller's instructions to the delegation, December 14, 1818, Records of the Cherokee Indian Agency in Tennessee; Meigs to Calhoun, December 19, 1818, Letters Received by the Secretary of War; Cotterill, *The Southern Indians*, pp. 205–6, 206 n.40.

11. James Barbour to John Q. Adams, December 29, 1825, and Calhoun to the Cherokee delegation, February 11, 1819, U.S., House, "Message from the President . . . on Cherokee Treaty of 1819," 19th Cong., 1st sess., *Executive Document 21* (serial 133), pp. 5, 7–8; Charles Hicks to Calhoun, February 12, 17, 19, and March 5, 1819, Letters Received by the Secretary of War; Royce, "The Cherokee Nation of Indians," part 2, pp. 225–26.

12. Royce, "The Cherokee Nation of Indians," part 2, pp. 219–28; *American State Papers*, Indian Affairs, 2: 187–88.

13. Survey of Ross's reservation, September 15, 1819, Special File 131, Office of Indian Affairs, National Archives. (For Ross's request for his reservation see Ross to Meigs, June 17, 1819, Cherokee Collection, Georgia Department of Archives and History, Atlanta. For a list of the reserves, see U.S., House, "Reservations under the Cherokee Treaty," 20th Cong., 1st sess., *Executive Document 104* (serial 171), pp. 6–7.) Williams to Calhoun, February 25, 1819, in Robert L. Meriwether, W. Edwin Hemphill, and Clyde N. Wilson, eds., *The Papers of John C. Calhoun*, 10 vols. to date (Columbia, S.C.: University of South Carolina Press, 1959–), 3: 616; Tennessee Land Grants, Hiawassee District, Tennessee State Library and Archives.

14. Miscellaneous Notes, Payne Papers, Newberry Library; Charles Hicks to Meigs, March 11, 1819, Records of the Cherokee Indian Agency in Tennessee; Rachel Caroline Eaton, *John Ross and the Cherokee Indians* (Menasha, Wis.: George Banta, 1914), pp. 32–33.

15. Malone, *Cherokees of the Old South*, p. 100; Ross to Calvin Jones, July 3, 1819, Cherokee Collection, Tennessee State Library and Archives

16. Elias Cornelius, *The Little Osage Captive, an Authentic Narrative: To Which Are Added Some Interesting Letters, Written by Indians* (York, England: W. Alexander and Son, 1821), pp. 64–74; Cephas Washburn, *Reminiscences of the Indians* (Richmond, Va.: Presbyterian Committee of Publication, 1869), pp. 130–31; Meigs to Calhoun, October 10, 1819, Letters Received by the Secretary of War; "Journal of the Arkansas Mission by Alfred Finney and Cephas Washburn," Foreman Collection, Gilcrease Institute; *Panoplist* (*Missionary Herald*), July 1819, pp. 322–23, February, 1820, pp. 82–83, and March 1820, p. 123; Pathkiller to Meigs, September 9, 1819, Records of the Cherokee Indian Agency in Tennessee.

17. McKenney, *History of the Indian Tribes of North America*, 2: 299; Jackson to Calhoun, June 15 and July 9, 1820, in John Spencer Bassett, ed., *Correspondence of Andrew Jackson*, 7 vols. (Washington, D.C.: Carnegie Institute of Washington, 1926–35), 3: 25–26, 29; Hicks to Meigs, September 12, 1820, Records of the Cherokee Indian Agency in Tennessee; Calhoun to Meigs, April 20 [1820?], Payne Papers, Newberry Library.

18. *Laws of the Cherokee Nation Adopted by the Council at Various Periods*, pp. 11–12, 14–15; Cotterill, *The Southern Indians*, p. 212.

19. Resolution of the Cherokee Committee and Council, October 23, 1822, and Meigs to Hicks, December 5, 1822, in Annie Heloise Abel, "The Cherokee Negotiations of 1822–1823," *Smith College Studies in History*, 1, no. 4 (July 1916), pp. 203–4, 206–7; Ross et al. to Calhoun, October 24, 1822, Letters Received by the Secretary of War; McMinn to Calhoun, April 18 and July 4, 1823, Records of the Cherokee Agency in Tennessee.

20. Mooney, "Myths of the Cherokees," part 2, p. 114; Calhoun to the Commissioners, June 15, 1822, *American State Papers*, Indian Affairs, 2: 464–65.

21. Ross et al. to McMinn, April 25, 1823, Meriwether and Campbell to McMinn, June 16, 1823, and McMinn to Meriwether and Campbell, July 7, 1823, in Abel, "The Cherokee Negotiations of 1822–1823," pp. 211–18; Cotterill, *The Southern Indians*, pp. 215–17.

22. Hicks and Ross to McMinn, July 22, 1823, Records of the Cherokee Indian Agency in Tennessee; Ross to McMinn, October 8, 1823, Campbell and Meriwether to the Cherokee Council, October 16 and 21, 1823, and Cherokee Council to Campbell and Meriwether, October 20, 1823, *American State Papers*, Indian Affairs 2: 466–70; Annie Heloise Abel, "The History of Events Resulting in Indian Consolidation West of the Mississippi," *Annual Report of the American Historical Association for the Year 1906*, 2 vols. (Washington, D.C.: Government Printing Office, 1908), 1: 324–25.

23. McIntosh to Ross, October 21, 1823, in Abel, "The Cherokee Negotiations of 1822–1823," p. 220.

24. Ibid.

25. John Quincy Adams, *Memoirs of John Quincy Adams*, ed. Charles Francis Adams, 12 vols. (Philadelphia: J. B. Lippincott and Company, 1874–77), 6; 229; Calhoun to Ross et al., January 5, 1824, Letters Sent by the Secretary of War; Ross et al. to Monroe, January 19, 1824, Calhoun to Ross et al., January 30, 1824, and Ross et al. to Calhoun, February 11, 1824, *American State Papers*, Indian Affairs, 2: 473–74.

26. Calhoun to Ross et al., January 30, 1824, and Ross et al. to Calhoun, February 11, 1824, *American State Papers*, Indian Affairs, 2: 473–74.

27. Adams, *Memoirs of John Quincy Adams*, 6: 255–56, 268, 271–72; message of Monroe to the Senate and House of Representatives, March 30, 1824, in James D. Richardson, comp., *A Compilation of the Messages and Papers of the Presidents, 1789–1902*, 10 vols. (New York: Bureau of National Literature and Art, 1897–1904), 2: 234–37; Ross et al. to the Senate, April 16, 1824, *American State Papers*, Indian Affairs, 2: 502.

28. Ross et al. to Calhoun, February 25, 1824, Cherokee Agency East Letters Received; Calhoun to Ross et al., February 6, 1824, Letters Sent by the Secretary of War. For McMinn's answers see McMinn to Calhoun, June 9, 1824, Cherokee Agency East Letters Received.

29. Ross et al. to Calhoun, February 25, 1824, Ross to McMinn, October 6, 1823, Ross et al. to McKenney, May 7, 1824, McMinn to Calhoun, June 24, 1824, and Montgomery to McKenney, May 10, 1825, Cherokee Agency East Letters Received; Montgomery to McKenney, April 23, 1825, U.S., House, "Intrusions on Cherokee Lands," 21st Cong., 2nd sess., *Executive Document 89* (serial 197) p. 2; Cotterill, *The Southern Indians*, p. 214.

30. Ross et al. to Calhoun, February 13, 1824, and Charles Cutts to Calhoun, April 13, 1824, U.S., House, "Message from the President of the United States," 18th Cong., 2nd sess., *Executive Document 19* (serial 114), pp. 16–17; Calhoun to Ross et al., February 6, 1824, Letters Sent by the Secretary of War; Ross et al. to McKenney, May 17, 1824, Cherokee Agency East Letters Received; Memorial of Ross et al., February 10, 1829, U.S., House, "Memorial of John Ross and Others, in Behalf of the Cherokee Nation," 20th Cong., 2nd sess., *Executive Document 124* (serial 186), pp. 1–2; Cotterill, *The Southern Indians*, pp. 217–19. This was Ross's first encounter with McKenney, the first commissioner of Indian affairs. Despite many differing views they became lifelong friends.

31. Memorial of Ross et al., February 10, 1829, U.S., House, "Memorial of John Ross and Others, in Behalf of the Cherokee Nation," *Executive Document 124* (serial 186), pp. 1–15; Ross et al. to McKenney, May 28 and June 1, 1824, Cherokee Agency East Letters Received; Adams, *Memoirs of John Quincy Adams*, 6: 373.

32. Schwarze, *Moravian Missions*, pp. 174–75; *Laws of the Cherokee Nation Adopted by the Council at Various Periods*, pp. 32–44.

33. McKenney to Ross et al., February 22, 1825, memorial of Ross et al.,

February 10, 1829, and Hugh L. White to Ross, April 26, 1824, U.S., House, "Memorial of John Ross and Others, in Behalf of the Cherokee Nation," *Executive Document 124* (serial 186), pp. 1–2; Ross et al. to McKenney, March 11, 1825, Cherokee Agency East Letters Received.

34. Ross et al. to Calhoun, February 17, 1825, and Ross et al. to McKenney, March 14, 1825, Cherokee Agency East Letters Received.

35. Ross et al. to Adams, March 12, 1825, ibid.; Adams, *Memoirs of John Quincy Adams*, 7: 411.

36. *Laws of the Cherokee Nation Adopted by the Council at Various Periods*, pp. 45–46.

37. Govan and Livingood, *The Chattanooga Country, 1540–1951*, pp. 80–81; Allen, "John Ross' Log Mansion"; Diary of S. A. Worcester, 1824–30, Robertson Collection, University of Tulsa Library; George M. Batty, Jr., *A History of Rome and Floyd County*, 2 vols. (Atlanta, Ga.: Webb and Vary Company, 1922), 1: 26, 36–37.

38. Appraisal of John Ross's possessions, September 21, 1836, Special File 75, Office of Indian Affairs; Anson West, *A History of Methodism in Alabama* (Nashville, Tenn.: Publishing House, Methodist Episcopal Church, South, 1893), pp. 395–96; *Cherokee Phoenix*, October 1, 1830, and January 15, 1831. Ross had also served as postmaster at Rossville from 1817 until 1823 (Registers of Appointments of Postmasters, Records of the Post Office Department, National Archives).

39. Malone, *Cherokees of the Old South*, pp. 56, 94, 127; Miscellaneous Notes, Payne Papers, Newberry Library; McMinn to Calhoun, January 26, 1819, *American State Papers*, Indian Affairs, 2: 482–83; Starkey, *The Cherokee Nation*, p. 51; Schwarze, *Moravian Missions*, pp. 180–81.

40. Adams, *Memoirs of John Quincy Adams*, 7: 136; Montgomery to Hicks et al., September 26, 1826, and Hicks and Ross to Montgomery, December 11, 1826, U.S., House, "Cherokee Council to Col. H. Montgomery," 20th Cong., 2nd sess., *Executive Document 6* (serial 184), pp. 12–13.

41. *Laws of the Cherokee Nation Adopted by the Council at Various Periods*, pp. 73–76, 118–30; *Niles' Register*, June 9, 1827, p. 255; Cotterill, *The Southern Indians*, pp. 235–36.

42. *Laws of the Cherokee Nation Adopted by the Council at Various Periods*, pp. 118–30; Miscellaneous Notes, Payne Papers, Newberry Library.

43. Report of a joint committee of the Georgia legislature, December 19, 1827, and John Forsyth to John Quincy Adams, January 26, 1828, U.S., House, "Cherokee Government," 20th Cong., 1st sess., *Executive Document 211* (serial 173), pp. 7–18; U.S., House, "Indian Governments," 20th Cong., 1st sess., *Report 67* (serial 177), pp. 1–2.

44. McKenney to James Barbour, November 29, 1827, U.S., House, "Report of the Commissioner of Indian Affairs, 1827," 20th Cong., 1st sess., *Executive Document 2*, pp. 194–95; Adams, *Memoirs of John Quincy Adams*, 7: 411, 426; Barbour to Montgomery, February 23, 1818, U.S.,

House, "Cherokee Government," *Executive Document 211* (serial 173), p. 19; William Hicks and Ross to Montgomery, April 16, 1828, in *Cherokee Phoenix*, April 24, 1828.

45. Cotterill, *The Southern Indians*, p. 235.

CHAPTER 3

1. Journal of the Commission, July 3–7, 1827, and Cocke et al. to James Barbour, undated [1827?], U.S., House, "Negotiations for Cherokee Lands," 20th Cong., 1st sess., *Executive Document 106* (serial 171), pp. 8–9, 5.

2. Journal of the Commission, August 15 and 22, September 18–22, 1827, Ross and Ridge to Gray, Cocke, and Davidson, September 15, 1827, and Journal of the Commission, September 24, 1827, ibid., pp. 9, 14–16, 18.

3. Ross and Ridge to Cocke, Gray, and Davidson, September 27, 1827, Cocke, Gray, and Davidson to Ross and Ridge, October 4 and 11, 1827, and Cocke, Davidson, and Gray to committee and council of the Cherokee Nation, undated [1827?], ibid., pp. 19–29; William Hicks and Ross to Francis W. Armstrong, July 19, 1828, in *Cherokee Phoenix*, July 30, 1828; McKenney to P. B. Porter, November 1, 1828, "Report of the Commissioner of Indian Affairs, 1828," U.S., Senate, 20th Cong., 2nd sess., *Document 1*, p. 95.

4. Annual message of Hicks and Ross, October 13, 1828, in *Cherokee Phoenix*, October 22, 1828.

5. McKenney to Montgomery, May 27, 1828, U.S., House, "Articles of Cession between the United States and Georgia, and the Treaty with the [Western] Cherokee Indians," 20th Cong., 2nd sess., *Executive Document 95* (serial 186), pp. 2–4.

6. Malone, *Cherokees of the Old South*, pp. 155–57.

7. Ibid., pp. 157–59; *Laws of the Cherokee Nation Adopted by the Council at Various Periods*, p. 47; Diary of S. A. Worcester, 1824–30, Robertson Collection, University of Tulsa Library; Miscellaneous Notes, Payne Papers, Newberry Library; Althea Bass, *Cherokee Messenger* (Norman: University of Oklahoma Press, 1936), p. 79.

8. Annual message of Hicks and Ross, October 13, 1828, in *Cherokee Phoenix*, October 22, 1828; Miscellaneous Notes, Payne Papers, Newberry Library; *Laws of the Cherokee Nation Adopted by the Council at Various Periods*, p. 144.

9. *Cherokee Phoenix*, October 22, 1828; Miscellaneous Notes, Payne Papers, Newberry Library; Ross to president of the National Committee [Lewis Ross], November 15, 1828, and Lewis Ross to Ross, November 15, 1828, in *Cherokee Phoenix*, November 19, 1828.

10. Ross et al. to P. B. Porter, January 21, 1829, and Coffee to John Eaton, January 21, 1830, Cherokee Agency East Letters Received; Ross et al. to

Andrew Jackson, March 6, April 6, and June 24, 1829, Ross Papers, Gilcrease Institute.

11. Starkey, *The Cherokee Nation*, p. 136; Carl Jackson Vipperman, "Wilson Lumpkin and the Cherokee Removal" (Master's thesis, University of Georgia, 1961), p. 47; E. Merton Coulter, *A Short History of Georgia* (Chapel Hill: University of North Carolina Press, 1933), p. 232; Eaton to Ross et al., April 18, 1829, in [Jeremiah Evarts?], *Essays on the Present Crisis in the Condition of the American Indians: First Published in the National Intelligencer under the Signature of William Penn* (Boston: Perkins and Marvin, 1829), pp. 102–3.

12. U.S., House, "Memorial of John Ross and Others, Representatives of the Cherokee Nation of Indians," *Document 145* (serial 187), pp. 1–3.

13. Royce, "The Cherokee Nation of Indians," part 2, pp. 229–30; McKenney to Eaton, November 17, 1829, and Eaton to Carroll and Coffee, May 30, 1829, U.S., House, "Report of the Commissioner of Indian Affairs, 1829," *Executive Document 2*, pp. 164–66, 178–80.

14. Carroll to Eaton, August 15 and September 2, 1829, and Coffee to Eaton, October 14, 1829, U.S., House, "Report of the Commissioner of Indian Affairs, 1829," *Executive Document 2*, pp. 181–84; Carroll to Ross, August 29, 1829, and Ross to Carroll, August 29, 1829, in *Cherokee Phoenix*, September 10, 1829.

15. Eaton to Forsyth, October 14, 1829, U.S., House, "Report of the Commissioner of Indian Affairs, 1829," *Executive Document 2*, pp. 186–91; Ross to Coffee, December 13, 1829, Ross Papers, Gilcrease Institute; Ross to Coffee, December 29, 1829, Cherokee Agency East Letters Received; Ross to Montgomery, September 3, 1829, and Montgomery to Ross, September 3, 1829, U.S., House, "Intrusions on Cherokee Lands," *Executive Document 89* (serial 197), pp. 16–17; Ross's annual message, October 14, 1829, in *Niles' Register*, November 14, 1829, pp. 189–90.

16. Ross to George Lowrey et al., November 27, 1829, John Ross Papers, Indian Archives Division, Oklahoma Historical Society.

17. Gilmer to Eaton, February 15, 1830, Montgomery to Eaton, February 18, 1830, Ross to Montgomery, February 19, 1830, Lowrey et al. to Jackson, February 25, 1830, Maj. Gen. Alexander Macomb to the commanding officer at Fort Mitchell, February 25, 1830, and James Williams to Montgomery, March 4, 1830, "Intrusions on Cherokee Lands," *Executive Document 89* (serial 197), pp. 29–37.

18. Ross to the Cherokee Delegation, March 3, 1830, ibid., p. 44; Lowrey et al. to Jackson, March 20, 1830, Cherokee Agency East Letters Received; Lowrey et al. to the Senate and House of Representatives, May 3, 1830, U.S., House, "Memorial of a Delegation of the Cherokee Nation of Indians," 21st Cong., 1st sess., *Report 397* (serial 201), pp. 1–4; Coulter, *History of Georgia*, p. 233; Abel, "Indian Consolidation West of the Mississippi," pp. 396–97.

19. McKenney to Montgomery, June 9, 1830, U.S., Senate, "Correspondence on the Subject of the Emigration of Indians," 23rd Cong., 1st sess., *Document 512* (serial 245), 2: 14–15; Randolph to Montgomery, June 18, 1830, U.S., Senate, "Memorial of the Cherokee Delegation," 24th Cong., 1st sess., *Document 340* (serial 283), p. 6; Montgomery to Ross, July 10, 1830, and Ross to Montgomery, July 20, 1830, in *Cherokee Pheonix*, July 24, 1830.

20. Ross to the General Council, July 17, 1830, Lester Hargrett Collection of Imprints, Gilcrease Institute; resolution of the General Council, July 16, 1830, and remonstrance of the Cherokees, July 17, 1830, Ross Papers, Gilcrease Institute.

21. Message of Jackson to the Senate, December 8, 1829, in Richardson, comp., *Messages and Papers of the Presidents*, 2: 456–59; [Evarts?], *Condition of the American Indians*, passim; Joseph C. Burke, "The Cherokee Cases: A Study in Law, Politics, and Morality," *Stanford Law Review*, 21, no. 3 (February 1969), pp. 505–6; Abel, "Indian Consolidation West of the Mississippi," pp. 377–78.

22. Abel, "Indian Consolidation West of the Mississippi," pp. 378–81; Burke, "The Cherokee Cases," pp. 506–7.

23. Ross to David Crockett, January 13, 1831, Ross Papers, Newberry Library.

24. "Cherokees," *Missionary Herald*, December 1830, p. 382; Eaton to Montgomery, July 29, 1830, in *Niles' Register*, November 13, 1830, p. 198; Ross to David Crockett, January 13, 1831, Ross Papers, Newberry Library; Ross to Montgomery, November 25, 1830, and Montgomery to Ross, November 25, 1830, in *Cherokee Phoenix*, December 5, 1830; U.S., House, "Memorial of a Delegation from the Cherokee Indians," 21st Cong., 2nd sess., *Document 57* (serial 208) p. 4; Eaton to Jackson, February 21, 1831, U.S., Senate, "Message from the President of the United States," 21st Cong., 2nd sess., *Document 65* (serial 204), pp. 5–6.

25. Jeremiah Evarts to Ross, July 20, 1830, Ross Papers, Gilcrease Institute; Burke, "The Cherokee Cases," pp. 508–11; George Rockingham Gilmer, *Sketches of Some of the First Settlers of Upper Georgia, of the Cherokee, and the Author* (New York: D. Appleton and Company, 1855), p. 354.

26. Wirt to Ross, June 4, 1830, Ross Papers, Gilcrease Institute; William Wirt, *An Opinion on the Claims for Improvements by the State of Georgia on the Cherokee Nation under the Treaties of 1817 and 1828* (New Echota, Ga.: Office of the *Cherokee Phoenix and Indians' Advocate*, 1830), passim; William Wirt, *Opinion on the Right of the State of Georgia to Extend Her Laws over the Cherokee Nation* (Baltimore: F. Lucas, Jr., 1830), passim; Wirt to Ross, September 22, 1830, and Ross to Wirt, October 30, 1830, Ross Papers, Gilcrease Institute.

27. Ross to Wirt, January 1, 1831, William Wirt Papers, Maryland Historical Society, Baltimore, Maryland; Ross to Gilmer, December 20, 1830, Cherokee Collection, Georgia Archives; Gilmer, *Sketches*, p. 378.

28. Burke, "The Cherokee Cases," pp. 513–18; Abel, "Indian Consolidation West of the Mississippi," pp. 386–87; Ross's annual message, October 24, 1831, in *Cherokee Phoenix*, November 19, 1831.

29. Ross to the General Council, October 30, 1834, Payne Papers, Newberry Library; Hansell to Joel R. Poinsett, March 16, 1837, U.S., Senate, "Report from the Secretary of War . . . in Relation to the Cherokee Treaty of 1835," 25th Cong., 2nd sess., *Document 120* (serial 315), pp. 796–97; Ross to D. Russell, July 13, 1840, Robertson Collection, University of Tulsa Library.

30. Ross to Wirt, May 10 and November 11, 1831, Wirt Papers, Maryland Historical Society; Montgomery to Eaton, May 18, 1831, Cherokee Agency East Letters Received; Henry Clay to John Gunter, June 6, 1831, U.S., Senate, "Report from the Secretary of War . . . in Relation to the Cherokee Treaty of 1835," *Document 120* (serial 315), pp. 678–79.

31. *Cherokee Phoenix*, October 1, 1830; "Cherokees," *Missionary Herald*, March 1831, pp. 79–84; Vipperman, "Wilson Lumpkin and Cherokee Removal," pp. 51–52, 54; Abel, "Indian Consolidation West of the Mississippi," pp. 396–98.

32. Abel, "Indian Consolidation West of the Mississippi," pp. 397–400; "Arrest of the Missionaries of the Board in the Cherokee Nation," *Missionary Herald*, May 1831, pp. 165–66; "Arrest of the Missionaries in the Cherokee Nation," *Missionary Herald*, July 1831, p. 229; *Missionary Herald*, February 1832, p. 46; Burke, "The Cherokee Cases," pp. 519–20; Bass, *Cherokee Messenger*, p. 146; Ross to Wirt, October 7, 1831, Wirt Papers, Maryland Historical Society.

33. Burke, "The Cherokee Cases," pp. 521–31; Edwin A. Miles, "After John Marshall's Decision: *Worcester* v. *Georgia* and the Nullification Crisis," *Journal of Southern History*, 39, no. 4 (November 1973), pp. 527–28; "Trial of Rev. Samuel A. Worcester, and Doct. Elizur Butler," *Missionary Herald*, November 1831, pp. 363–65; "Release of Messrs. Worcester and Butler," *Missionary Herald*, December 1832, pp. 460–61; B. B. Wisner to Ross, December 27, 1832, Ross Papers, Oklahoma Historical Society; McLean to Ross, May 23, 1832, Ross Papers, Gilcrease Institute; Ross to Wirt, June 8, 1832, Wirt Papers, Maryland Historical Society.

34. Gilmer to Montgomery, May 31, 1831, and Gilmer to Sanford, June 15, 1831, in Gilmer, *Sketches*, pp. 400–402; Sanford to Gilmer, August 10, 1831, Cherokees, Eastern Band, Gilcrease Institute; Worcester to William Shorey Coodey, March 15, 1830, in *Missionary Herald*, May 1830, p. 155.

35. Miscellaneous Notes, Payne Papers, Newberry Library; Ross's annual message, October 24, 1831, in *Cherokee Phoenix*, November 19, 1831; Ross

to Martin, Ridge, and Coodey, December 1, 1831, Payne Papers, Newberry Library.

36. *Cherokee Phoenix*, January 21, 1832. This is Ross's account.

37. Miscellaneous Notes, Payne Papers, Newberry Library; John Ridge to Ross, January 12 and April 3, 1832, Ross Papers, Gilcrease Institute; Starkey, *The Cherokee Nation*, pp. 168–69; proclamation of Ross, July 3, 1832, in *Cherokee Phoenix*, July 14, 1832.

38. Cass to the Cherokees, April 17, 1832, U.S., Senate, "Correspondence on the Subject of the Emigration of Indians," *Document 512* (serial 245), 2: 816–17; Chester to Cass, June 9, 1832, ibid. (serial 246), 3: 372–73; Ross to Wirt, June 8, 1832, Wirt Papers, Maryland Historical Society; Starkey, *The Cherokee Nation*, pp. 143, 181.

39. Ross to Wirt, November 11, 1831, Wirt Papers, Maryland Historical Society; Chester to Ross, July 20, 31 [two letters], and August 3, 1832, Ross to Chester, July 31 and August 3 [two letters], 1832, Cherokee General Council to Cass, August 6, 1832, and Chester to Cass, August 11, 1832, U.S., Senate, "Correspondence on the Subject of the Emigration of Indians," *Document 512* (serial 246), 3: 421–27, 418–19.

40. Chester to Ross, October 16 and 30, 1832, Ross to Chester, October 30, 1832 [two letters], Chester to Cass, October 27, 1832, Ross to Montgomery, October 30, 1832, and Montgomery to Cass, October 31, 1832, U.S., Senate, "Correspondence on the Subject of the Emigration of Indians," *Document 512* (serial 246), 3: 520–22, 510–11, 513–14; Ross's annual message, October 10, 1832, in *Cherokee Phoenix*, October 27, 1832.

41. Ross to Cass, January 8, 1833, U.S., Senate, "Correspondence on the Subject of the Emigration of Indians," *Document 512* (serial 247), 4: 13; Ross et al. to Cass, January 28, February 14, and March 8, 1833, Cass to Ross et al., February 2 and 20, 1833, and Elbert Herring to Ross et al., February 14 and March 14, 1833, U.S., Senate, "Memorial of John Ross, and Others," 23rd Cong., 1st sess., *Document 386* (serial 242), pp. 7–17; Andrew J. Donelson to Ross, March 1, 1833, in *Cherokee Phoenix*, August 17, 1833.

42. John Walker, Jr., to Montgomery, November 12, 1832, Cherokee Agency East Letters Received; Ross et al. to Cass, February 26, 1833, U.S., Senate, "Correspondence on the Subject of the Emigration of Indians," *Document 512* (serial 247), 4: 119; Ross to Thomas Foreman et al., April 18, 1832, U.S., Senate, "Correspondence on the Subject of the Emigration of Indians," *Document 512* (serial 246), 3: 314–16.

43. U.S., Senate, "Documents in Relation to the Validity of the Cherokee Treaty of 1835," 25th Cong., 2nd sess., *Document 121* (serial 315), pp. 3–11.

44. John Ridge to Ross, February 2, 1833, Ross Papers, Gilcrease Institute.

45. Ross to the General Council, May 13, 1833, in *Niles' Register*, October 19, 1833, p. 121; Benjamin Currey to Elbert Herring, May 3 and 23, 1833, Cherokee Agency East Letters Received; Herring to Ross et al., March 14, 1833, and John Robb to Ross, June 20, 1833, U.S., Senate, "Memorial of

John Ross, and Others," *Document 386* (serial 242), pp. 17, 19; John Ridge et al. to Cass, April 5, 1833, U.S., Senate, "Correspondence on the Subject of the Emigration of Indians," *Document 512* (serial 247), 4: 169–70; Herring to Ridge et al., May 1, 1833, in *Niles' Register*, June 1, 1833, p. 231.

46. Ross to "My Friends," August 9, 1833, Cherokee Collection, Georgia Archives.

47. Ross's annual message, October 15, 1833, in *Cherokee Phoenix*, November 23, 1833; Act of the General Council, October 31, 1833, General Council to Montgomery, October 31, 1833, and Montgomery to Ross, December 21, 1833, U.S., Senate, "Memorial of John Ross, and Others," *Document 386* (serial 242), pp. 20–22.

CHAPTER 4

1. Miscellaneous Notes, Payne Papers, Newberry Library; Ross et al. to Cass, February 6, 1834, U.S., Senate, "Memorial of John Ross, and Others," *Document 386* (serial 242), pp. 22–23; Currey to Herring, May 23, 1833, U.S., Senate, "Correspondence on the Subject of the Emigration of Indians," *Document 512* (serial 247), 4: 411–15; Grant Foreman, *Indian Removal: The Emigration of the Five Civilized Tribes of Indians* (Norman: University of Oklahoma Press, 1932), pp. 235–36.

2. Cass to Ross et al., February 13, 1834, Ross et al. to Jackson, March 12, 1834, and Cass to Ross et al., March 13, 1834, U.S., Senate, "Memorial of John Ross, and Others, *Document 386* (serial 242), pp. 23–26.

3. Ross et al. to Jackson, March 28, 1834, Ross et al. to Cass, April 29, 1834, Herring to Ross et al., May 1, 1834, and Ross et al. to the Senate and House of Representatives, May 17, 1834, ibid., pp. 1–3, 26–28, 30–31.

4. Ross et al. to the Seneca Delegation, April 14, 1834, Ross Papers, Gilcrease Institute.

5. Ross et al. to Cass, May 14, 1834, and Lewis Ross to Ross et al., April 28, 1834, U.S., Senate, "Memorial of John Ross and Others," 23rd Cong., 2nd sess., *Document 71* (serial 268), pp. 3–4; Wilkins, *Cherokee Tragedy*, pp. 251–53.

6. Protest of the Cherokee, 1834, Cass to Ross et al., June 12, 1834, Andrew Ross et al. to Herring, June 2, 1834, Ross et al. to Cass, June 16, 1834, Eaton to Ross, May 26, 1834, and Ross to Eaton, May 29, 1834, U.S., Senate, "Memorial of John Ross and Others," *Document 71* (serial 268), pp. 4–8.

7. Andrew Ross et al. to the Senate, June 25, 1834, U.S., Senate, "Memorial of a Delegation from the Cherokees," 23rd Cong., 1st sess., *Document 486* (serial 243), pp. 1–2; Articles of Agreement between Eaton and the Cherokee Delegation [Andrew Ross et al.], June 19, 1834, U.S., House, "Memorial and Protest of the Cherokee Nation," *Document 286* (serial 292), pp. 133–40.

8. Ross to Underwood, August 12, 1834, and Edward Harden to Ross et al., April 7, 1834, Ross Papers, Gilcrease Institute; Coulter, *History of Georgia*, p. 235; Vipperman, "Wilson Lumpkin and the Cherokee Removal," pp. 74–75, 80–81, 88–89, 91–92, 96; Lumpkin to James M. Wayne, February 1, 1834, in Wilson Lumpkin, *The Removal of the Cherokee Indians from Georgia . . . 1827–1841*, 2 vols. (New York: Dodd, Mead and Company, 1907), 1: 238–39; *Charges against the Hon. John W. Hooper, Judge of the Superior Courts of the Cherokee Circuit* (Milledgeville, Ga.: Office of the *Federal Union*, 1835), p. 69, passim.

9. Currey to Cass, September 15, 1834, Cherokee Agency East Letters Received.

10. Ibid.; Currey to Herring, August 25, 1834, and Andrew Ross to Currey, August 17, 1834, ibid.; Jackson to Currey and Montgomery, September 3, 1834, and Ross to Jackson, September 15, 1834, in Jackson, *Correspondence of Andrew Jackson*, 5: 288, 292–93. Tom Foreman and his half-brother, A. Springton, were later arrested for the murder of Walker but, since the Tennessee courts did not have jurisdiction over Indians, they soon were released (Currey to Jackson, November 10, 1834, Cherokee Agency East Letters Received).

11. Ross to John Ridge, September 12, 1834, Ross Papers, Gilcrease Institute.

12. Currey to Herring, October 2, 1834, Cherokee Agency East Letters Received; Ross to William H. Underwood, October 9, 1834, Ross Papers, Gilcrease Institute; Miscellaneous Notes, Payne Papers, Newberry Library.

13. Ross's annual message, October 13, 1834, Payne Papers, Newberry Library.

14. Ross et al. to Currey, October 23, 1834, Currey to Ross et al., October 24, 1834, and Resolutions of the Cherokees, November 3, 1834, U.S., Senate, "Memorial of John Ross and Others," *Document 71* (serial 268), pp. 2–3, 14–17; Ross to the General Council, October 28, 1834, Payne Papers, Newberry Library.

15. Currey to Jackson, November 10, 1834, and John Ridge to Currey, November, 1834, Cherokee Agency East Letters Received; Edward Harden to Ross et al., December 17, 1834, Ross Papers, Gilcrease Institute.

16. Ross et al. to Cass, January 14, 1835, U.S., Senate, "Memorial of John Ross and Others," *Document 71* (serial 268), pp. 17–18; Ross et al. to Jackson, January 23, 1835, in Jackson, *Correspondence of Andrew Jackson*, 5: 319–20.

17. Ross et al. to Cass, February 14, 1835, and Cass to Ross et al., February 16, 1835, U.S., House, "Memorial and Protest of the Cherokee Nation," *Document 286* (serial 292), pp. 129–33.

18. Ross et. al. to Cass, February 25, 1835, ibid., pp. 126–29.

19. Cass to Ross et al., February 27, 1835, and "Memorandum B, for Mr.

Ross and his party," February 28, 1835, U.S., Senate, "Report from the Secretary of War . . . in Relation to the Cherokee Treaty of 1835," *Document 120* (serial 315), pp. 96–97; Miscellaneous Notes, Payne Papers, Newberry Library; Ross et al. to Cass, February 27 and 28, 1835, and Memorial of the Cherokee Delegation, March 3, 1835, U.S., House, "Memorial and Protest of the Cherokee Nation," *Document 286* (serial 292), pp. 129, 141, 124–25.

20. Memorial of the Cherokee Delegation, March 3, 1835, Ross to Theodore Frelinghuysen, March 3, 1835, Cass to Ross et al., March 6 and 7, 1835, and Ross et al. to Cass, March 6 and 9, 1835, U.S., House, "Memorial and Protest of the Cherokee Nation, *Document 286* (serial 292), pp. 124–26, 142–46.

21. Ross to Roenne, March 5, 1835, Ross Papers, Oklahoma Historical Society; Roenne to Lanzas, March 6, 1835, and Ross to Lanzas, March 22, 1835, Ross Papers, Gilcrease Institute.

22. Bishop to Ross, March 17, 1835, John Drew Papers, Gilcrease Institute; James F. Smith, *The Cherokee Land Lottery* (New York: Harper and Brothers, 1838), p. 40; John Morgan Wooten, *A History of Bradley County* (Nashville, Tenn.: Tennessee Historical Commission, 1949), p. 71; Ross et al. to the Senate and House of Representatives, June 21, 1836, U.S., House, "Memorial and Protest of the Cherokee Nation," *Document 286* (serial 292), pp. 5–6. Ross's lot, number 244, district 23, section 3, was drawn by Stephen Carter of Fayette County; it is now the site of Rome, Georgia (Official Records of the Georgia Surveyor General Department, Office of the Secretary of State, Atlanta, Ga.).

23. Lumpkin to Boudinot, August 6, 1835, in Lumpkin, *Removal of the Cherokee Indians*, 1: 362–63; Currey to Herring, January 15, 1835, and Currey to Lewis Ross, April 14, 1835, Cherokee Agency East Letters Received; Vipperman, "Wilson Lumpkin and the Cherokee Removal," p. 103; Wilkins, *Cherokee Tragedy*, p. 241.

24. Currey's notice, April 16, 1835, and Ross to Currey, April 26, 1835, U.S., House, "Memorial and Protest of the Cherokee Nation," *Document 286* (serial 292), pp. 44–45; Currey to Herring, May 6, 1835, U.S., Senate, "Report from the Secretary of War . . . in Relation to the Cherokee Treaty of 1835," *Document 120* (serial 315), p. 368.

25. Cherokee Resolution, May 12, 1835, U.S., Senate, "Memorial of the Cherokee Delegation," *Document 340* (serial 283), p. 6; Ross to the General Council, May 18, 1835, Payne Papers, Newberry Library; Currey to Herring, May 23, 1835, and Underwood and Ridge to Cass, May 13, 1835, U.S., Senate, "Report from the Secretary of War . . . in Relation to the Cherokee Treaty of 1835," *Document 120* (serial 315), pp. 368–71.

26. Ross to Schermerhorn and Currey, July 7, 1835, Schermerhorn to Ross, July 7 and 9, 1835, and Currey to Ross, July 9, 1835, U.S., House, "Memorial and Protest of the Cherokee Nation," *Document 286* (serial

292), pp. 46–48; R. J. Meigs, the younger, "Journal Kept While Serving as Secretary of John F. Schermerhorn," typescript, Southern Historical Collections, University of North Carolina, Chapel Hill.

27. Meigs, the younger, "Journal," University of North Carolina; Miscellaneous Notes, Payne Papers, Newberry Library; Schermerhorn to Herring, August 3, 1835, and Currey to Herring, July 27 and 30, 1835, U.S., Senate, "Report from the Secretary of War . . . in Relation to the Cherokee Treaty of 1835," Document 120, pp. 450–51, 390–91, 395–97.

28. Meigs, the younger, "Journal," University of North Carolina; Miscellaneous Notes, Payne Papers, Newberry Library, Schermerhorn to Herring, August 3, 1835, and Currey to Herring, July 27 and 30 [with enclosure], 1835, U.S., Senate, "Report from the Secretary of War . . . in Relation to the Cherokee Treaty of 1835," Document 120 (serial 315), pp. 451–61, 391–92, 397–98, 448.

29. Schermerhorn to Herring, August 3, 1835, U.S., Senate, "Report from the Secretary of War . . . in Relation to the Cherokee Treaty of 1835," Document 120 (serial 315), p. 461; Ross to Schermerhorn, July 24, 1835, U.S., House, "Memorial and Protest of the Cherokee Nation," Document 286 (serial 292), p. 55.

30. Ross to Major Ridge and John Ridge, July 30, 1835, and Major Ridge and John Ridge to Ross, July 31, 1835, U.S., House, "Memorial and Protest of the Cherokee Nation," Document 286 (serial 292), pp. 60–61; Miscellaneous Notes, Payne Papers, Newberry Library.

31. Ross to Schermerhorn and Currey, August 22, 1835, Currey to Ross, September 9 and October 27, 1835, and Ross to Currey, October 27 and 28, 1835, U.S., House, "Memorial and Protest of the Cherokee Nation," Document 286 (serial 292), pp. 61–63, 82–83; Ross et al. to Cass, April 22, 1836, Cherokee Agency East Letters Received.

32. Payne to [?], October 11, 1835, U.S., Senate, "Report from the Secretary of War . . . in Relation to the Cherokee Treaty of 1835," Document 120 (serial 315) p. 574.

33. Ibid., p. 578.

34. Ross's annual message, October 12, 1835, U.S., House, "Removal of the Cherokees West of the Mississippi," 27th Cong., 2nd sess., Report 1098 (serial 411), pp. 41–43.

35. Carroll to Schermerhorn, October 13, 1835, Schermerhorn to the Cherokee Nation, October 17, 1835, and Ross to the General Council, October 22, 1835, U.S., House, "Memorial and Protest of the Cherokee Nation," Document 286 (serial 292), pp. 89, 65–79.

36. James William Van Hoeven, "Salvation and Indian Removal: The Career Biography of John Freeman Schermerhorn, Indian Commissioner" (Ph.D. diss., Vanderbilt University, 1972), pp. 205–6.

37. Ross to Major Ridge and John Ridge, October 19, 1835, Major Ridge and John Ridge to Ross, October 19, 1835, and agreement of the two parties,

October 24, 1835, U.S., House, "Memorial and Protest of the Cherokee Nation," *Document 286* (serial 292), pp. 81–82.

38. Ross et al. to Schermerhorn, October 27 and 28, 1835, Schermerhorn to Ross et al., October 27 and 30, 1835, and Schermerhorn's proposed treaty, October 28, 1835, ibid., pp. 87–88, 93–99, 90–91.

39. John Howard Payne, "The Captivity of John Howard Payne," *North American Quarterly Magazine*, 7, no. 33 (January 1836), pp. 107–24; claim of John Ross [undated], Ross Papers, Oklahoma Historical Society. Ross claimed an indemnity of $100,000 for this indignity, but it is unlikely that he ever received it (ibid.).

40. Ross to Gilmer, November 13, 1835, and Payne to Ross, [November 20, 1835?], Ross Papers, Gilcrease Institute; Payne to Ross, January 4 and 15, 1836, and Ross to Payne, January 7, 1836, John Howard Payne Papers, Gilcrease Institute.

41. Boudinot to [?], May 16, 1836, U.S., Senate, "Documents in Relation to the Validity of the Cherokee Treaty of 1835," *Document 121* (serial 315), pp. 15–17; Ross to the General Council, October 24, 1835, resolution of the General Council, October 24, 1835, Boudinot to Ross, November 25, 1835, John Ridge to Ross, December 1835, and Ross to John Ridge, December 4, 1835, U.S., House, "Memorial and Protest of the Cherokee Nation," *Document 286* (serial 292), pp. 83–84, 101–2; John Howard Payne, *John Howard Payne to His Countrymen*, ed. Clemens de Baillou (Athens: University of Georgia Press, 1961), pp. 49–61.

42. Currey to Ross et al., November 30, 1835, and Ross et al to Currey, December 2, 1835, U.S., House, "Memorial and Protest of the Cherokee Nation," *Document 286* (serial 292), p. 103; Cass to Schermerhorn, September 26, 1835, U.S., Senate, "Report from the Secretary of War . . . in Relation to the Cherokee Treaty of 1835," *Document 120* (serial 315), p. 124.

CHAPTER 5

1. Notice of Carroll and Schermerhorn, November 3, 1835, U.S., Senate, "Report from the Secretary of War . . . in Relation to the Cherokee Treaty of 1835," *Document 120* (serial 315), p. 518; Royce, "Cherokee Nation of Indians," part 2, p. 281.

2. Schermerhorn to Herring, December 19 and 31, 1835, U.S., Senate, "Report from the Secretary of War . . . in Relation to the Cherokee Treaty of 1835," *Document 120* (serial 315), pp. 494–97; James J. Trott to Cherokee Delegation, January 6, 1836, and minutes and resolutions of the New Echota Council, December 22, 1836, U.S., House, "Memorial and Protest of the Cherokee Nation," *Document 286* (serial 292), pp. 120–21, 112–14.

3. Fries and Rights, eds., *Records of the Moravians in North Carolina*, 8:

4177; Ross to John Howard Payne, January 7, 1836, Payne Papers, Gilcrease Institute; Ross et al. to Cass, January 2, 1836, and Ross et al. to the Senate, March 8, 1836, U.S., House, "Memorial and Protest of the Cherokee Nation," *Document 286* (serial 292), pp. 27, 104–5.

4. Ross et al. to Cass, January 14, 1836, Major Ridge et al. to Ross et al., February 6, 1836, and Ross et al. to the Senate, March 8, 1836, U.S., House, "Memorial and Protest of the Cherokee Nation," *Document 286* (serial 292), pp. 28–29, 106–7, 111–12.

5. Ross et al. to Cass, February 9, 1836, and Herring to Ross et al., February 13, 1836, ibid., pp. 107–10; Ridge and Watie to Schermerhorn, February 26, 1836, U.S., Senate, "Report from the Secretary of War . . . in Relation to the Cherokee Treaty of 1835," *Document 120* (serial 315), pp. 528–31; Ross, *Letter in Answer to Inquiries from a Friend*, p. 13.

6. Currey to Herring, January 27 and February 5, 1836, Cherokee Agency Letters Received; Cherokee resolution and protest, February 3, 1836, U.S., House, "Memorial and Protest of the Cherokee Nation," *Document 286* (serial 292), pp. 114–15. The figure 14,000 is based on the count of the secretary of the Senate; the Cherokees estimated 12,000 signatures (ibid.). Ross et al. to Cass [with accompanying documents], February 29, 1836, ibid., pp. 115–20; Schermerhorn to Herring, December 31, 1835, U.S., Senate, "Report from the Secretary of War . . . in Relation to the Cherokee Treaty of 1835," *Document 120* (serial 315), pp. 496–97.

7. Royce, "Cherokee Nation of Indians," part 2, pp. 253–58.

8. "Memo of Documents for reference," undated, and "Objections to the instrument negotiated by John F. Schermerhorn," undated, Ross Papers, Gilcrease Institute; Ross et al. to the Senate, March 8, 1836, U.S., House, "Memorial and Protest of the Cherokee Nation," *Document 286* (serial 292), p. 31, passim.

9. Davis to Cass, March 5, 1836, U.S., House, "Memorial and Protest of the Cherokee Nation," *Document 286* (serial 292), pp. 148–54.

10. George Lowrey to Ross, February 11, 1836, ibid., pp. 118–19.

11. Ross et al. to Cass, February 24, March 5 and 24, and April 18, 1836, and Herring to Ross et al., March 9, 1836, U.S., Senate, "Memorial of the Cherokee Delegation," *Document 340* (serial 283), pp. 7–12; "Estimate of expenses . . . [for treaty delegation]," undated [1836?], Cherokee Agency Letters Received.

12. Ross et al. to the Senate and House of Representatives, April 28, 1836, U.S., Senate, "Memorial of the Cherokee Delegation," *Document 340* (serial 283), pp. 1–5; Herring to Cass, May 9, 1836, U.S., Senate, untitled, 24th Cong., 1st sess., *Document 371* (serial 283), pp. 2–3; report of J. A. Slade and J. T. Bender, U.S., House, "Moneys Due the Cherokee Nation," 53rd Cong., 3rd sess., *Executive Document 182* (serial 3323), pp. 2–3.

13. Robert A. Rutland, "Political Background of the Cherokee Treaty of

New Echota," *Chronicles of Oklahoma*, 27, no. 4 (Winter 1949–50), pp. 405–6; Thomas Hart Benton, *Thirty Years' View*, 2 vols. (New York: D. Appleton and Company, 1893), 1: 624–26.

14. Coodey to Currey, July 8, 1836, Ross Papers, Gilcrease Institute; Ross to Lowrey, May 26, 1836, U.S., Senate, "Report from the Secretary of War . . . in Relation to the Cherokee Treaty of 1835," *Document 120* (serial 315), pp. 679–80.

15. Ross, *Letter in Answer to Inquiries from a Friend*, pp. 4–6; Wilkins, *Cherokee Tragedy*, p. 284.

16. Ross, *Letter in Answer to Inquiries from a Friend*, pp. 10–11; Ross to Meigs, June 17, 1819, Cherokee Collection, Georgia Archives; Miscellaneous Notes, Payne Papers, Newberry Library; statement of John Watts, March 9, 1838, Ross Papers, Gilcrease Institute; Boudinot to Ross, November 25, 1836, U.S., Senate, "Documents in Relation to the Validity of the Cherokee Treaty of 1835," *Document 121* (serial 315), pp. 32–33.

17. Fries and Rights, eds., *Records of the Moravians in North Carolina*, 8: 4218; [Ross?] to Wool, September 2, 1836, and Major Ridge et al. to Ross, August 17, 1836, Ross Papers, Gilcrease Institute; Wilkins, *Cherokee Tragedy*, p. 285; Wool to Cass, September 10, 1836, U.S., Senate, "Report from the Secretary of War . . . in Relation to the Cherokee Treaty of 1835," *Document 120* (serial 315), pp. 29–30.

18. Wool to Butler, November 6, 1836, U.S., House, "Message on the Case of General Wool," 25th Cong., 1st sess., *Executive Document 46* (serial 311), p. 62 and passim; Wool to General R. Jones, September 12, 1836, U.S., Senate, "Report from the Secretary of War . . . in Relation to the Cherokee Treaty of 1835," *Document 120* (serial 315), p. 31; Currey to C. A. Harris, September 30, 1836, Cherokee Emigration Letters Received, Office of Indian Affairs, National Archives; Ross et al. to Wool, September 30, 1836, U.S., House, "Message on the Case of General Wool," *Executive Document 46* (serial 311), pp. 74–75.

19. Resolution of the Cherokee Council, September 28, 1836, U.S., Senate, "Report from the Secretary of War . . . in Relation to the Cherokee Treaty of 1835," *Document 120* (serial 315), pp. 797–99; Wool's General Order Number 74, Payne Papers, Newberry Library.

20. C. A. Harris to Currey, July 25, 1836, U.S., Senate, "Report from the Secretary of War," 25th Cong., 3rd sess., *Document 277* (serial 342), pp. 88–90; Vipperman, "Wilson Lumpkin and the Cherokee Removal," pp. 118–22; Harris to B. F. Butler, December 1, 1836, U.S., House, "Report of the Commissioner of Indian Affairs, 1836," 24th Cong., 2nd sess., *Executive Document 2*, pp. 384–86; entry of Heinrich Gottlieb and Elisabeth Clauder, August 29, 1836, in Adelaide Fries, trans., extracts from "The Diary of the Moravian Missions among the Cherokee Indians, 1833–1838," typescript, Oklahoma Historical Society, p. 26; Ross to Crawford, July 10, 1840, Cher-

okee Agency Letters Received; Boudinot to Ross, November 25, 1836, U.S., Senate, "Documents in Relation to the Validity of the Cherokee Treaty of 1835," *Document 121* (serial 315), pp. 40–41; valuations of Ross's properties, September 21, 1836, Special File 75, Office of Indian Affairs, National Archives; various Cherokee valuations, undated, U.S., Senate, "Report from the Secretary of War," *Document 277* (serial 342), passim. This latter document shows Ross's claims as $17,965.75; the difference of $5,700 probably derives from the dispute over Ross's ferry. The larger amount was the final settlement.

21. Harris to Armstrong, October 12, 1836, and Armstrong to Harris, February 3, 1837, U.S., Senate, "Report from the Secretary of War . . . in Relation to the Cherokee Treaty of 1835," *Document 120* (serial 315), pp. 184, 774–75; Armstrong to Harris, November 17, 1836, Foreman Collection, Gilcrease Institute; John Ross, *Letter from John Ross, the Principal Chief of the Cherokee Nation, to a Gentleman of Philadelphia* (n. p., 1837), pp. 14–15; Ross's annual message, August 3, 1837, Division of Manuscripts, Western History Collections, University of Oklahoma; resolutions of the Western Cherokees, December 8, 1836, U.S., House, "Memorial of a Delegation of the Cherokee Nation," 25th Cong., 2nd sess., *Document 99* (serial 325), pp. 14–15.

22. "Extract from Governor Stokes's letter," undated [1837?], U.S., Senate, "Report from the Secretary of War . . . in Relation to the Cherokee Treaty of 1835," *Document 120* (serial 315), pp. 775; Lewis Ross to Ross, January 13, 1837, Ross Papers, Gilcrease Institute; Elizur Butler to John Howard Payne, January 25, 1837, Payne Papers, Newberry Library; Ross to Joel R. Poinsett, May 4, 1837, U.S., House, "Memorial of a Delegation of the Cherokee Nation," *Document 99* (serial 325), pp. 24–25.

23. Ross's annual message, August 3, 1837, Division of Manuscripts, Western History Collections, University of Oklahoma; H. G. Clauder to John Howard Payne, February 8, 1837, Payne Papers, Newberry Library; Fries and Rights, eds., *Records of the Moravians in North Carolina*, 8: 4263; Ross et al. to B. F. Butler, February 13, 1837, and Butler to Ross et al., February 24, 1837, in Ross, *Letter to a Gentleman of Philadelphia*, pp. 27, 31; Ross et al. to Butler, February 22 and 28, 1837, and Butler to Ross et al., March 11, 1837, U.S., Senate, "Report from the Secretary of War . . . in Relation to the Cherokee Treaty of 1835," *Document 120* (serial 315), pp. 249–50, 785–87.

24. Ross et al. to Poinsett, March 16, 1837, Ross et al. to the president, March 16, 1837, and Poinsett to Ross et al., March 24, 1837, U.S., House, "Memorial of a Delegation of the Cherokee Nation," *Document 99* (serial 325), pp. 17–24; Ross's annual message, August 3, 1837, Division of Manuscripts, Western History Collections, University of Oklahoma; Ross to Poinsett, March 25, 1837, Cherokee Agency Letters Received; Harris to

Poinsett, March 29, 1837, U.S., Senate, "Report from the Secretary of War . . . in Relation to the Cherokee Treaty of 1835," *Document 120* (serial 315), pp. 254–55.

25. J. R. Tyson to Ross, December 12, 1837, and Ross to Tyson, January 19, 1838, Ross Papers, Gilcrease Institute; Ross to Claudia Arguelles, April 15, 1837, Ross Papers, Oklahoma Historical Society; Ross, *Letter to a Gentleman of Philadelphia*, pp. 18–20; Thomas L. McKenney, *Memoirs, Official and Personal* (New York: Paine and Burgess, 1846), pp. 267–68; testimony of John H. Payne, August 6, 1842, U.S., House, "Removal of the Cherokees West of the Mississippi," *Report 1098* (serial 411), p. 39; Ross to Poinsett, May 4, 1837, and Poinsett to Ross, May 6, 1837, U.S., House, "Memorial of a Delegation of the Cherokee Nation," *Document 99* (serial 325), pp. 24–27.

26. Nathaniel Smith to Harris, April 20 and 24, May 10, and June 24, 1837, Special File 31, Office of Indian Affairs.

27. Lumpkin and John Kennedy to Harris, June 5, 1837, in Lumpkin, *Removal of the Cherokee Indians*, 2: 111–13; Smith to Harris, June 24 and July 1, 1837, Special File 31, Office of Indian Affairs; Wool's General Order Number 74, Payne Papers, Newberry Library; Royce, "Cherokee Nation of Indians," part 2, p. 289.

28. Lindsay to Poinsett, June 26, 1837, Cherokee Agency Letters Received; Ross to Poinsett, June 22, 1837, Lindsay to Ross, July 24 and 25, 1837, and Ross to Lindsay, July 25 and 26, 1837, U.S., House, "Memorial of a Delegation of the Cherokee Nation," *Document 99* (serial 325), pp. 26–29; Poinsett to Lindsay, July 12, 1837, and Harris to Smith, July 12, 1837, Letters Sent, Office of Indian Affairs.

29. Ross's annual message, August 3, 1837, Division of Manuscripts, Western History Collections, University of Oklahoma; Lindsay to Ross, August 4, 1837, U.S., House, "Memorial of a Delegation of the Cherokee Nation," *Document 99* (serial 325), pp. 30–31; Poinsett to Mason, July 15, 1837 [two letters], U.S., Senate, "Report from the Secretary of War . . . in Relation to the Cherokee Treaty of 1835," *Document 120* (serial 315), pp. 289–93.

30. G. W. Featherstonhaugh, *A Canoe Voyage up the Minnay Sotor with an Account of . . . the Cherokee Country*, 2 vols. (London: Richard Bentley, 1847), 2: 228–32, 240–41.

31. Ibid., pp. 236–38.

32. Ibid., pp. 242–43; Mason's address, August 7, 1837, and Mason to Poinsett, September 25, 1837, U.S., House, "Cherokee Indians," 25th Cong., 2nd sess., *Document 82* (serial 325), pp. 2–7.

33. Resolution of the General Council, August 8, 1837, U.S., House, "Memorial of a Delegation of the Cherokee Nation," *Document 99* (serial 325), pp. 15–17; resolution of the General Council, August 12, 1837, Ross

Papers, Gilcrease Institute; Ross to John Looney et al., August 15, 1837, Cherokee Collection, Tennessee State Library and Archives.

CHAPTER 6

1. Ross et al. to Poinsett, October 7, 1837, and Poinsett to Ross et al., October 7, 1837, U.S., House, "Memorial of a Delegation of the Cherokee Nation," *Document 99* (serial 325), p. 39; Ross to Lewis Ross, October 12, 1837, Ross Papers, Gilcrease Institute. Besides Ross, the delegation included Edward Gunter, Richard Taylor, James Brown, Samuel Gunter, Elijah Hicks, Sitawakee, and White Path.

2. Sherburne to Ross, July 8 and August 10, 1837, Ross Papers, Gilcrease Institute; Ross to Sherburne, September 18, 1837, Ross Papers, Oklahoma Historical Society.

3. Ross to Hair Conrad et al., October 20, 1837, and Ross to the chiefs, headmen, and warriors of the Seminoles, October 18, 1837, U.S., House, "Seminole and Cherokee Indians," 25th Cong., 2nd sess., *Document 285* (serial 328), pp. 4–9.

4. Grant Foreman, ed., "Report of the Cherokee Deputation into Florida," *Chronicles of Oklahoma*, 9, no. 4 (December 1931), pp. 428, 431, passim; Edwin C. McReynolds, *The Seminoles* (Norman: University of Oklahoma Press, 1957), pp. 197–200; Ross to Poinsett, March 5 and 8, 1838, U.S., House, "Seminoles and Cherokee Indians," *Document 285* (serial 328), pp. 14–19.

5. Ross to Poinsett, January 2, 1838, and Poinsett to Ross, March 2, 7, and 17, 1838, U.S., House, "Seminole and Cherokee Indians," *Document 285* (serial 328), pp. 11–15, 20; McReynolds, *The Seminoles*, p. 200; Ross to C. A. Harris, June 12, 1838, Cherokee Collection, Tennessee State Library and Archives.

6. Ross to Lewis Ross, October 30 and November 11, 1837, and Ross to James C. Martin, November 5, 1837, Ross Papers, Gilcrease Institute; Ross and Gunter to Mason, November 14, 1837, U.S., House, "Memorial of a Delegation of the Cherokee Nation," *Document 99* (serial 325), pp. 40–42.

7. Mason to Ross and Gunter, November 24, 1837, Ross and Gunter to Mason, December 6, 1837, and Poinsett to Ross et al., U.S., House, "Memorial of a Delegation of the Cherokee Nation," *Document 99* (serial 325), pp. 42–49.

8. Ross to Coodey, December 1837, and Ross to Lowrey, January 27, 1838, Ross Papers, Gilcrease Institute; Harris to Armstrong, January 3, 1838, Letters Sent, Office of Indian Affairs; Ross et al. to the Senate and House of Representatives, December 15, 1837, U.S., House, "Memorial of a Delegation of the Cherokee Nation," *Document 99* (serial 325), pp. 1–3; C. E.

Haynes to Harris, January 29, 1838, Cherokee Agency Letters Received; Adams, *Memoirs of John Quincy Adams*, 9: 473–74.

9. Smith to Harris, December 4 and 20, 1837, and February 1 and 19, 1838, Special File 31, Office of Indian Affairs; Harris to Smith, December 13, 1837, and Ross to Poinsett, January 16, 1838, Cherokee Agency Letters Received; Harris to Ross, January 18, 1838, Letters Sent, Office of Indian Affairs; Poinsett to Gilmer, December 16, 1837, in Gilmer, *Sketches*, p. 537; Smith et al. to the Cherokees, December 28, 1837, U.S., House, "Memorial of the Cherokee Delegation," 25th Cong., 2nd sess., *Document 316* (serial 329), pp. 4–7; Ross et al. to Van Buren, April 13, 1838, Cherokee Agency Letters Received.

10. Ross to Payne, January 27, 1838, Ross Papers, Gilcrease Institute; Ross to Payne, February 10, 1838, Payne Papers, Gilcrease Institute.

11. Araminta Ross to Ross, January 19, 1838, Robert Ross to Ross, March 16, 1838, John McDonald Ross to Ross, February 2, 1838, and William P. Ross to Ross, January 20 and March 2, 1838, Ross Papers, Gilcrease Institute; R. J. Mulford, notes on the history of Lawrenceville Academy, John Dixon Library, Lawrenceville School, Lawrenceville, New Jersey.

12. Lewis Ross to Ross, March 5 and 22, 1838, Ross Papers, Gilcrease Institute; Smith to Harris, March 22, 1838, Special File 31, Office of Indian Affairs.

13. Gilmer to Poinsett, March 3, 1838, Cherokee Agency Letters Received; Gilmer to Ross, March 9, 1838, in Gilmer, *Sketches*, pp. 534–36; Ross to Gilmer, April 6, 1838, Ross Papers, Gilcrease Institute.

14. Hildebrand to Ross, March 10, 1838, and Ross et al. to the Senate and House of Representatives, March 12, 1838, U.S., House, "Memorial of the Cherokee Delegation," *Document 316* (serial 329), pp. 1–4, 7; Ross to Lewis Ross, March 15, 28, and April 5, 1838, and Harris to John Kennedy et al., March 27, 1838, Ross Papers, Gilcrease Institute.

15. Ross et al. to Van Buren, April 13, 1838, and Ross to Cooper, April 16, 1838, Cherokee Agency Letters Received; Cooper to Ross et al., April 14, 1838, Special File 158, Office of Indian Affairs; Cooper to Ross, April 17, 1838, Ross Papers, Gilcrease Institute.

16. Ross to Samuel Webb and John M. Truman, May 3 and 14, 1838, Ross Papers, Gilcrease Institute. John Ridge was in the East during May visiting his wife's relatives and he "found that the religious community were entirely bewildered by John Ross." Despite Ridge's explanations, the religious groups continued to support the antiremoval cause (Ridge to Lumpkin, May 7, 1838, in Lumpkin, *Removal of the Cherokee Indians*, pp. 201–5). O. S. Fowler to Ross, March 28, 1838, Ross Papers, Gilcrease Institute.

17. Poinsett to Ross et al., May 18, 1838, U.S., House, "Cherokee Indians," 25th Cong., 2nd sess., *Executive Document 376* (serial 330), pp. 2–4; Poinsett to R. M. Johnson, May 25, 1838, U.S., Senate, "Report from the

Secretary of War," 25th Cong., 2nd sess., *Document 461* (serial 318), unpaged [only one page].

18. Poinsett to Johnson, May 25, 1838, U.S., Senate, "Report from the
Secretary of War," *Document 461* (serial 318); Ross to Hugh L. White, May
28, 1838, Hugh L. White to Ross, May 28, 1838, and "Memorandum of Estimates regarding the Removal of the Cherokee Nation," undated [May
1838?], Samuel L. Southard Papers, Princeton University Library, Princeton,
New Jersey; Poinsett to James K. Polk, May 25, 1838, U.S., House, "Removal of the Cherokees," 25th Cong., 2nd sess., *Executive Document 401*
(serial 330), unpaged [only one page]; report of J. A. Slade and J. T. Bender,
April 28, 1894, U.S., House, "Moneys Due the Cherokee Nation," *Executive Document 182* (serial 3323), pp. 9–10, 17; statement of moneys paid the
Cherokees, August 18, 1842, U.S., House, "Removal of the Cherokees West
of the Mississippi," *Report 1098* (serial 411), p. 69; Report of the Committee
on Indian Affairs, June 5, 1838, U.S., Senate, untitled, 25th Cong., 2nd sess.,
Document 466 (serial 318), pp. 1–2.

19. Ross to Lewis Ross, April 5, 1838, Ross Papers, Gilcrease Institute;
Alexander Macomb to Scott, April 6 and May 3, 1838, Scott to Poinsett,
May 18, 1838, Scott's address to the Cherokees, May 10, 1838, Scott's Order
Number 25, May 17, 1838, Scott to R. Jones, May 22, 1838, and Scott to
Smith, June 6, 1838, U.S., House, "Removal of the Cherokees," 25th Cong.,
2nd sess., *Executive Document 453* (serial 331), pp. 1–2, 7–13, 21–22.

20. Poinsett to Scott, May 23, and June 1, 3, 25, and 27, 1838, Scott to
Poinsett, June 7, 15, and 18, 1838, and Scott to Smith, June 8, 1838, U.S.,
House, "Removal of the Cherokees," *Executive Document 453* (serial 331),
pp. 2–6, 18–23, 25–26; Mooney, "Myths of the Cherokee," part 2, pp. 130–
31.

21. Scott to Poinsett, June 18, 1838, U.S., House, "Removal of the Cherokees," *Executive Document 453* (serial 331), p. 26; Scott to Lowrey et al.,
June 19, 1838, U.S., House, "Memorial—Indians—Cherokee Delegation,"
26th Cong., 1st sess., *Document 129* (serial 365), p. 33; Smith to Harris, June
21 and July 3, 1838, Special File 31, Office of Indian Affairs.

22. Ross to Payne, July 5 and 9, 1838, Payne Papers, Gilcrease Institute;
Fries, trans., "Diary," Oklahoma Historical Society; Scott to Poinsett, July
13, 1838, and Scott to Jones, July 17, 1838, Cherokee Emigration Letters
Received; resolution of the General Council, July 21, 1838, U.S., House,
"Memorial—Indians—Cherokee Delegation," *Document 129* (serial 365),
p. 34. Scott to Ross et al., July 28, 1838, U.S., Senate, "Report of the Commissioner of Indian Affairs, 1838," 25th Cong., 3rd sess., *Document 1*, pp.
462–63.

23. Ross et al. to Scott, July 31 and August 2, 1838, and Scott to Ross et al.,
August 1 and 2, 1838, U.S., Senate, "Report of the Commissioner of Indian
Affairs, 1838," *Document 1*, pp. 463–66; report of J. A. Slade and J. T.

Bender, April 28, 1894, U.S., House, "Moneys Due the Cherokee Nation," *Executive Document 182* (serial 3323), p. 9; Scott to Ross et al., August 31, 1838, Cherokee Emigration Letters Received.

24. Agreement between Removal Committee and Lewis Ross, August 10, 1838, and Smith to Harris, August 16, 1838, Special File 31, Office of Indian Affairs. Smith was assured that his functions were not superseded by Ross, and he maintained his position until removal was completed (See Harris to Smith, September 8, 1838, ibid., and T. Hartley Crawford to Smith, January 17, 1839, Letters Sent, Office of Indian Affairs). N. A. Bryan et al. to Lewis Ross and John McGhee, August 18, 1838, and Lewis Ross to N. A. Bryan et al., August 18, 1838, Cherokee Emigration Letters Received; Foreman, *Indian Removal*, p. 299; John A. Bell et al. to Scott, August 20, 1838, and Scott to Ross et al., August 22, 1838, U.S., House, "Removal of the Cherokees West of the Mississippi," *Report 1098* (serial 411), pp. 31–38.

25. Ross et al. to Scott, August 25, 1838, and Deas to Harris, October 27, November 24, and December 3, 1838, Cherokee Emigration Letters Received.

26. Foreman, *Indian Removal*, p. 300, 300 n.14; remarks of General Scott, June 17, 1841, U.S., House, "Removal of the Cherokees West of the Mississippi," *Report 1098* (serial 411), pp. 27–28; Scott to Ross, August 1, 1838, U.S., Senate, "Report of the Commissioner of Indian Affairs, 1838," *Document 1*, pp. 464–65.

27. Ross's certificates of detachment expenses [May 18, 1840?], U.S., House, "Removal of the Cherokees," 27th Cong., 3rd sess., *Report 288* (serial 429), pp. 57–70; John Page to Harris, September 4, October 6 and 22, 1838, Cherokee Emigration Letters Received; Foreman, *Indian Removal*, pp. 302–12.

28. Lucy Butler to John Howard Payne, January 26, 1839, Payne Papers, Newberry Library; Scott to Poinsett, November 13, 1838, Cherokee Emigration Letters Received.

29. Foreman, *Indian Removal*, pp. 302–12; reminiscence of H. B. Henegar [October 25, 1897?], in Wooten, *A History of Bradley County*, pp. 58–59; Mooney, "Myths of the Cherokee," part 2, pp. 132–33.

30. Foreman, *Indian Removal*, pp. 310–12.

31. Page to Crawford, November 24 and December 4, 1838, Cherokee Emigration Letters Received; Lucy Butler to John Howard Payne, January 26, 1839, Payne Papers, Newberry Library; story of John G. Burnett, December 11, 1890, Cherokee Papers, Museum of the Cherokee Indian, Cherokee, North Carolina; *Arkansas Gazette*, February 6, 1839.

32. Report of J. A. Slade and J. T. Bender, April 28, 1894, U.S., House, "Moneys Due the Cherokee Nation," *Executive Document 182* (serial 3323), pp. 9–10. The 125 days as given for the average time of emigration by the 13 parties was not based on actual movement but from the date a party

was organized with its conductor and other leaders until the detachment reached the Cherokee Nation in the West. The actual time on the road is undetermined.

33. Ross to Scott, November 9, 1838, Ross Papers, Gilcrease Institute; Ross's certificates of detachment expenses [May 18, 1840?], U.S., House, "Removal of the Cherokees," *Report 288* (serial 429), p. 56.

34. Crawford to Poinsett, August 8, 1840, U.S., House, "Removal of the Cherokees," *Report 288* (serial 429), pp. 12–17.

35. Ibid., pp. 17–24.

36. Van Buren's statement, September 2, 1840, Clarke to Scott, November 3, 1840 [Scott's answers accompany the questions asked by Clarke in this letter], statement of Scott, June 17, 1841, Clarke to Van Buren, January 7, 1841, ibid., pp. 24–26, 32–35, 37.

37. Report of the Committee on Indian Affairs, March 2, 1843, Tyler to Ross et al., September 20, 1841, statement of Scott, June 17, 1841, ibid., pp. 2, 36–40, 49–50.

38. Decision of Secretary Bell, September 6, 1841, ibid., pp. 27–31; report of J. A. Slade and J. T. Bender, April 28, 1894, U.S., House, "Moneys Due the Cherokee Nation," *Executive Document 182* (serial 3323), p. 11; statement of the second auditor, August 18, 1842, U.S., House, "Removal of the Cherokees West of the Mississippi," *Report 1098* (serial 411), p. 70.

39. Testimony of Samuel C. Stambaugh [1842?], and Ross's annual message, October [28?], 1840, U.S., House, "Removal of the Cherokees West of the Mississippi," *Report 1098* (serial 411), pp. 53, 46; testimonies of Gideon Morgan, January 1, 1841, R. E. Clements, August 6, 1842, Gideon F. Morris [1842?], Gary Hinant [1842?] and J. K. Rodgers, February 24, 1843, U.S., House, "Removal of the Cherokees," *Report 288* (serial 429), pp. 40–49, 70; *Parks* v. *Ross* (11 Howard 362); Ross's annual message, October 3, 1843, Ross Papers, Gilcrease Institute, Ross to the Committee and Council, December 20, 1842, U.S., House, "Cherokee Disturbances," 29th Cong., 1st sess., *Document 185* (serial 485), pp. 106–8; *The Constitution and Laws of the Cherokee Nation: Passed at Tahlequah, Cherokee Nation, 1839–51* (Tahlequah, Cherokee Nation: *Cherokee Advocate* Office, 1852), pp. 75–76, 106. Ross overpaid $24,427.98 in the $125,000 settlement, all but $1,500 of which he claimed personally. Ross requested that the amount be returned after a final settlement was determined, but it seems he was never repaid (see "The Cherokee Nation in account with John Ross Superintending Agent of Cher. Removal," [1845?] and affidavit of James Brown, November 2, 1858, Ross Papers, Gilcrease Institute, and Ross to the National Council, October 25, 1861, Ross Papers, Oklahoma Historical Society).

40. Report of J. A. Slade and J. T. Bender, April 28, 1894, U.S., House, "Moneys Due the Cherokee Nation," *Executive Document 182* (serial 3323), pp. 7, 9–10, 19–20.

41. Crawford to Poinsett, August 8, 1840, and statement of Gideon F.

Morris [1842?], U.S., House, "Removal of the Cherokees," *Report 288* (serial 429), pp. 16, 44; Foreman, *Indian Removal*, pp. 295, 299, 302.

42. Thomas N. Clark, Jr., to Ross, November 15, 1838, Foreman Collection, Gilcrease Institute; Foreman, *Indian Removal*, p. 304; report of J. A. Slade and J. T. Bender, April 28, 1894, U.S., House, "Moneys Due the Cherokee Nation," *Executive Document 182* (serial 3323), p. 11; statement of Thomas C. Hindman, [1840?], Ross Papers, Gilcrease Institute.

CHAPTER 7

1. Silas Ross to Ross, June 13, 1840, and George and Silas to Ross, May 6, 1842, Ross Papers, Gilcrease Institute.

2. Daniel H. Ross to Ross, June 17, 1840, Ross to Daniel and William, August 19, 1841, and William to Ross, July 16, 1842, ibid. Ross received notices of William's progress from the academy at Lawrenceville; they were always the highest. H. and S. M. Hamill to Ross, June 20, 1839, ibid.

3. George Hicks and Collins McDonald to Ross, March 15, 1839, and Ross to Stokes, April 5, 1839, ibid.; Ross to Arbuckle, April 19, 1839, and Armstrong to Crawford, April 25, 1839, U.S., House, "Frauds upon Indians—Rights of the President to Withhold Papers," 27th Cong., 3rd sess., *Report 271* (serial 428), pp. 147–50.

4. Ross to Arbuckle, April 23, 1839, Glasgow and Harrison to Crawford, April 25, 1839, Crawford to Armstrong, June 12, 1839, and E. A. Hitchcock to J. C. Spencer, August 3, 1842, U.S., House, "Frauds upon Indians—Rights of the President to Withhold Papers," *Report 271* (serial 428), pp. 145–47, 151–55, 166–67; Grant Foreman, *The Five Civilized Tribes* (Norman: University of Oklahoma Press, 1934), pp. 285–88.

5. M.C.M. Hammond to Arbuckle, April 25, 1839, Arbuckle to Ross, April 26, 1839, and George A. McCall to Arbuckle, May 3, 1839, U.S., House, "Memorial—Indians—Cherokee Delegation," *Document 129* (serial 365), pp. 39–43; Ross to W. P. Rowles, April 27, 1839, Ross Papers, Gilcrease Institute.

6. Foreman, *The Five Civilized Tribes*, p. 291; Morris L. Wardell, *A Political History of the Cherokee Nation, 1838–1907* (Norman: University of Oklahoma Press, 1938), pp. 13–14; Evan Jones to John Howard Payne, July 24, 1839, Payne Papers, Newberry Library.

7. Wardell, *History of the Cherokee Nation*, pp. 14–15; Ross to the General Council, June 10, 1839, U.S., House, "Memorial—Indians—Cherokee Delegation," *Document 129* (serial 365), pp. 48–49.

8. Brown, Looney, and Rogers to Ross and Lowrey, June 11, 1839, Ross and Lowrey to Brown, Looney, and Rogers, June 13, 1839, resolution of the Eastern Cherokee Council, June 13, 1839, and Brown, Looney, and Rogers to Ross and Lowrey, June 14, 1839, U.S., House, "Memorial—Indians—Cher-

okee Delegation," *Document 129* (serial 365), pp. 49–52; Evan Jones to John Howard Payne, July 22, 1839, Payne Papers, Newberry Library; statement of Thomas C. Hindman [1840?], Ross Papers, Gilcrease Institute.

9. Wardell, *History of the Cherokee Nation*, p. 15; Ross and Lowrey to the General Council of the Eastern Cherokees, June 15, 1839, resolution of the General Council, August 1, 1838, and resolution of Eastern and Western Cherokees, June 20, 1839, U.S., House, "Memorial—Indians—Cherokee Delegation," *Document 129* (serial 365), pp. 37, 52–53. This document erroneously sets the date for the Illinois Camp Ground conference as July 31.

10. Wardell, *History of the Cherokee Nation*, pp. 16–17; John A. Bell and Stand Watie to the editor, July 8, 1839, in *Arkansas Gazette*, August 21, 1839; Grant Foreman, ed., "The Murder of Elias Boudinot," *Chronicles of Oklahoma*, 12, no. 1 (March 1934), pp. 19–24; Jones to Payne, July 22, 1839, Payne Papers, Newberry Library.

11. Ross to Arbuckle, June 22, 23, and 24, 1839, and Arbuckle to Ross, June 23 and 24, 1839, U.S., House, "Memorials—Indians—Cherokee Delegation," *Document 129* (serial 365), pp. 54–57; statement of Thomas C. Hindman [1840?] Ross Papers, Gilcrease Institute. Although he carried the same family name, John G. Ross does not appear to have been related to Chief Ross except by marriage. He married Chief Ross's older sister Elizabeth about 1817 or 1819.

12. Wardell, *History of the Cherokee Nation*, pp. 17–18; *Laws of the Cherokee Nation Adopted by the Council at Various Periods*, pp. 136–37; statement of H. B. Henegar [October 25, 1897?], in Wooten, *A History of Bradley County*, pp. 59–60; Schermerhorn to the editor of the *Utica Observer*, July 17, 1839, in *Niles' Register*, September 14, 1839, p. 42; Stokes to Poinsett, June 24, 1839, U.S., Senate, "Report of the Commissioner of Indian Affairs, 1839," 26th Cong., 1st sess., *Document 1*, pp. 354–55.

13. Arbuckle to Gen. R. Jones, June 26, 1839, Brown, Looney, and Rogers to Ross et al., June 28, 1839, Arbuckle and Stokes to Ross et al., June 29, 1839, Ross et al. to Arbuckle and Stokes, June 30, 1839, and George A. McCall to Arbuckle, July 3, 1839, U.S., Senate, "Report of the Commissioner of Indian Affairs, 1839," *Document 1*, pp. 358, 364–70.

14. Ross et al. to the chiefs of the Western Cherokees, June 30, 1839, Ross to Armstrong, June 30, 1839, George Guess to Brown, Looney, and Rogers, July 2, 1839, Ross to Brown, Looney, and Rogers, July 5, 1839, and Brown, Looney, and Rogers to Ross, July 6, 1839, U.S., House, "Memorial—Indians—Cherokee Delegation," *Document 129* (serial 365), pp. 62–67; Arbuckle to Ross et al., July 8, 1839, and Ross et al. to Arbuckle, July 9, 1839, U.S., Senate, "Report of the Commissioner of Indian Affairs, 1839," *Document 1*, pp. 371–73.

15. John R. Nicholson to [Ross?], May 13, 1839, Ross Papers, Gilcrease Institute; Andrew Buckhanan and Mark Bean to Ross, July 30, 1839, Ross et al. to Stokes, August 7, 1838, Stokes to Lowrey et al., August 9, 1839, and

testimonies of Daniel McCoy, William Williams, Looney Price, Joseph Coodey, Eleanor Bevert, and Larkin Bevert, August 9, 1839, U.S., House, "Memorial—Indians—Cherokee Delegation," *Document 129* (serial 365), pp. 95–98; statement of Thomas C. Hindman [1840?], Ross Papers, Gilcrease Institute.

16. Armstrong to Crawford, July 12, 1839, and Cherokee Decree, July 7/13, 1839, U.S., Senate, "Report of the Commissioner of Indian Affairs, 1839," *Document 1*, pp. 363–64, 390, 392.

17. Cherokee Decree, July 10, 1839, U.S., House, "Cherokee Disturbances," *Document 185* (serial 485), p. 111; Wardell, *History of the Cherokees*, p. 53.

18. Cherokee Act of Union, July 12, 1839, Ross et al. to Arbuckle, July 12, 13, 15, 19, and 20, 1839, and Arbuckle to Ross et al., July 14, 17, 18, and 22, 1839, U.S., Senate, "Report of the Commissioner of Indian Affairs, 1839," *Document 1*, pp. 389–90, 394–401, 403–4; John Rogers to Arbuckle, July 17, 1839, U.S., House, "Memorial—Indians—Cherokee Delegation," *Document 129* (serial 365), p. 78.

19. Wardell, *History of the Cherokees*, pp. 29–30; Ross et al. to George Guess et al., July 23, 1839, and Ross et al. to John Martin et al., July 27, 1839, Ross Papers, Gilcrease Institute; Ross et al. to Arbuckle, July 24, 1839, Arbuckle to Ross et al., July 29 and August 4, 1839, Brown, Looney, and Rogers to Ross et al., August 2, 1839, and Ross et al. to Brown, Looney, and Rogers, August 6, 1839, U.S., Senate, "Report of the Commissioner of Indian Affairs, 1839," *Document 1*, pp. 376–82.

20. Ross to William S. and Daniel R. Coodey, August 9, 1839, Ross Papers, Gilcrease Institute; Ross et al. to Arbuckle, August 7, 1839, U.S., Senate, "Report of the Commissioner of Indian Affairs, 1839," *Document 1*, pp. 382–83.

21. Old Settlers [Ross adherents] to John Drew and William Shorey Coodey, August 16, 1839, U.S., House, "Indians—Cherokees," 26th Cong., 1st sess., *Document 222* (serial 368), pp. 21–22; Old Settlers resolutions [Ross adherents], August 23, 1839, U.S., Senate, "Report of the Commissioner of Indian Affairs, 1839," *Document 1*, pp. 386–88; Arbuckle to Ross, October 14, 1839, U.S., House, "Memorial—Indians—Cherokee Delegation," *Document 129* (serial 365), pp. 114–15.

22. Resolutions of the Treaty Party, August 20, 1839, Treaty Party Committee to Poinsett, August 20, 1839, and Eastern Cherokee resolution, August 28, 1839, U.S., Senate, "Report of the Commissioner of Indian Affairs, 1839," *Document 1*, p. 405–11; statement of Thomas C. Hindman [1840?], Ross Papers, Gilcrease Institute.

23. Wardell, *History of the Cherokee Nation*, pp. 33–34; constitution of the Cherokee Nation, adopted September 6, 1839, in *The Constitution and Laws of the Cherokee Nation*, pp. 5–15; Ross et al. to John Bell, April 20, 1840, U.S., House, "Indians—Cherokees," *Document 222* (serial 368), p. 2.

24. Ross to the National Council, September 12 and 28, 1839, Daniel But-

rick to Ross, September 20, 1839, Ross Papers, Gilcrease Institute; *The Constitution and Laws of the Cherokee Nation,* pp. 17–39; Ross to the National Council, September 27, 1839, John Ross Papers, Cherokee Collection, John Vaughn Library, Northeastern Oklahoma State University, Tahlequah, Oklahoma; Cherokee resolution, October 2, 1839, U.S., House, "Memorial—Indians—Cherokee Delegation," *Document 129* (serial 365), pp. 110–13.

25. Arbuckle and Armstrong to Ross, September 28, 1839, and Ross to Arbuckle and Armstrong, September 30, 1839, U.S., House, "Memorial—Indians—Cherokee Delegation," *Document 129* (serial 365), pp. 107–8; Arbuckle to Jones, October 2 and 8, 1839, Crawford to Armstrong, October 8, 1839, and Poinsett to Arbuckle, October 12, 1839, U.S., Senate, "Report of the Commissioner of Indian Affairs, 1839," *Document 1*, pp. 414–17, 422–24.

26. Arbuckle to Jones, October 8, 1839, and Armstrong to Crawford, October 10, 1839, U.S., Senate, "Report of the Commissioner of Indian Affairs, 1839," *Document 1*, pp. 422–24; Ross et al. to the chiefs of the Creek Nation, July 1, 1839, and Ross et al. to the chiefs of the Senecas, Shawnees, Delawares, and Quapaws, July 29, 1839, U.S., House, "Indians—Cherokees," *Document 222* (serial 368), pp. 15–16; R. A. Callaway to Arbuckle, October 15, 1839, Arbuckle to Ross, November 2, 1839, and Ross to Arbuckle, November 4, 1839, U.S., House, "Cherokee Indians," 26th Cong., 1st sess., *Document 188* (serial 366), pp. 14–17, 21.

27. Stokes to the Western Cherokees, November 11, 1839, resolution of the Western Cherokees, November 5, 1839, Rogers et al. to Arbuckle, November 7, 1839, Arbuckle to Rogers et al., November 10, 1839, Arbuckle to Jones, November 24, 1839, Rogers et al. to Stokes, November 22, 1839, and Crawford to Armstrong, January 2, 1840, U.S., House, "Cherokee Indians," *Document 188* (serial 366), pp. 17–21, 23–26.

28. Arbuckle to Vann, December 5, 14, and 24, 1839, Vann to Arbuckle, December 6 and 24, 1839, agreement between Stokes and the Eastern Cherokees, December 20, 1839, call for Cherokee assembly, December 20, 1839, Rogers et al. to Arbuckle and Stokes, December 27, 1839, revocation of the amnesty decree and ratification of the constitution, January 16, 1840, Arbuckle to Poinsett, January 22 and 28, 1840, and Armstrong to Crawford, January 22, 1840, ibid., pp. 28–29, 31–37, 43–45, 53, 56.

29. William Shorey Coodey to Ross, January 22, 1840, Ross Papers, Gilcrease Institute; Stokes to Poinsett, January 22, 1840, U.S., House, "Cherokee Indians," *Document 188* (serial 366), pp. 50–51.

30. William Shorey Coodey to Ross, January 2, 1840, Ross Papers, Gilcrease Institute; Arbuckle to Poinsett, February 8 and 10, 1840, report of the select committee of Western Cherokees, February 7, 1840, Crawford to Stokes, March 7, 1840, Poinsett to Arbuckle, March 7, 1840, U.S., House, "Cherokee Indians," *Document 188* (serial 366), pp. 56–59, 64.

31. Arbuckle to Poinsett, April 13, May 6 and 27, 1840, Cherokee Agency Letters Received; delegation to Vann, March 22, 1840, Ross Papers, Gilcrease Institute; Arbuckle's address, April 21, 1840, Eastern Cherokee response, April 22, 1840, Old Settler response, April 25, 1840, Vann to Arbuckle, April 24, 1840, and Arbuckle to Vann, May 11 and 24, 1840, U.S., Senate, "Report of the Commissioner of Indian Affairs, 1840," 26th Cong., 2nd sess., *Document 1*, pp. 262–69.

32. Arbuckle to Poinsett, June 9 and 28, 1840, Arbuckle to Vann, June 2, 1840, Vann et al. to Arbuckle, June 3, 1840, and Act of Union, June 26, 1840, U.S., Senate, "Report of the Commissioner of Indian Affairs, 1840," *Document 1*, pp. 269–72.

33. Lewis Ross to Ross, January 3, 1840, and Ross to Elijah Parker, January 23, 1840, Ross Papers, Gilcrease Institute; Ross et al. to Poinsett, December 31, 1839, Poinsett to Lynch et al., January 2 and 4, 1840, Lynch et al. to Poinsett, January 3, 1840, and Ross to Poinsett, January 3, 1840, Crawford to Poinsett, March 30, 1840, U.S., House, "Cherokee Indians," *Document 188* (serial 366), pp. 38–40.

34. Arbuckle to Poinsett, February 10, 1840, Rogers et al. to Poinsett, January 22, 1840, and Crawford to Poinsett, March 27, 1840, U.S., House, "Cherokee Indians," *Document 188* (serial 366), pp. 42–43, 62, 64; memorial of Dutch et al. [March 1840?], U.S., House, "Indians—Cherokee Nation," 26th Cong., 1st sess., *Document 162* (serial 366), pp. 1–15; Foreman, *The Five Civilized Tribes*, p. 304 n.14.

35. Ross to the National Council, October [28?], 1840, U.S., House, "Removal of the Cherokees West of the Mississippi," *Report 1098* (serial 411), p. 45; Ross to Payne, January 22, 1840, Ross Papers, Gilcrease Institute; Foreman, *The Five Civilized Tribes*, p. 311, 311 n.2; Ross et al. to the Senate and House of Representatives, February 28, 1840, U.S., House, "Memorial—Indians—Cherokee Delegation," *Document 129* (serial 365), passim.

36. Coodey to Ross, March 5, 1840, U.S., House, "Memorial—Indians—Cherokee Delegation," *Document 129* (serial 365), pp. 10–11; Crawford to Poinsett, March 30, 1840, U.S., House, "Cherokee Indians," *Document 188* (serial 366), p. 11; William Shorey Coodey to the Committee on Indian Affairs, April 22, 1840, U.S., House, "Indians—Cherokees," *Document 222* (serial 368), pp. 17–21.

37. Delegation to Vann, March 22, 1840, Ross Papers, Gilcrease Institute; Crawford to the delegation, July 21, 1840, Crawford to Ross, July 15 and 17, 1840, Letters Sent, Office of Indian Affairs; Ross et al. to Crawford, July 10, 13, 16, and 27, 1840, Cherokee Agency Letters Received; E. Hicks to Poinsett, August 21, 1840, and Crawford to Poinsett, August 22, 1840, U.S., Senate, "Report of the Commissioner of Indian Affairs, 1840," *Document 1*, pp. 272–75; Ross to the National Council, October [28?], 1840, U.S., House, "Removal of the Cherokees West of the Mississippi," *Report 1098* (serial 411), p. 45.

38. Ross to the National Council, October [28?], 1840, U.S., House, "Removal of the Cherokees West of the Mississippi," *Report 1098* (serial 411), pp. 44–47; Grant Foreman, *Advancing the Frontier, 1830–1860* (Norman: University of Oklahoma Press, 1933), p. 319; resolutions of the National Council, November 13 and 14, 1840, Ross Papers, Gilcrease Institute.

39. Arbuckle to the General Council, October 24, 1840, Armstrong to Crawford, October 25, 1840, Arbuckle to R. Jones, October 27, 1840, William Shorey Coodey et al. to Arbuckle, November 6, 1840, and Poinsett to Crawford, November 11, 1840, Cherokee Agency Letters Received; H. B. Gaither to Ross, January 6, 1841, and Crawford to Stokes, October 21, 1840, Ross Papers, Gilcrease Institute; Arbuckle to Tyler, May 26, 1841, Foreman Collection, Gilcrease Institute; Foreman, *The Five Civilized Tribes*, p. 318.

CHAPTER 8

1. Bell to Ross, March 22, 1841, Letters Sent, Office of Indian Affairs; Ross et al. to Bell, March 27, 1841, Cherokee Agency Letters Received.

2. Ross to Bell, May 15, 1841, Cherokee Agency Letters Received; statement of moneys paid to the Cherokee Nation, August 18, 1842, U.S., House, "Removal of the Cherokees West of the Mississippi," *Report 1098* (serial 411), p. 70.

3. Ross to E. Milligan, April 10, 1838, Anne Milligan to Ross, May 27, 1841, and Ross to Anne Milligan, May 27, 1841, J. L. Hargett Collection, Western History Collections, University of Oklahoma; Thomas C. Hindman to Ross, April 14, 1841, Ross Papers, Oklahoma Historical Society.

4. Ross to Elizabeth, September 5, 1841, Hargett Collection, Western History Collections, University of Oklahoma.

5. Ross to Elizabeth, September 5, 1841, and September 19, 1842, ibid. The proposal letter went through a number of revisions, many more than Ross usually made, indicating, perhaps, that the decision was not firm. Another encounter was with a certain Mary Connelly of Bethlehem, Pennsylvania. A friend of Ross's niece, Miss Connelly wrote Eliza Jane Ross of "the first and only that I could ever love." Ross did not reciprocate her love (Eliza Jane to Ross, June 8, 1844, Ross Papers, Gilcrease Institute. See also Mary Connelly to Ross, May 30, 1844, and Ross to Mary Connelly, September 12, 1841, ibid.).

6. Ross to Bell, July 8, 1841, Cherokee Agency Letters Received; William Shorey Coodey to Ross, July 19, 1841, Ross Papers, Gilcrease Institute.

7. Ross et al. to Bell, August 26, 1841, Cherokee Agency Letters Received; statement of moneys paid to the Cherokee Nation, August 18, 1842, and Tyler to Ross, September 20, 1841, U.S., House, "Removal of the Cherokees West of the Mississippi," *Report 1098* (serial 411), pp. 70–72.

8. Elijah Hicks to Ross, July 28, 1841, Ross Papers, Gilcrease Institute;

A. M. Vann to Bell, September 10, 1841, and Ethan Allen Hitchcock to J. C. Spencer, November 28, 1841, Cherokee Agency Letters Received; *The Constitution and Laws of the Cherokee Nation*, p. 54.

9. Ross to the National Council, November 29, 1841, Cherokee Agency Letters Received; Ethan Allen Hitchcock, *A Traveler in Indian Territory: The Journal of Ethan Allen Hitchcock*, ed. Grant Foreman (Cedar Rapids, Iowa: Torch Press, 1930), p. 38.

10. Hitchcock, *Traveler in Indian Territory*, p. 234.

11. Ibid., p. 39; Ross to the National Council, November 29, 1841, Ross Papers, Gilcrease Institute.

12. Ross to Butler, December 28, 1841, Ross Papers, Gilcrease Institute; Hitchcock to Spencer, December 7, 1841, and Butler to Crawford, March 4, 1842, Cherokee Agency Letters Received; *The Constitution and Laws of the Cherokee Nation*, pp. 59–61.

13. Carolyn Thomas Foreman, "Pierce Mason Butler," *Chronicles of Oklahoma*, 30, no. 1 (Spring 1952), p. 10; Butler to Crawford, March 4, 1842, Cherokee Agency Letters Received.

14. Ross to Sarah F. Stapler, April 2, 1842, Ross Papers, Gilcrease Institute.

15. Ross to Spencer, May 13 and June 2, 6, 14, and 28, 1842, Special File 75, Office of Indian Affairs; John H. Eaton and Edward H. Hubley to James M. Porter, November 17, 1843, and Minority Opinion, March 29, 1844, U.S., House, "Claims Arising under the Cherokee Treaty," 28th Cong., 1st sess., *Report 391* (serial 446), pp. 13–14, 18.

16. Ross et al. to Spencer, August 12, 1842, and Butler to Spencer, August 24, 1842, Special File 75, Office of Indian Affairs.

17. *The Constitution and Laws of the Cherokee Nation*, pp. 62–63, 74, passim; Ross to Butler, December 11, 1842, Cherokee Agency Letters Received.

18. Butler to Crawford, January 16, 1843, Cherokee Agency Letters Received; *The Constitution and Laws of the Cherokee Nation*, pp. 68–69.

19. William H. Goode, *Outposts of Zion with Limnings of Mission Life* (Cincinnati, Ohio: Poe and Hitchcock, 1863), pp. 28–30, 69–72; Hannah Hitchcock, "Cycle of Indian Territory History—the '40's," typescript, Robertson Collection, University of Tulsa Library.

20. Goode, *Outposts of Zion*, pp. 71–74.

21. *The Constitution and Laws of the Cherokee Nation*, pp. 87–89.

22. "Cherokee Indians," *Niles' Register*, September 16, 1843, p. 36. The election returns of at least one district have been preserved. Curiously, Ross and Lowrey were listed as "Whigs," while Vann and Adair were noted as "Loco[focos]" (David Vann and Isaac Bushyhead to A. Campbell and Jack Spears, August 7, 1843, Ross Papers, Gilcrease Institute).

23. Foreman, *The Five Civilized Tribes*, pp. 326–27; Ross's annual message, October 3, 1843, Ross Papers, Gilcrease Institute.

24. Duval to Crawford, August 12, 1843, Cherokee Agency Letters Received; statement of David Carter, December 31, 1844, Ross to General Zachary Taylor, September 29, 1843, and W. W. S. Bliss to Ross, October 3, 1843, U.S., Senate, "Report of the Secretary of War," 28th Cong., 2nd sess., *Document 140* (serial 457), pp. 113–14, 122–23.

25. Ross's annual message, October 3, 1843, and David Greene to Ross, September 30, 1842, Ross Papers, Gilcrease Institute; *The Constitution and Laws of the Cherokee Nation*, pp. 81–82, 102.

26. *The Constitution and Laws of the Cherokee Nation*, pp. 95–99, 104.

27. Ross to Wilkins, April 19, 1844, Wilkins to Ross, April 20, 1844, Ross et al. to Wilkins, May 6, 1844, and Wilkins to Ross et al., May 9, 1844, in *Cherokee Advocate*, November 28, 1844.

28. John Rogers et al. to Wilkins, May 6, 1844, ibid.; U.S., House, "Memorial of the 'Treaty Party' of the Cherokee Indians," 28th Cong., 1st sess., *Document 234* (serial 443), passim; U.S., House; "Cherokee Indians," 28th Cong., 1st sess., *Document 235* (serial 443), passim; *The Constitution and Laws of the Cherokee Nation*, pp. 67–68; Ross to Butler, November 18, 1843, Cherokee Agency Letters Received.

29. Ross et al. to Wilkins, May 14, 30, and June 4, 1844, and Wilkins to Ross et al., May 27, June 3 and 17, 1844, in *Cherokee Advocate*, November 28, 1844.

30. Wilkins to Ross et al., July 8, 1844, and Ross et al. to Wilkins, July 17, 1844, U.S., Senate, "Memorial of John Ross and Others," 27th Cong., 1st sess., *Document 331* (serial 476), pp. 46–55.

31. Ross to Sarah F. Stapler, April 2, 1842, Ross Papers, Gilcrease Institute; William Wade Hinshaw, *Encyclopedia of American Quaker Genealogy*, 3 vols. (Ann Arbor, Mich.: Genealogical Publishers, 1936–40), 2: 768; J. Mortimer Levering, *A History of the Moravian Seminary for Young Ladies at Bethlehem* (Bethlehem, Pa.: New Era Printing Company, 1901), p. 430.

32. Mary to Ross, May 3, 1844, and Ross to Mary, May 9, 1844, Ross Papers, Gilcrease Institute.

33. Mary to Ross, May 22, 1844, ibid.; Ross to Mary, June 16, 1844, Ross Papers, Oklahoma Historical Society. John W. Stapler later married Grave Levy (Genealogical File, Historical Society of Delaware, Wilmington, Delaware).

34. Mary to Ross, June 17, 26 and July 14, 1844, Ross Papers, Gilcrease Institute; Ross to Mary, June 16, 1844, Ross Papers, Oklahoma Historical Society.

35. Mary to Ross, June 26, 1844, and Ross to Mary, June 27/July 1, 1844, Ross Papers, Gilcrease Institute.

36. Ross to Mary, July 19 and 25, 1844, Mary to Ross, July 28, 1844; Ross to Mary, July 30, 1844, Mary to Ross, August 1, 1844, Ross to Mary, July 27

and August 2, 1844, Mary to Ross, August 6, 1844, and Ross to Mary, August 13/14, 1844, ibid.

37. Ross to John Stapler, August 14, 1844, and Ross to Sarah, August 14, 1844, ibid.; Mary to Ross, August 26, 1844, Hargett Collection, Western History Collections, University of Oklahoma; Sarah to Ross, August 17, 1844, Ross Papers, Gilcrease Institute.

38. Ross to Mary, August 13 and 14, 1844, and July 25, 1845, Ross and Mary's marriage license, September 2, 1844, Mrs. Dolly Madison to Mary, undated, and Ross to McKenney, August 25, 1844, Ross Papers, Gilcrease Institute; Ross to McKenney, July 3, 1844, Ross Papers, Oklahoma Historical Society; Carolyn Thomas Foreman, *Park Hill* (Muskogee, Okla.: Star Printery, 1948), pp. 28–29.

39. Grant Foreman, "John Howard Payne and the Cherokee Indians," *The American Historical Review*, 37, no. 4 (July 1932), pp. 723–30; Ross to McKenney, September 6, 1844, Ross Papers, Gilcrease Institute. Ross may have located where his relative, Charles Coodey, an Old Settler, lived. He purchased Coodey's house, stock, and improvements near the Illinois River for $2,900 (Statement of Charles Coodey, November 14, 1839, Ross Papers, Gilcrease Institute). Goode, *Outposts of Zion*, p. 176.

40. Foreman, *Park Hill*, pp. 30–31; J. M. Stanley, "Catalogue of Portraits of North American Indians, with Sketches of Scenery, etc.," Smithsonian Institution, *Miscellaneous Collections*, 153 vols. (Washington, D.C.: Smithsonian Institution, 1862–), 2: 15; "An Account . . . of Family [of Miles Vogler] . . . in 1854," Records of the Moravian Mission Among the Indians of North America, Archives of the Moravian Church, Bethlehem, Pennsylvania; R. R. Meigs interview, Grant Foreman, ed., "Indian Pioneer History," 113 vols., (typescripts), 108: 207–11, Indian Archives Division, Oklahoma Historical Society; Emily V. Mason to [?], March 1845, Stephen T. Mason Papers, Burton Historical Collection, Detroit Public Library, Detroit, Michigan; *Cherokee Advocate*, March 9, 1852.

41. Ross's message, November 18, 1844, in *Cherokee Advocate*, November 28, 1844; *The Constitution and Laws of the Cherokee Nation*, pp. 113–15, 121–23.

42. Jones to Wilkins, November 17, 1844, Cherokee Agency Letters Received; Ross to Jones, November 29, 1844, minutes of the commission, December 17–24, 1844, and statement submitted by the committee of the Treaty Party, December 21, 1844, U.S., Senate, "Report of the Secretary of War," *Document 140* (serial 457), pp. 15–30, 94–96, 133.

43. Ross to Butler, December 6, 1844, Cherokee Agency Letters Received; Looney et al. to Jones, Mason, and Butler, December 13, 1844, and minutes of the commission, December 17 and 18, 1844, U.S., Senate, "Report of the Secretary of War," *Document 140* (serial 457), pp. 19–20, 23, 136.

44. Answers of the Cherokee authorities, January 10, 1845, U.S., Senate,

"Report of the Secretary of War," *Document 140* (serial 457), pp. 35–48.

45. Report of the commissioners, January 17, 1845, ibid., pp. 5–14.

46. Ibid.; Butler to Spencer, March 17, 1844, Special File 75, Office of Indian Affairs.

47. Foreman, *The Five Civilized Tribes*, pp. 335–36, 349; Crawford to Ross et al., August 1, 1845, Marcy to Ross, August 14, 1845, and Crawford to Butler, September 13, 1845, Letters Sent, Office of Indian Affairs; Ross et al. to Marcy, August 27, 1845, Cherokee Agency Letters Received.

CHAPTER 9

1. Wardell, *History of the Cherokee Nation*, pp. 54–55, 62–66; Foreman, *Five Civilized Tribes*, pp. 327–28, 347; Ross's annual message, October 3, 1843, Ross Papers, Gilcrease Institute.

2. Foreman, *Five Civilized Tribes*, pp. 338, 342, 347; Wardell, *History of the Cherokee Nation*, p. 65. Meigs married Ross's oldest daughter Jane in 1838 and died of cholera near the Salt Lake on August 6, 1850, while enroute to the California gold fields (Starr, *History*, p. 411, and *Cherokee Advocate*, December 3, 1850).

3. Stambaugh and Kendall to Marcy, October 4, November 1, November [?], December 26 and 30, 1845, and January 16, 1846, U.S., House, "Cherokee Disturbances," *Document 185* (serial 485), pp. 19–73.

4. George W. Adair et al. to William Medill, March [?], 1846, J. A. Bell and Ezekiel Starr to the Senate and House of Representatives, April 13, 1844, and "Argument in Behalf of the Treaty Party of Cherokees," [April or May?], 1844, ibid., pp. 73–105, 116–49; report of J. A. Slade and J. T. Bender, April 18, 1894, U.S., House, "Moneys Due the Cherokee Nation," *Document 182* (serial 3323), p. 18.

5. The Ross delegation as finally formed included Ross, Richard Taylor, Richard Fields, David Vann, C. V. McNair, Stephen Foreman, T. Walker, John Thorn, and John Looney. Ross et al. to the president, November 8, 1845, and Cherokee Petition, February 4, 1846, U.S., House, "Cherokee Disturbances," *Document 185* (serial 485), pp. 149–60.

6. Ross et al. to the Senate and House of Representatives, April 30, 1846, and Ross et al. to the president, April 11, 1846, U.S., Senate, "Memorial of John Ross and Others," *Document 331* (serial 476), pp. 1–19, 44–46; James K. Polk, *The Diary of James K. Polk during His Presidency, 1845 to 1849*, ed. Milo Milton Quaife, 4 vols. (Chicago: A. C. McClurg and Company, 1910), 1: 301–2; John Thorn to John Drew, March 31, 1846, Drew Papers, Gilcrease Institute.

7. Medill to Marcy, March 31, 1846, and Polk to the Senate and House of Representatives, April 13, 1846, U.S., House, "Cherokee Disturbances," *Document 185* (serial 485), pp. 1–19; report of the Committee on Indian

Affairs, June 2, 1846, U.S., House, "Cherokee Indians," 29th Cong., 1st sess., *Report 683* (serial 490), pp. 1–5.

8. Ross et al. to Armstrong, June 16, 1846, G. W. Adair et al. to Armstrong, June 17, 1846, Armstrong to Medill, June 23, 1846, Burke, Armstrong, and Parris to Polk, July 8, 1846, and Ross et al. to Burke, Armstrong, and Parris, July 8, 1846, Cherokee Agency Letters Received; Wardell, *History of the Cherokee Nation*, pp. 71–73, 353–54; Richardson, comp., *Messages and Papers of the Presidents*, 458–59; Polk, *Diary*, 2: 80–82.

9. Royce, "The Cherokee Nation of Indians," part 2, pp. 298–300; Kappler, comp. and ed., *Indian Affairs*, 2: 561–65.

10. Report of the Committee on Indian Affairs, February 19, 1847, U.S., Senate, untitled, 29th Cong., 2nd sess., *Document 157* (serial 495), pp. 1–5; Ross to Richard Taylor and Robert D. Ross, November 16, 1847, Ross Papers, Gilcrease Institute; report of J. A. Slade and J. T. Bender, April 28, 1894, U.S., House, "Moneys Due the Cherokee Nation," *Document 182* (serial 3323), pp. 12–13, 13 n.2, 21–22; A. K. Parris and P. Clayton to the president of the Senate, December 3, 1849, U.S., Senate, "Report of the Second Comptroller and Second Auditor of the Treasury," 31st Cong., 1st sess., *Executive Document 6* (serial 554), pp. 1–4; report of the Committee on Indian Affairs, August 8, 1850, U.S., Senate, untitled, 31st Cong., 1st sess., *Report 176* (serial 565), pp. 1–7.

11. John Drennen to Luke Lea, October 20, 1851, U.S., Senate, "Report of the Commissioner of Indian Affairs, 1851," 32nd Cong., 1st sess., *Executive Document 1*, pp. 363–66; *The Constitution and Laws of the Cherokee Nation*, pp. 234–35; Ross to Drennen, March 9 and 22, 1852, and Ross to Lea, March 22, 1852, Cherokee Agency Letters Received; Drennen to Lea, October 15, 1852, U.S., Senate, "Report of the Commissioner of Indian Affairs, 1852," 32nd Cong., 2nd sess., *Executive Document 1*, pp. 390–93; *Cherokee Advocate*, May 5, 1852.

12. Ross's annual message, October 4, 1852, in *Cherokee Advocate*, October 27, 1852; protest of the National Council, November 29, 1851, Ross Papers, Gilcrease Institute; report of J. A. Slade and J. T. Bender, April 28, 1894, U.S., House, "Moneys Due the Cherokee Nation," *Document 182* (serial 3323), pp. 22–23, 29–32.

13. *Cherokee Advocate*, July 8, 1847, February 19, April 16, September 24, October 8, 1849, February 11, July 29, 1851, and May 5, 1852; Ross's Memo Book, various dates, 1851–53, unpaged, and Account of Stapler and Ross, January 23, 1860, Ross Papers, Gilcrease Institute; Nell Stapler Bradshaw interview, Foreman, ed., "Indian Pioneer History," 104:132–44; Ross's Account List, various dates (1849–51), Ross Papers, Cherokee Collection, John Vaughn Library, Northeastern Oklahoma State University; Starr, *History*, pp. 410–12; "Cherokee Records," 730 vols., manuscripts, 215:52–53, Indian Archives Division, Oklahoma Historical Society.

14. These blacks were almost equally divided between male and female,

while approximately twelve of them were under the age of ten. The average age was about thirty. Ross also maintained eleven slave houses for their quarters ("Arkansas and the Indian Lands," Eighth Census, 1860, National Archives). At least one record exists of a slave transaction by Ross. In April 1850 he purchased an 18-year-old boy, Peter, for $400 (statement of Susan Coodey, April 19, 1850, Ross Papers, Gilcrease Institute). Receipt of Lorenzo Delano, March 26, 1849, Ross Papers, Gilcrease Institute; "An Account . . . of Family [of Miles Vogler] . . . in 1854," Records of the Moravian Mission Among the Indians of North America, Archives of the Moravian Church; John G. Ross to Ross, June 3, 1841, Ross Papers, Gilcrease Institute. Mary closed one of her letters to Ross: "Remembrances from . . . the blacks" (June 7, 1864, Ross Papers, Gilcrease Institute); Ross to Annie, September 18, 1865, Cherokee Collection, Tennessee State Library and Archives.

15. Stanley, "Portraits of North American Indians," 2: 15; Evan Jones to Ross, November 13, 1846, Ross Papers, Gilcrease Institute. At a meeting of the Tahlequah Missionary Society a roll was taken of the contributing members with a normal contribution of fifty cents recorded. One local merchant, Lorenzo Delano, offered a dollar and, not to be outdone, Ross gave two (Cherokee Advocate, October 1, 1849). Nor did the chief forget his Scottish heritage. As famine swept the Scottish isles in 1847, Ross called for contributions to relieve the suffering, raising altogether one hundred ninety dollars (Cherokee Advocate, April 29 and July 15, 1847).

16. Ross's annual message, November 12, 1846, Cherokee Advocate, November 19, 1846; The Constitution and Laws of the Cherokee Nation, pp. 34–35, 174–75, 218–19; Cherokee Advocate, December 10, 1850. Wardell notes a six-hundred-dollar decrease in Ross's salary rather than a hundred-dollar cut. It is doubtful that Ross would have been receiving a thousand dollars a year during those depressed times (Wardell, History of the Cherokee Nation, p. 88). Compare Wardell, History of the Cherokee Nation, p. 99 n.11.

17. Ross's annual message, October 1, 1849, in Cherokee Advocate, October 8, 1849; proclamation of Ross, October 24, 1849, ibid., October 29, 1849; Cherokee Advocate, November 19, 1849; Ross's annual message, October 5, 1851, ibid., October 14, 1851; Ross to the National Council, November 20, 1851, Ross Papers, Gilcrease Institute; The Constitution and Laws of the Cherokee Nation, pp. 192–234; George Butler to Thomas S. Drew, September 13, 1853, U.S., Senate, "Report of the Commissioner of Indian Affairs, 1853," 33rd Cong., 1st sess., Executive Document 1, p. 383. A bill was introduced for individual taxation in 1853 but gained little interest in the Cherokee National Council (George Butler to Thomas S. Drew, September 27, 1854, U.S., Senate, "Report of the Commissioner of Indian Affairs, 1854," 33rd Cong., 2nd sess., Executive Document 1, pp. 322–23.

18. George Butler to Drennen, September 14, 1851, U.S., Senate, "Report of the Commissioner of Indian Affairs, 1851," Executive Document 1, p.

380; Ross's annual message, October 3, 1859, Ross Papers, Gilcrease Institute; Wardell, *History of the Cherokee Nation*, p. 86.

19. *The Constitution and Laws of the Cherokee Nation*, pp. 192, 223, 230–31, 238–39; Ross to the National Council, November 20, 1851, Ross Papers, Gilcrease Institute; Ross's annual message, October 4, 1852, *Cherokee Advocate*, October 27, 1852.

20. Vann et al. to Lea, July 7, 1852, Alexander H. H. Stuart to Lea, July 16, 1852, Elijah Hicks et al. to Lea, February 14, 1853, Hicks to Manypenny, July 27, 1853, John Thomas et al. to Manypenny, December 28, 1854, [Manypenny?] to McClelland, January 15, 1855, conference notes, January 8, 1855, conference with the Cherokee Delegation, January 15, 1855, Cherokee Agency Letters Received; Lea to Stuart, November 30, 1852, U.S., Senate, "Report of the Commissioner of Indian Affairs, 1852," *Executive Document 1*, p. 298; Ross's instructions to the Cherokee Delegation, January 7, 1853, and November 22, 1854, Ross Papers, Gilcrease Institute; Butler to C. W. Dean, September 10, 1856, U.S., Senate, "Report of the Commissioner of Indian Affairs, 1856," 34th Cong., 3rd sess., *Executive Document 1*, p. 689.

21. Dean to Manypenny, April 16, 1856, and January 17, 1857, Butler to Dean, August 9, 1856, Butler to Charles Mix, October 12, 1857, and R. J. Cowart to A. B. Greenwood, November 9, 1860, Cherokee Agency Letters Received.

22. Ross's annual message, October 5, 1857, and Butler to Elias Rector, September 8, 1857, U.S., Senate, "Report of the Commissioner of Indian Affairs, 1857," 35th Cong., 1st sess., *Executive Document 1*, pp. 500, 509–10, Butler to Mix, January 24, 1858, and Ross to Greenwood, April 2, 1860, Cherokee Agency Letters Received; Butler to Rector, September 10, 1858, U.S., Senate, "Report of the Commissioner of Indian Affairs, 1858," 35th Cong., 2nd sess., *Executive Document 1*, p. 493; Butler to Rector, September 10, 1859, and Rector to Greenwood, September 20, 1859, U.S., Senate, "Report of the Commissioner of Indian Affairs, 1859," 36th Cong., 1st sess., *Executive Document 1*, pp. 531, 540–41.

23. Ross's annual message, October 7, 1850, in *Cherokee Advocate*, October 12, 1850; Ross's annual message, October 5, 1851, ibid., October 14, 1851; *The Constitution and Laws of the Cherokee Nation*, pp. 221–22; Butler to Drennen, September 14, 1851, U.S., Senate, "Report of the Commissioner of Indian Affairs, 1851," *Executive Document 1*, p. 380.

24. James McKisick to Samuel M. Rutherford, September 29, 1847, U.S., Senate, "Report of the Commissioner of Indian Affairs, 1847," 30th Cong., 1st sess., *Executive Document 1*, p. 883; Foreman, *The Five Civilized Tribes*, pp. 408–9; *The Constitution and Laws of the Cherokee Nation*, pp. 157–62.

25. Reports from the two seminaries, September 5 and 8, 1854, U.S., Senate, "Report of the Commissioner of Indian Affairs, 1854," *Executive*

Document 1, pp. 330–32; Ross's annual message, October 3, 1859, Ross Papers, Gilcrease Institute.

26. Foreman, *The Five Civilized Tribes*, p. 414; Ross's annual message, October 5, 1857, U.S., Senate, "Report of the Commissioner of Indian Affairs, 1857," *Executive Document 1*, pp. 508–9; Ross's annual message, October 3, 1859," Ross Papers, Gilcrease Institute. The financial strain on the Cherokees during the 1850s also caused the demise of the *Cherokee Advocate* in 1853 (*Laws of the Cherokee Nation Passed at the Annual Sessions of the National Council, 1852–3* [Tahlequah, Cherokee Nation: *Cherokee Advocate* Office, 1853], p. 20).

27. Butler to Drennen, September 30, 1852, U.S., Senate, "Report of the Commissioner of Indian Affairs, 1852," *Executive Document 1*, p. 401; Ross to Butler, September 8, 1854, and Ross to P. M. Butler, February 14, 1844, Cherokee Agency Letters Received; Bass, *Cherokee Messenger*, p. 230.

28. Jefferson Davis to McClelland, January 13, 1855, and Ross to James W. Denver, June 6, 1857, Cherokee Agency Letters Received; Ross's annual message, October 5, 1857, U.S., Senate, "Report of the Commissioner of Indian Affairs, 1857," *Executive Document 1*, p. 511; Ross's annual message, October 3, 1859, Ross Papers, Gilcrease Institute; Butler to Rector, September 10, 1858, U.S., Senate, "Report of the Commissioner of Indian Affairs, 1858," *Executive Document 1*, p. 493.

29. "Results of Election—August 2, 1847," *Cherokee Advocate*, August 12, 1847; Wardell, *History of the Cherokee Nation*, p. 114; Ross to Thomas S. Drew, September 26, 1853, Cherokee Agency Letters Received; Manypenny to McClelland, November 26, 1853, U.S., Senate, "Report of the Commissioner of Indian Affairs, 1853," *Executive Document 1*, pp. 253–54; George Butler to Rector, September 10, 1859, U.S., Senate, "Report of the Commissioner of Indian Affairs, 1859," *Executive Document 1*, p. 541.

30. *Cherokee Advocate*, January 22, 1849, and April 29, 1851; *Friend*, 32 (1859), p. 120; Ross to Mrs. M. B. Stapler, December 31, 1860/January 1, 1861, and January 18, 1861, Hargett Collection, Western History Collections, University of Oklahoma; extracts from the autobiography of Charles Cutler Torrey (unpublished), "Life among the Cherokees, 1855–1861," Foreman, ed., "Indian Pioneer History," 53: 400–422, Indian Archives Division, Oklahoma Historical Society; Elizabeth Ross interview, Foreman, "Indian Pioneer History," 52: 447–48, Indian Archives Division, Oklahoma Historical Society; Foreman, *Park Hill*, p. 114.

31. Proposed bill in the National Council, October 24, 1855, note attached to the proposed bill, [October, 1855?], and Butler to Mix, October 12, 1858, Cherokee Agency Letters Received; Greenwood to Rector, June 4, 1860, Letters Sent, Office of Indian Affairs.

32. Wardell, *History of the Cherokee Nation*, pp. 116, 119–23.

33. Instructions for negotiations at Washington, November 3, 4, 11, and 14, 1859, Ross Papers, Gilcrease Institute; Annie B. Ross to Lizzie Meigs,

March 14, 1860, Andrew Nave Papers, Cherokee Collection, John Vaughn Library, Northeastern Oklahoma State University; Ross to Greenwood, April 2, 1860, Cherokee Agency Letters Received; Greenwood to Ross et al., April 12, 1860, Letters Sent, Office of Indian Affairs.

34. Ross to Sarah Stapler, April 19, 1860, Ross Papers, Gilcrease Institute; Ross to Mary, May 1, 1860, in Foreman, comp., "Copies of Letters . . . and Miscellaneous Documents Relative to the Cherokee and Creek Indians."

CHAPTER 10

1. Cyrus Harris to Ross, January 5, 1861, and act of the Chickasaw legislature, January 5, 1861, Ross Papers, Gilcrease Institute; Ross to Harris, February 9, 1861, Cherokee Agency Letters Received. The delegation included William P. Ross, Thomas Pegg, John Spears, and Lewis Downing (Ross to William P. Ross et al., February 12, 1861, ibid.). The Creek Nation was to designate the time and place; therefore, the acting Creek chief, Jacob Derrysaw, set February 17, 1861, at the General Council Ground (Derrysaw to Ross, February 4, 1861, ibid.). The meeting concluded generally on the sentiments Ross had expressed (William P. Ross et al. to Ross, March 15, 1861, ibid.).

2. Rector to Ross, January 29, 1861, and Ross to Rector, February 22, 1861, U.S., Department of War, *War of the Rebellion: A Compilation of the Official Records of the Union and Confederate Armies*, 70 vols., 128 books, ser. 1, 13: 490–92; Ross to Editor of Van Buren *Press*, February 1, 1861, Van Buren *Press*, February 8, 1861; Ogden to Ross, February 15, 1861, and Ross to Ogden, February 28, 1861, Cherokee Agency Letters Received.

3. James E. Harrison et al. to Edward Clark, April 23, 1861, U.S., Department of War, *Official Records*, ser. 4, 1: 322–25; Mark Bean et al. to Ross, May 9, 1861, Kannady to Ross, May 15, 1861, Ross to Kannady, May 17, 1861, Ross to Mark Bean et al., May 18, 1861, and Ross's proclamation to the Cherokees, May 17, 1861, ibid., ser. 1, 13: 489–90, 492–95. Ross called a meeting of the Cherokee Executive Council three days before the proclamation to gain the support of the members. The Executive Council at this time was composed of James Brown, John Drew, and William P. Ross, all Ross's staunch supporters (Ross to John Drew, May 9, 1861, Drew Papers, Gilcrease Institute).

4. Pike to Robert Toombs, May 29, 1861, U.S., Department of War, *Official Records*, ser. 4, 1: 359–61; Pike to Ross, June 6, 1861, Cherokee Nation Papers, Western History Collections, University of Oklahoma; Ross to Pike, July 1, 1861, Cherokee Agency Letters Received; Walter L. Brown, "Albert Pike, 1809–1891" (Ph.D. dissertation, University of Texas, 1955), p. 553. Ross may have known Pike as early as 1839. When Quatie died near the end of the removal process, she was buried at Little Rock in an unmarked grave.

In 1843 Mount Holly Cemetery came into service, and Quatie's remains sup-posedly were transferred to the Pike family plot there. A marker now stands as her memorial on the Albert Pike lot. This tenuous connection was not ap-parent in the Ross-Pike correspondence.

5. John B. Luce to Ross, May 29, 1861, Ross Papers, Gilcrease Institute; McCulloch to Walker, May 28 and June 12, 1861, U.S., Department of War, *Official Records*, ser. 1, 3: 587–88, 590–91; McCulloch to Ross, June 12, 1861, U.S., Department of War, *Official Records*, ser. 1, 13: 495.

6. Hubbard to Ross, June 12, 1861, U.S., Department of War, *Official Records*, ser. 1, 13: 497–98.

7. Ross to McCulloch, June 17, 1861, ibid., pp. 495–97; McCulloch to Walker, June 22, 1861, ibid., ser. 1, 3: 595–96; Ross to Hubbard, June 17, 1861, ibid., ser. 1, 13: 499.

8. Ross and Joseph Vann to John Drew, July 2, 1861, Ross Papers, Gil-crease Institute.

9. Executive Council notes, July 2, 1861, Cherokee Agency Letters Re-ceived; minutes of Executive Council, August 1, 1861, Ross Papers, Gil-crease Institute; Ross's address, August 21, 1861, and resolutions of the Cherokees, August 21, 1861, U.S., Department of War, *Official Records*, ser. 1, 3: 673–76.

10. Ross to McCulloch, August 24, 1861, U.S., Department of War, *Offi-cial Records*, ser. 1, 3: 673; Ross to James Brown, September 10, 1861, Ross to Pike, September 25, 1861, and Ross's annual message, October 9, 1861, Ross Papers, Gilcrease Institute.

11. Brown, "Albert Pike, 1809–1891," pp. 585, 588–91; Confederate Cherokee treaty, October 7, 1861, U.S., Department of War, *Official Rec-ords*, ser. 4, 1: 669–86; Pike to Dennis N. Cooley, February 17, 1866, in Joseph Thoburn, ed., "The Cherokee Question," *Chronicles of Oklahoma*, 2, no. 2 (June 1924), p. 176. A comparison of the treaty with the proposals Pike had suggested to Ross on June 6, 1861, indicates much similarity.

12. McCulloch to Ross, September 1, 1861, U.S., Department of War, *Official Records*, ser. 1, 3: 690–91; Evan Jones to William P. Dole, October 31, 1861, U.S., Senate, "Report of the Commissioner of Indian Affairs, 1861," 37th Cong., 2nd sess., *Executive Document 1*, pp. 658–59; Evan Jones to Dole, November 2, 1861, Cherokee Agency Letters Received.

13. Pike to Dennis N. Cooley, February 17, 1866, in Thoburn, ed., "The Cherokee Question," p. 174; William P. Adair to Stand Watie, August 29, 1861, Edward Everett Dale and Gaston Litton, eds., *Cherokee Cavaliers: Forty Years of Cherokee History As Told in the Correspondence of the Ridge-Watie-Boudinot Family* (Norman: University of Oklahoma Press, 1939), pp. 108–9. Adair evidently did not understand the full meaning of the convention, as he thought the meeting did not support an alliance with the South. He urged Watie to "place us if possible at least on an honorable

equity with this old Dominant party" (Dale and Litton, *Cherokee Cavaliers*, p. 109).

14. Pike to Ross, August 1, 1861, in Smith Christie et al., *Communication from the Delegation of the Cherokee Nation to the President of the United States* (Washington: Gibson Brothers, 1866), pp. 45–48; Ross to James Brown, September 10, 1861, Ross Papers, Gilcrease Institute; Confederate Cherokee treaty, October 7, 1861, U.S., Department of War, *Official Records*, ser. 4, 1: 669–86; Pike to J. P. Benjamin, December 25, 1861, ibid., ser. 1, 8: 720. McCulloch also concurred on this point (McCulloch to Walker, September 2, 1861, ibid., ser. 1, 3: 692). The defeat of the federals at Bull Run on the same date also likely influenced Ross at the August 21 convention at Tahlequah.

15. Ross Speech, August 21, 1861, U.S., Department of War, *Official Records*, ser. 1, 3: 674; Ross's annual message, October 9, 1861, Ross Papers, Gilcrease Institute; Christie et al., *Communication from the Cherokee Nation to the President*, p. 10.

16. Wardell, *History of the Cherokee Nation*, p. 130; Ross to the chiefs and headmen of the Creek Nation, August 24, 1861, and Opothleyahola to Ross, August 24, 1861, Ross Papers, Gilcrease Institute; Ross to Opothleyahola, September 19 and October 8, 1861, U.S., House, "Report of the Commissioner of Indian Affairs, 1865," 39th Cong., 1st sess., *Executive Document 1*, pp. 537–38; Ross to Kennard, October 4, 20, and November 28, 1861, Ross Papers, Gilcrease Institute.

17. Evan Jones to Dole, January 21, 1862, Ross Papers, Gilcrease Institute; McIntosh to S. Cooper, January 4, 1861, U.S., Department of War, *Official Records*, ser. 1, 8: 732.

18. Wardell, *History of the Cherokee Nation*, pp. 142–47; Ross to Jefferson Davis, May 10, 1862, U.S., Department of War, *Official Records*, ser. 1, 13: 826.

19. U.S., Department of War, *Official Records*, ser. 1, 13: 825; Ross to Hindman, June 25, 1862, ibid., pp. 950–51; Robert Lipscomb Duncan, *Reluctant General: The Life and Times of Albert Pike* (New York: E. P. Dutton and Company, 1961), pp. 239–40.

20. Coffin to Ross, June 16, 1862, Cherokee Nation Papers, Western History Collections, University of Oklahoma; Weer to Thomas Moonlight, June 13, 1862, U.S., Department of War, *Official Records*, ser. 1, 13: 431.

21. Weer to Ross, July 7, 1862, Ross to Weer, July 8, 1862, Blunt to E. M. Stanton, July 21, 1862, and Blunt to Weer, July 12, 1862, U.S., Department of War, *Official Records*, ser. 1, 13: 464, 486–89. Ross sent his proclamation of neutrality of May 17, 1861, his correspondence with Rector, Kannady, McCulloch, Hubbard, and certain Arkansans, the proclamation of the Cherokee Nation, August 21, 1861, his message to the Cherokee Nation, October 9, 1861, and the Cherokee declaration, October 28, 1861, ibid., pp.

489–505; Greeno to Weer, July 15 and 17, 1862, and Weer to Moonlight, July 16, 1862, ibid., pp. 160–62, 473; Carruth and Martin to Coffin, July 19, 1862, U.S., House, "Report of the Commissioner of Indian Affairs, 1862," 37th Cong., 3rd sess., *Executive Document 1*, pp. 302–4; Journal and Letters of Stephen Foreman, Cherokee Minister, typescript, Western History Collection, University of Oklahoma.

22. Blunt to Lincoln, August 13, 1862, U.S., Department of War, *Official Records*, ser. 1, 13: 565–66. Col. Frederick Salomon, Weer's second in command, arrested his superior on July 18, 1861, and forced the retreat into Kansas near Fort Scott, from where Ross was escorted to Blunt by Col. William F. Cloud (Ross to William P. Dole, October 13, 1862, Ross Papers, Gilcrease Institute). Wardell, *History of the Cherokee Nation*, pp. 155–56; Ross to Sarah, April 30, 1863, John Ross, Jr. to Ross, May 5, 1864, and Ross to Sarah, April 4, 1866, Ross Papers, Gilcrease Institute; Ross to Mary, June 6, 1864, Hargett Collection, Western History Collections, University of Oklahoma; Mary to Ross, June 7, 1864 [two letters of this date], Hargett Collection, Western History Collections, University of Oklahoma, and Ross Papers, Gilcrease Institute.

23. Ross to Lincoln, September 16, 1862, Ross Papers, Gilcrease Institute.

24. Lincoln to Ross, September 25, 1862, and Lincoln to Curtis, October 10, 1862, in Roy P. Basler, ed., *The Collected Works of Abraham Lincoln*, 9 vols. (New Brunswick, N.J.: Rutgers University Press, 1953–55), 5: 439–40, 456, 456 n.1; Dole to Ross, January 26, 1866, Cherokee Agency Letters Received; Wendell Holmes Stephenson, *The Political Career of General James H. Lane* (Topeka: Kansas State Printing Plant, 1930), pp. 118–22; Dole to John P. Usher, October 31, 1863, U.S., House, "Report of the Commissioner of Indian Affairs, 1863," 38th Cong., 1st sess., *Executive Document 1*, p. 114; Dole to Usher, November 15, 1864, U.S., House, "Report of the Commissioner of Indian Affairs, 1864," 38th Cong., 2nd sess., *Executive Document 1*, p. 175.

25. Dole to Usher, October 31, 1863, U.S., House, "Report of the Commissioner of Indian Affairs, 1863," *Executive Document 1*, p. 144; Ross to Sarah, September 22, 1863, and February 12, 1864, and Ross to countrymen, January 13, 1863, Ross Papers, Gilcrease Institute.

26. F. W. Sumner to Ross, November 29, 1863, Hargett Collection, Western History Collections, University of Oklahoma; obituary of James McDonald Ross, undated, and E. Jane Ross to Ross, December 31, 1864, Foreman, comp., "Copies of Letters . . . and Miscellaneous Documents Relative to the Cherokee and Creek Indians"; Allen, Silas, and George Ross's service records, Adjutant General's Office, National Archives; Ross to Lizzie, December 3/5, 1863, Foreman Collection, Gilcrease Institute; Mary to Ross, December 4, 1863, Ross Papers, Gilcrease Institute.

27. Dole to Ross et al., November 19, 1863, Ross et al. to Dole, November 21, 1863, and May 23 and 25, 1864, Ross Papers, Gilcrease Institute.

28. Act of the National Council, February 18, 1863, ibid.; Ross to Dole,

April 2, 1863, and Ross's oath of office, April 5, 1863, Cherokee Agency Letters Received; Wardell, *History of the Cherokee Nation*, pp. 171–72, 183.

29. Ross to Dole, October 13, 1862, Ross Papers, Gilcrease Institute; Ross to Dole, November 19, 1862, April 2 and May 4, 1863, August 26, 1864, E. B. French to Dole, June 19, 1863, Ross to Charles E. Mix, September 13, 1863, and Usher to Dole, December 12, 1863, Cherokee Agency Letters Received; Dole to Ross, January 10, April 4, and May 6, 1863, and Dole to French, June 20, 1863, Letters Sent, Office of Indian Affairs; report of the Committee on Claims, April 20, 1870, U.S., Senate, untitled, 41st Cong., 2nd sess., *Report 113* (serial 1409), p. 8.

30. Ross to Dole, July 29, 1864, and Usher to Dole, August 25, 1864, U.S., Senate, untitled, *Report 113* (serial 1409), p. 8; Ross to Dole, September 29, 1864, Ross Papers, Gilcrease Institute; Dole to Ross, August 27 and October 14, 1864, Letters Sent, Office of Indian Affairs; Ross to Mary, October 13, 1864, Hargett Collection, Western History Collections, University of Oklahoma.

31. Mix to Ross, July 2, 1863, and Dole to Ross, July 30, 1863, Letters Sent, Office of Indian Affairs; Ross to Mix, July 3 and August 7, 1863, and Ross to Dole, July 17, 28, and 31, 1863, Cherokee Agency Letters Received; Ross to Dole, December 10, 1863, Ross Papers, Gilcrease Institute. There is no evidence that Ross received this money (Ross to Mix, June 24, 1864, and Usher to Dole, July 25, 1864, Cherokee Agency Letters Received). The delegation obtained twenty-five hundred dollars at the time and the remainder in December (Dole to Ross, December 22, 1864, Letters Sent, Office of Indian Affairs).

32. Proposed treaty at Washington, June, 1864, Ross Papers, Gilcrease Institute. The similarities between this proposal and the Confederate Cherokee treaty of 1861 are astonishing. That the Cherokee delegates thought they could acquire such a favorable pact is quite surprising, especially since the legitimacy of their government was not fully accepted.

33. The delegation consisted of Ross, Evan Jones, and D. H. Ross (Ross et al. to Dole, February 7 and 18, 1865, Ross Papers, Gilcrease Institute); Coffin to Dole, July 8, 1864, Indian Division Letters Received, Office of the Secretary of the Interior; Dole to Ross et al., February 14 and March 20, 1865, and Dole to Coffin, March 28, 1865, Letters Sent, Office of Indian Affairs; Ross to Dole, February 23, 1864, Cherokee Agency Letters Received. There are two letters of this date, one giving the amount of $133,571.55 due up to January 1, 1864, and the other showing $153,403.04 due up to July 1, 1864 (Cherokee Agency Letters Received). Ross et al. to Usher, March 22, 1865, and Usher to Dole, March 30, 1865, Cherokee Agency Letters Received.

34. Coffin to Dole, July 8, 1864, Southern Superintendency Letters Received, Office of Indian Affairs; Coffin to Dole, June 16, 1864, U.S., House, "Report of the Commissioner of Indian Affairs, 1864," *Executive Document*

1, pp. 486–87; Ross to Dole, August 26, 1864, and Ross to Dennis N. Cooley, May 4, 1866, Cherokee Agency Letters Received. See also the testimony of Daniel H. Ross who owned the Fort Gibson store (affidavit of Daniel H. Ross, May 10, 1866, Cherokee Agency Letters Received).

35. Mary to Ross, January 10, 1865, and June 4, 1864, Ross Papers, Gilcrease Institute; Mary to Ross, September 26, 1863, and June 2 and 7, 1864, Hargett Collection, Western History Collections, University of Oklahoma; Ross to Sarah, April 19, 1860, Ross Papers, Gilcrease Institute; Ross to Mary, May 1, 1860, October 13, 1862, and June 6, 1864, Hargett Collection, Western History Collections, University of Oklahoma.

36. Ross to Mary, July 25, 1845, Ross Papers, Gilcrease Institute. Mary was baptized in May 1850 by the Reverend J. H. Garner in the Cherokee Nation. Ross, Annie, and John, Jr., were baptized in December 1855 in the Cherokee Nation by a certain Reverend John Harrell (statement of Mary B. Ross, August 1, 1863, Hargett Collection, Western History Collections, University of Oklahoma). Mary to A.E.W. Robertson, March 11, 1850, Alice Robertson Collection, University of Tulsa Library.

37. Ross to Mary, June 27/July 1, 1844, and December 22, 1863, Ross Papers, Gilcrease Institute.

38. Mary to Ross, December 4, 1863, ibid.; *Philadelphia Daily Evening Bulletin*, July 20, 1865, and July 22, 1865; obituary, undated and hand copied, Anne Ross Piburn Collection, Western History Collections, University of Oklahoma.

CHAPTER 11

1. Justin Harlan to Elijah Sells, October 1, 1865, U.S., House, "Report of the Commissioner of Indian Affairs, 1865," *Executive Document 1*, pp. 468–72.

2. Ross to Sarah, August 30, 1865, Ross Papers, Gilcrease Institute; Ross to Annie, September 18, 1865, Hargett Collection, Western History Collections, University of Oklahoma.

3. Cooley's report of the Fort Smith Council, October 30, 1865, U.S., House, "Report of the Commissioner of Indian Affairs, 1865," *Executive Document 1*, p. 480; Charles E. Mix's report of the Fort Smith Council, [October 1865?], ibid., pp. 497, 531.

4. Ibid., pp. 519–20.

5. Ibid., pp. 510–11.

6. Dole to Caleb B. Smith, November 27, 1861, U.S., Senate, "Report of the Commissioner of Indian Affairs, 1861," *Executive Document 1*, p. 627; Dole to Usher, November 15, 1864, U.S., House, "Report of the Commissioner of Indian Affairs, 1864," *Executive Document 1*, p. 177.

7. Cooley's report of the Fort Smith Council, October 30, 1865, U.S., House, "Report of the Commissioner of Indian Affairs, 1865," *Executive Document 1*, pp. 488–89; report of Wilson of the *New York Herald*, September 15, 1865, Special File 125, Office of Indian Affairs.

8. Report of Wilson of the *New York Herald*, September 15, 1865, Special File 125, Office of Indian Affairs; Cooley's report of the Fort Smith Council, October 30, 1865, U.S., House, "Report of the Commissioner of Indian Affairs, 1865," *Executive Document 1*, pp. 490–91, 496.

9. Mix's report of the Fort Smith Council [October 1865?], U.S., House, "Report of the Commissioner of Indian Affairs, 1865," *Executive Document 1*, pp. 521, 530–31.

10. Cooley to Harlan, September 16, 1865, and Harlan to Cooley, September 18, 1865, Cherokee Agency Letters Received.

11. Wardell, *History of the Cherokee Nation*, pp. 105–7, 184–85; Ross to George Butler, January 1, 1860, Cherokee Agency Letters Received.

12. Act of the National Council, November 7, 1865, and Ross to Sarah, October 28 and November 12, 1865, Ross Papers, Gilcrease Institute. Ross's niece Eliza Jane, who saw him when he returned to Park Hill, observed his health and commented: "How much of earthly sorrow has that father of your's been called to endure—how indomitable his energy & will!" (E. Jane to Annie Ross, September 6, 1865, Hargett Collection, Western History Collections, University of Oklahoma).

13. Smith Christie et al., *Memorial of the Delegates of the Cherokee Nation to the President of the United States and the Senate and House of Representatives in Congress* (Washington: Chronicle Print, 1866, passim.

14. Christie et al., *Communication from the Cherokee Nation to the President*, pp. 6, 7, 10, 13.

15. Boudinot and Adair to Cooley, January 12, 1866, Cherokee Agency Letters Received. It is interesting that Boudinot and Adair in their letter had originally used the sum $150,000 but marked that out and substituted $250,000 (ibid.). Pike to Cooley, February 17, 1866, in Thoburn, ed., "The Cherokee Question," 2: 178; Brown, "Albert Pike," p. 635; Stapler to Harlan, April 28,1866, Cherokee Agency Letters Received; Ross's annual message, October 3, 1859, Ross Papers, Gilcrease Institute.

16. J. B. Jones to Harlan, August 8, 1866, Grant Foreman Collection, Indian Archives Division, Oklahoma Historical Society.

17. E. C. Boudinot and W. P. Adair, *Reply of the Southern Cherokees to the Memorial of Certain Delegates from the Cherokee Nation* (Washington: McGill and Witherow, 1866), pp. 9–10; John R. Ridge et al., *Comments on the Objections of Certain Cherokee Delegates to the Proposition of the Government to Separate the Hostile Parties of the Cherokee Nation* (Washington: Intelligencer Printing House, 1866), pp. 6–7; James McDaniel et al., *Reply of the Delegates of the Cherokee Nation to the Demands of the Commissioner of Indian Affairs* (Washington: Gibson Brothers, 1866), p. 13.

18. Cooley to Johnson, February 25, 1866, Special File 125, Office of Indian Affairs. For the entire pamphlet with documentation refuting the major part of the commissioner's arguments, see Thoburn, ed., "The Cherokee Question," 2: 141–242. Smith Christie et al., *Reply of the Delegates of the Cherokee Nation to the Pamphlet of the Commissioner of Indian Affairs* (Washington: no imprint, 1866), pp. 5, 11, 12.

19. Ross to Sarah, February 22, 1866, Ross Papers, Gilcrease Institute.

20. Ibid.; Annie Heloise Abel, *The American Indian under Reconstruction* (Cleveland: Arthur H. Clark Company, 1925), pp. 353, 353–54, n.623.

21. Abel, *The American Indian under Reconstruction*, pp. 354–55. Ross to Sarah, March 18, 1866, Ross Papers, Gilcrease Institute; proposed treaty (Northern Cherokees), March 15, 1866, Special File 125, Office of Indian Affairs; J. B. Jones to Jennie Jones, March 17, 1866, Foreman Collection, Oklahoma Historical Society.

22. Ross to Sarah, January 19, March 18 and 30, and April 4, 1866, and Ross to G. Bishop, April 10, 1866, Ross Papers, Gilcrease Institute.

23. Daniel H. Ross to William P. Ross, April 3, 1866, ibid.

24. Stand Watie et al. to Cooley et al., April 7, 1866, Special File 125, Office of Indian Affairs; Ross et al., to Johnson, May 13, 1866, Cherokee Nation Papers, Western History Collections, University of Oklahoma; Wardell, *History of the Cherokee Nation*, p. 195.

25. J. W. Washbourne to J. A. Scales, June 1, 1866, in Dale and Litton, eds., *Cherokee Cavaliers*, p. 244; proposed treaty (Southern Cherokees), June 13, 1866, Special File 125, Office of Indian Affairs.

26. W. A. Phillips to William H. Seward, June 14, 1866, Cherokee Agency Letters Received; *New York Tribune*, May 21, 1866, May 28, 1866, and June 5, 1866; Smith Christie et al. to Cooley, July 9, 1866, Cherokee Nation Papers, Western History Collections, University of Oklahoma; Harlan to Cooley, July 10, 1866, Cherokee Agency Letters Received; Abel, *The American Indian under Reconstruction*, pp. 359–61. For the treaty itself, see Kappler, comp., *Indian Affairs*, 2: 942–50. Ross's medical expenses came to a considerable amount during the last few months of his life. In all the cost from April until his death in August came to nearly two thousand dollars, which included doctors' bills, medical supplies, extra food, and intensive care by Sarah and the children. One notation includes expenses for forty-five visits from May 9 to June 22, 1866, by Doctors J. C. Hall and J. W. Nairu (statement of expenses of John Ross, April 9 to August 1, 1866, Cherokee Agency Letters Received). It appears that the United States government paid these expenses as part of the settlement of the Treaty of 1866 (Elijah Sells to Dennis N. Cooley, August 21, 1866, Cherokee Agency Letters Received).

27. Last will of John Ross, Ross Papers, Gilcrease Institute; Jane Nave to James Harlan, August 30, 1866, and Jane Nave to O. H. Browning, September 21, 1866, Cherokee Agency Letters Received; report of the Committee on Claims, April 20, 1870, U.S., Senate, untitled, *Report 113*, passim.

28. Description of Ross's funeral at Wilmington, August, 1866, Foreman Collection, Gilcrease Institute; *Delaware Republican*, August 6, 1866.

29. Ross, ed., *The Life and Times of Honorable William P. Ross of the Cherokee Nation*, pp. 254–55.

30. Ibid., pp. 260, 264–65; Schwarze, *Moravian Missions*, pp. 292–93; *Fort Smith Herald*, May 11, 1867; "Notes of Travel through a Portion of the Indian Country and the Borders of Arkansas," *Fort Smith Herald*, June 6, 1867.

BIBLIOGRAPHY

PRIMARY

ATLANTA, GEORGIA.
Georgia Department of Archives and History. Cherokee Collection.
Surveyor-General Department. Official Records of the Georgia Surveyor-General.
BALTIMORE, MARYLAND. Maryland Historical Society. William Wirt Papers.
BETHLEHEM, PENNSYLVANIA. Archives of the Moravian Church. Records of the Moravian Mission among the Indians of North America.
CAMBRIDGE, MASSACHUSETTS. Harvard University. Houghton Library. Cherokee Mission Papers.
CHAPEL HILL, NORTH CAROLINA. University of North Carolina. Southern Historical Collections, R. J. Meigs, the younger. "Journal Kept While Serving as Secretary of John F. Schermerhorn." Typescript.
CHATTANOOGA, TENNESSEE. Penelope Johnson Allen. Private Collection.
CHEROKEE, NORTH CAROLINA. Museum of the Cherokee Indian. Cherokee Papers.
CHICAGO, ILLINOIS. Newberry Library. Ayer Collection.
  John Howard Payne Papers.
  John Ross Papers.
DETROIT, MICHIGAN. Detroit Public Library. Burton Historical Collection. Steven T. Mason Papers.
HANOVER, NEW HAMPSHIRE. Dartmouth College Library. Moses Fisk Papers.
LAWRENCEVILLE, NEW JERSEY. Lawrenceville School John Dixon Library. Mulford, R. J. Notes on the history of Lawrenceville Academy.
NASHVILLE, TENNESSEE. Tennessee State Library and Archives.
  Cherokee Collection.
  Tennessee Historical Society Collection. Miscellaneous File.
  Tennessee Land Grants.
NORMAN, OKLAHOMA. University of Oklahoma. Western History Collections.

Anne Ross Piburn Collection.

Cherokee Nation Papers.

Division of Manuscripts.

J. L. Hargett Collection.

Journal and Letters of Stephen Foreman, Cherokee Minister. Typescript.

OKLAHOMA CITY, OKLAHOMA. Oklahoma Historical Society.

Foreman, Grant, comp. "Copies of Letters . . . and Miscellaneous Documents Relative to the Cherokee and Creek Indians, 1836–1933."

Fries, Adelaide, trans. Extracts from "The Diary of the Moravian Missions among the Cherokee Indians, 1833–1838." Typescript.

Indian Archives Division.

"Cherokee Records." 730 vols.

Foreman, Grant, ed. "Indian Pioneer History." 113 vols. Typescripts.

Grant Foreman Collection.

John Ross Papers.

"Indian Documents." 52 vols.

Litton, Gaston, comp. "Cherokee Papers, 1815–1874." Typescripts.

Starr, Emmet. Notes for *History of the Cherokee Indians.*

PRINCETON, NEW JERSEY. Princeton University Library. Samuel L. Southard Papers.

TAHLEQUAH, OKLAHOMA. Northeastern Oklahoma State University. John Vaughn Library. Cherokee Collection.

Andrew Nave Papers.

John Ross Papers.

TULSA, OKLAHOMA.

Thomas Gilcrease Institute of American History and Art.

Cherokees, Eastern Band.

Grant Foreman Collection of Notes, Typescripts, Photostats, and United States Government Publications.

John Drew Papers.

John Howard Payne Papers.

John Ross Papers.

Lester Hargett Collection of Imprints.

University of Tulsa Library. Alice Robertson Collection.

WASHINGTON, D. C.

Library of Congress. Manuscript Division. Indian Collection.

Return J. Meigs. "Memorandum Book of Occurrences in the Cherokee . . . Country, 1796–1807."

National Archives.

Adjutant General's Office. Military Service Records. Record Group 94.

Eighth Census, 1860. "Arkansas and the Indian Lands." Record Group 29.

Office of Indian Affairs. Record Group 75.

Cherokee Agency East Letters Received.

Cherokee Agency Letters Received.

Cherokee Emigration Letters Received.
Letters Received by the Secretary of War.
Letters Sent.
Letters Sent by the Secretary of War.
Records of the Cherokee Indian Agency in Tennessee.
Southern Superintendency Letters Received.
Special Files.
Records of the Bureau of Land Management. Record Group 49.
Records of the Office of the Secretary of the Interior. Record Group 48.
Records of the Post Office Department. Registers of Appointments of Postmasters. Record Group 28.
WILMINGTON, DELAWARE. Historical Society of Delaware. Genealogical Files.

GOVERNMENT DOCUMENTS

ABEL, ANNIE HELOISE. "The History of Events Resulting in Indian Consolidation West of the Mississippi." *Annual Report of the American Historical Association for the Year 1906.* 2 vols. Washington, D.C.: Government Printing Office, 1908.

KAPPLER, CHARLES J., ed. *Indian Affairs: Laws and Treaties.* 5 vols. Washington, D.C.: Government Printing Office, 1904–41.

MOONEY, JAMES. "Myths of the Cherokees." Bureau of American Ethnology, *Nineteenth Annual Report.* 2 parts. Washington, D.C.: Government Printing Office, 1900.

"REPORT OF THE COMMISSIONER OF INDIAN AFFAIRS."
(Note: In the instances where both House and Senate included the reports in their serial set, pagination remained identical.)

1827. 20th Cong., 1st sess., *Executive Document 2.* Serials 163 and 169.
1828. 20th Cong., 2nd sess., *Document 1.* Serials 181 and 184.
1829. 21st Cong., 1st sess., *Executive Document 2.* Serials 192 and 195.
1836. 24th Cong., 2nd sess., *Executive Document 2.* Serials 297 and 301.
1838. 25th Cong., 3rd sess., *Document 1.* Serials 338 and 344.
1839. 26th Cong., 1st sess., *Document 1.* Serials 354 and 363.
1840. 26th Cong., 2nd sess., *Document 1.* Serials 375 and 382.
1847. 30th Cong., 1st sess., *Executive Document 1.* Serials 503 and 515.
1851. 32nd Cong., 1st sess., *Executive Document 1.* Serials 613 and 636.
1852. 32nd Cong., 2nd sess., *Executive Document 1.* Serials 658 and 673.
1853. 33rd Cong., 1st sess., *Executive Document 1.* Serials 690 and 710.
1854. 33rd Cong., 2nd sess., *Executive Document 1.* Serials 746 and 777.
1856. 34th Cong., 3rd sess., *Executive Document 1.* Serials 875 and 893.
1857. 35th Cong., 1st sess., *Executive Document 1.* Serials 919 and 942.
1858. 35th Cong., 2nd sess., *Executive Document 1.* Serials 974 and 997.

1859. 36th Cong., 1st sess., *Executive Document 1*. Serial 1023.

1861. 37th Cong., 2nd sess., *Executive Document 1*. Serial 1117.

1862. 37th Cong., 3rd sess., *Executive Document 1*. Serial 1157.

1863. 38th Cong., 1st sess., *Executive Document 1*. Serial 1182.

1864. 38th Cong., 2nd sess., *Executive Document 1*. Serial 1220.

1865. 39th Cong., 1st sess., *Executive Document 1*. Serial 1248.

ROYCE, CHARLES C. "The Cherokee Nation of Indians." Bureau of American Ethnology, *Fifth Annual Report*. 2 parts. Washington, D.C.: Government Printing Office, 1887.

STANLEY, J. M. "Catalogue of Portraits of North American Indians, with Sketches of Scenery, etc." Smithsonian Institution, Miscellaneous Collections. 153 vols. Washington, D.C.: Smithsonian Institution, 1862–.

UNITED STATES CONGRESS. *American State Papers*, Indian Affairs. 2 vols. Washington, D.C.: Gales and Seaton, 1832–61.

UNITED STATES DEPARTMENT OF WAR. *War of the Rebellion: A Compilation of the Official Records of the Union and Confederate Armies*. 70 vols., 120 books. Washington, D.C.: Government Printing Office, 1880–1901.

UNITED STATES HOUSE OF REPRESENTATIVES. (Documents arranged in order of date.)

"Message from the President of the United States." 18th Cong., 2nd sess., *Executive Document 19*. Serial 114.

"Message from the President . . . on Cherokee Treaty of 1819." 19th Cong., 1st sess., *Executive Document 21*. Serial 133.

"Reservations under the Cherokee Treaty." 20th Cong., 1st sess., *Executive Document 104*. Serial 171.

"Negotiations for Cherokee Lands." 20th Cong., 1st sess., *Executive Document 106*. Serial 171.

"Cherokee Government." 20th Cong., 1st sess., *Executive Document 211*. Serial 173.

"Indian Governments." 20th Cong., 1st sess., *Report 67*. Serial 177.

"Cherokee Council to Col. H. Montgomery." 20th Cong., 2nd sess., *Executive Document 6*. Serial 184.

"Articles of Cession between the United States and Georgia, and the Treaty with the Cherokee Indians." 20th Cong., 2nd sess., *Executive Document 95*. Serial 186.

"Memorial of John Ross, and Others, in Behalf of the Cherokee Nation." 20th Cong., 2nd sess., *Executive Document 124*. Serial 186.

"Memorial of John Ross and Others, Representatives of the Cherokee Nation of Indians." 20th Cong., 2nd sess., *Document 145*. Serial 187.

"Intrusions on Cherokee Lands." 21st Cong., 1st sess., *Executive Document 89*. Serial 197.

"Memorial of a Delegation of the Cherokee Nation of Indians." 21st Cong., 1st sess., *Report 397*. Serial 201.

"Memorial of a Delegation from the Cherokee Indians." 21st Cong., 2nd sess., *Document 57*. Serial 208.

"Memorial and Protest of the Cherokee Nation." 24th Cong., 1st sess., *Document 286*. Serial 292.

"Message on the Case of General Wool." 25th Cong., 1st sess., *Executive Document 46*. Serial 311.

"Cherokee Indians." 25th Cong., 2nd sess., *Document 82*. Serial 325.

"Memorial of a Delegation of the Cherokee Nation." 25th Cong., 2nd sess., *Document 99*. Serial 325.

"Seminole and Cherokee Indians." 25th Cong., 2nd sess., *Document 285*. Serial 328.

"Memorial of the Cherokee Delegation." 25th Cong., 2nd sess., *Document 316*. Serial 329.

"Cherokee Indians." 25th Cong., 2nd sess., *Executive Document 376*. Serial 330.

"Removal of Cherokees." 25th Cong., 2nd sess., *Executive Document 401*. Serial 330.

"Removal of the Cherokees." 25th Cong., 2nd sess., *Executive Document 453*. Serial 331.

"Memorial—Indians—Cherokee Delegation." 26th Cong., 1st sess., *Document 129*. Serial 365.

"Indians—Cherokee Nation, West." 26th Cong., 1st sess., *Document 162*. Serial 366.

"Cherokee Indians." 26th Cong., 1st sess., *Document 188*. Serial 366.

"Indians—Cherokees." 26th Cong., 1st sess., *Document 222*. Serial 368.

"Removal of the Cherokees West of the Mississippi." 27th Cong., 2nd sess., *Report 1098*. Serial 411.

"Frauds upon Indians—Right of the President to Withhold Papers." 27th Cong., 3rd sess., *Report 271*. Serial 428.

"Removal of the Cherokees." 27th Cong., 3rd sess., *Report 288*. Serial 429.

"Memorial of the 'Treaty Party' of the Cherokee Indians." 28th Cong., 1st sess., *Document 234*. Serial 443.

"Cherokee Indians." 28th Cong., 1st sess., *Document 235*. Serial 443.

"Claims Arising under the Cherokee Treaty." 28th Cong., 1st sess., *Report 391*. Serial 446.

"Cherokee Disturbances." 29th Cong., 1st sess., *Document 185*. Serial 485.

"Cherokee Indians." 29th Cong., 1st sess., *Report 683*. Serial 490.

"Moneys Due the Cherokee Nation." 53rd Cong., 3rd sess., *Executive Document 182*. Serial 3323.

UNITED STATES SENATE. (Documents arranged in order of date.)

"Message from the President of the United States." 21st Cong., 2nd sess., *Document 65*. Serial 204.

"Memorial of John Ross, and Others." 23rd Cong., 1st sess., *Document 386*. Serial 242.

"Memorial of a Delegation from the Cherokees." 23rd Cong., 1st sess., *Document 486.* Serial 243.

"Correspondence on the Subject of the Emigration of Indians." 23rd Cong., 1st sess., *Document 512.* Serials 244, 245, 246, 247, and 248.

"Memorial of John Ross and Others." 23rd Cong., 2nd sess., *Document 71.* Serial 268.

"Memorial of the Cherokee Delegation." 24th Cong., 1st sess., *Document 340.* Serial 283.

Untitled. 24th Cong., 1st sess., *Document 371.* Serial 283.

"Report from the Secretary of War . . . in Relation to the Cherokee Treaty of 1835." 25th Cong., 2nd sess., *Document 120.* Serial 315.

"Documents in Relation to the Validity of the Cherokee Treaty of 1835." 25th Cong., 2nd sess., *Document 121.* Serial 315.

"Report from the Secretary of War." 25th Cong., 2nd sess., *Document 461.* Serial 318.

Untitled. 25th Cong., 2nd sess., *Document 466.* Serial 318.

"Report from the Secretary of War." 25th Cong., 3rd sess., *Document 277.* Serial 342.

"Report of the Secretary of War." 28th Cong., 2nd sess., *Document 140.* Serial 457.

"Memorial of John Ross and Others." 29th Cong., 1st sess., *Document 331.* Serial 476.

Untitled. 29th Cong., 2nd sess., *Document 157.* Serial 495.

"Report of the Second Comptroller and Second Auditor." 31st Cong., 1st sess., *Executive Document 6.* Serial 554.

Untitled. 31st Cong., 1st sess., *Report 176.* Serial 565.

Untitled. 41st Cong., 2nd sess., *Report 113.* Serial 1409.

NEWSPAPERS

Arkansas Gazette, 1839–66.
Cartersville Courant (Georgia), 1885.
Chattanooga Sunday Times, 1936.
Cherokee Advocate, 1844–53.
Cherokee Phoenix, 1828–34.
Christian Advocate, 1829.
Daily Evening Bulletin (Philadelphia), 1865.
Delaware Republican, 1866.
Fort Smith Herald, 1867.
New York Tribune, 1866.
Niles' Register, 1811–49.
Panoplist and *Missionary Herald,* 1805–53.
Van Buren Press (Arkansas), 1861.

PUBLISHED PRIMARY

ADAMS, JOHN QUINCY. *Memoirs of John Quincy Adams.* Edited by Charles Francis Adams. 12 vols. Philadelphia: J. P. Lippincott, 1874–77.

BASLER, ROY P., ed. *The Collected Works of Abraham Lincoln.* 9 vols. New Brunswick, N.J.: Rutgers University Press, 1953–55.

BASSETT, JOHN SPENCER, ed. *Correspondence of Andrew Jackson.* 7 vols. Washington, D.C.: Carnegie Institute of Washington, 1926–35.

BENTON, THOMAS HART. *Thirty Years' View.* 2 vols. New York: D. Appleton, 1893.

BOUDINOT, E. C., and W. P. ADAIR. *Reply of the Southern Cherokees to the Memorial of Certain Delegates from the Cherokee Nation.* Washington, D.C.: McGill and Witherow, 1866.

Charges against the Hon. John W. Hooper, Judge of the Superior Court of the Cherokee Circuit. Milledgeville, Ga.: Office of the *Federal Union,* 1835.

CHRISTIE, SMITH et al. *Communication from the Delegation of the Cherokee Nation to the President of the United States.* Washington, D.C.: Gibson Brothers, 1866.

———. *Memorial of the Delegates of the Cherokee Nation to the President of the United States and the House of Representatives in Congress.* Washington, D.C.: Chronicle Print, 1866.

———. *Reply of the Delegates of the Cherokee Nation to the Pamphlet of the Commissioner of Indian Affairs.* Washington, D.C.: no imprint, 1866.

The Constitution and Laws of the Cherokee Nation: Passed at Tahlequah, Cherokee Nation, 1839–51. Tahlequah, Cherokee Nation: *Cherokee Advocate* Office, 1852.

DALE, EDWARD EVERETT and GASTON LITTON, eds. *Cherokee Cavaliers: Forty Years of Cherokee History as Told in the Correspondence of the Ridge–Watie–Boudinot Family.* Norman: University of Oklahoma Press, 1939.

Documents Relative to the Judicial Administration of Hon. John W. Hooper. Milledgeville, Ga.: Office of the *Federal Union,* 1835.

[EVARTS, JEREMIAH?]. *Essays on the Present Crisis in the Condition of the American Indians: First Published in the National Intelligencer under the Signature of William Penn.* Boston: Perkins and Marvin, 1829.

FEATHERSTONHAUGH, G. W. *A Canoe Voyage up the Minnay Sotor with an Account of . . . the Cherokee Country.* 2 vols. London: Richard Bentley, 1847.

FOREMAN, GRANT, ed. "Report of the Cherokee Deputation into Florida." *Chronicles of Oklahoma,* 9, no. 4 (December 1931), pp. 423–38.

FRIES, ADELAIDE L., and DOUGLAS LETELL RIGHTS, eds. *Records of the Moravians in North Carolina.* 8 vols. Raleigh, N.C.: State Department of Archives and History, 1922–54.

GILMER, GEORGE ROCKINGHAM. *Sketches of some of the First Settlers of Upper Georgia, of the Cherokees and the Author.* New York: D. Appleton, 1855.

GOODE, WILLIAM H. *Outposts of Zion with Limnings of Mission Life.* Cincinnati: Poe and Hitchcock, 1863.

HITCHCOCK, ETHAN ALLEN. *A Traveler in Indian Territory, the Journal of Ethan Allen Hitchcock.* Edited by Grant Foreman. Cedar Rapids, Iowa: Torch Press, 1930.

Laws of the Cherokee Nation Adopted by the Council at Various Periods. Tahlequah, Cherokee Nation: *Cherokee Advocate* Office, 1852.

Laws of the Cherokee Nation Passed at the Annual Session of the National Council, 1852–3. Tahlequah, Cherokee Nation: *Cherokee Advocate* Office, 1853.

LOOMIS, AUGUSTUS. *Scenes in the Indian Country.* Philadelphia: Presbyterian Board of Publication, 1859.

LUMPKIN, WILSON. *The Removal of the Cherokee Indians from Georgia . . . 1827–1841.* 2 vols. New York: Mead, 1907.

MCDANIEL, JAMES et al. *Reply of the Delegates of the Cherokee Nation to the Demands of the Commissioner of Indian Affairs.* Washington, D.C.: Gibson Brothers, 1866.

MCKENNEY, THOMAS L. *History of the Indian Tribes of North America with Biographical Sketches and Anecdotes of the Principal Chiefs.* 3 vols. Philadelphia: Rice, Rutler, 1870.

————. *Memoirs, Official and Personal: with Sketches of Travels among Northern and Southern Indians.* New York: Paine and Burgess, 1846.

MERIWETHER, ROBERT L., W. EDWIN HEMPHILL, and CLYDE N. WILSON, eds., *The Papers of John C. Calhoun.* 10 vols. to date. Columbia: University of South Carolina Press, 1959–.

MORSE, JEDIDIAH. *A Report to the Secretary of War of the United States on Indian Affairs.* New Haven, Conn.: Howe and Spalding, 1822.

MOULTON, GARY E. " 'Voyage to the Arkansas': New Letters of Chief John Ross." *Tennessee Historical Quarterly,* 35, no. 1 (Spring 1976), pp. 46–50.

PASCHAL, GEORGE W. "The Trial of Stand Watie." Edited by Grant Foreman. *Chronicles of Oklahoma,* 12, no. 3 (September 1934), pp. 305–39.

PAYNE, JOHN HOWARD. "The Captivity of John Howard Payne." *North American Quarterly Magazine,* 7, no. 33 (January 1836), pp. 107–24.

————. *John Howard Payne to his Countrymen.* Edited by Clemens de Bailou. Athens: University of Georgia Press, 1961.

POLK, JAMES K. *The Diary of James K. Polk during His Presidency, 1845 to 1849.* Edited by Milo Milton Quaife. 4 vols. Chicago: A. C. McClurg, 1910.

RICHARDSON, JAMES D., comp. *A Compilation of the Messages and Papers of the Presidents, 1789–1902.* 10 vols. New York: Bureau of National Literature and Art, 1897–1904.

RIDGE, JOHN R., et al. *Comments on the Objections of Certain Cherokee Delegates to the Proposition of the Government to Separate the Hostile Parties of the Cherokee Nation.* Washington, D.C.: Intelligencer Printing House, 1866.

ROSS, JOHN. *Letter from John Ross, the Principal Chief of the Cherokee Nation, to a Gentleman of Philadelphia.* n.p., 1837.

———. *Letter from John Ross ... in Answer to Inquiries from a Friend Regarding the Cherokee Affairs with the United States.* n.p., 1836.

TIMBERLAKE, HENRY. *Memoirs, 1756–1765.* Edited by Samuel Cole Williams. Marietta, Ga.: Continental Book, 1948.

WASHBURN, CEPHAS. *Reminiscences of the Indians.* Richmond, Va.: Presbyterian Committee of Publication, 1869.

WIRT, WILLIAM. *An Opinion on the Claims for Improvements by the State of Georgia on the Cherokee Nation under the Treaties of 1817 and 1828.* New Echota, Ga.: Office of *Cherokee Phoenix and Indians' Advocate,* 1830.

———. *Opinion on the Right of the State of Georgia to Extend Her Laws over the Cherokee Nation.* Baltimore: F. Lucas, Jr., 1830.

PUBLISHED SECONDARY

ABEL, ANNIE HELOISE. *The American Indian as a Participant in the Civil War.* Cleveland: Arthur H. Clark, 1919.

———. *The American Indian as Slaveholder and Secessionist: An Omitted Chapter in the Diplomatic History of the Southern Confederacy.* Cleveland: Arthur H. Clark, 1915.

———. *The American Indian under Reconstruction.* Cleveland: Arthur H. Clark, 1925.

———. "The Cherokee Negotiations of 1822–1823." *Smith College Studies in History,* 1, no. 4 (July 1916), pp. 188–221.

ARMSTRONG, ZELLA. *History of Hamilton County, and Chattanooga, Tennessee.* Chattanooga: Lookout Mountain Publishing, 1931.

BASS, ALTHEA. *Cherokee Messenger.* Norman: University of Oklahoma Press, 1936.

BATTY, GEORGE M., JR. *A History of Rome and Floyd County.* 2 vols. Atlanta: Webb and Vary, 1922.

BROWN, JOHN P. "Cherokee Removal, an Unnecessary Tragedy." *East Tennessee Historical Society's Publications,* no. 11 (1939), pp. 11–19.

———. "Eastern Cherokee Chiefs." *Chronicles of Oklahoma,* 16, no. 1 (March 1938), pp. 3–35.

———. *Old Frontiers: The Story of the Cherokee Indians from Earliest Times to the Date of their Removal in the West, 1838.* Kingsport, Tenn.: Southern Publishers, 1938.

BROWN, WALTER L. "Albert Pike, 1809–1891." Ph.D. diss., University of Texas, 1955.

BRYCE, J. Y. "Beginning of Methodism in Indian Territory." *Chronicles of Oklahoma*, 7, no. 4 (December 1929), pp. 475–86.

BURKE, JOSEPH C. "The Cherokee Cases: A Study in Law, Politics, and Morality." *Stanford Law Review*, 21, no. 3 (February 1969), pp. 500–531.

Chief John Ross: His Life with Historic Notes on the State of Georgia, Walker County. Rossville, Ga.: North Georgia Publishing, 1937.

COLLINS, LINTON M. "The Activities of Missionaries among the Cherokees." *Georgia Historical Quarterly*, 6, no. 4 (December 1922), pp. 285–322.

CORNELIUS, ELIAS. *The Little Osage Captive, an Authentic Narrative to Which are Added Some Interesting Letters, Written by Indians.* New York, England: W. Alexander and Son, 1921.

COTTERILL, R. S. *The Southern Indians: The Story of the Civilized Tribes before Removal.* Norman: University of Oklahoma Press, 1954.

COULTER, E. MERTON. *A Short History of Georgia.* Chapel Hill: University of North Carolina Press, 1933.

DALE, EDWARD E. "Arkansas and the Cherokees." *Arkansas Historical Quarterly*, 8, no. 2 (Summer 1949), pp. 95–114.

DUNCAN, ROBERT LIPSCOMB. *Reluctant General: The Life and Times of Albert Pike.* New York: E. P. Dutton, 1961.

EATON, RACHEL CAROLINE. *John Ross and the Cherokee Indians.* Menasha, Wis.: George Banta, 1914.

FITZGERALD, O. P. *John B. McFerrin: A Biography.* Nashville, Tenn.: Publishing House, Methodist Episcopal Church, South, 1889.

FOREMAN, CAROLYN THOMAS. "A Cherokee Pioneer: Ella Flora Coodey Robinson." *Chronicles of Oklahoma*, 7, no. 4 (December 1929), pp. 364–74.

———. "Dr. William Butler and George Butler, Cherokee Agents." *Chronicles of Oklahoma*, 30, no. 2 (Summer 1952), pp. 160–72.

———. *Park Hill.* Muskogee, Okla.: Star Printery, 1948.

———. "Pierce Mason Butler." *Chronicles of Oklahoma*, 30, no. 1 (Spring 1952), pp. 6–26.

FOREMAN, GRANT. *Advancing the Frontier, 1830–1860.* Norman: University of Oklahoma Press, 1933.

———. *The Five Civilized Tribes.* Norman: University of Oklahoma Press, 1934.

———. *Indian Removal: The Emigration of the Five Civilized Tribes of Indians.* Norman: University of Oklahoma Press, 1953.

———. "John Howard Payne and the Cherokee Indians." *American Historical Review*, 27, no. 4 (July 1932), pp. 723–30.

———. "The Murder of Elias Boudinot." *Chronicles of Oklahoma*, 12, no. 1 (March 1934), pp. 19–24.

FOSTER, GEORGE EVERETT. *Literature of the Cherokees, also Bibliography and the Story of Their Genesis.* Ithaca, N.Y.: Office of the *Democrat,* 1889.

GABRIEL, RALPH HENRY. *Elias Boudinot, Cherokee, and His America.* Norman: University of Oklahoma Press, 1941.

GOVAN, GILBERT E. "Some Sidelights on the History of Chattanooga." *Tennessee Historical Quarterly,* 6, no. 2 (June 1947), pp. 148–60.

———, and James W. Livingood. *The Chattanooga Country, 1540–1951.* New York: E. P. Dutton, 1952.

HAMER, PHILIP M. "The British in Canada and the Southern Indians, 1790–1794." *East Tennessee Historical Society's Publications,* no. 2 (1930), pp. 107–34.

———. *Tennessee: A History, 1673–1932.* 4 vols. New York: American Historical Society, 1933.

HICKS, J. C. "The Rhetoric of John Ross." Ph.D. diss., University of Oklahoma, 1971.

HINSHAW, WILLIAM WADE. *Encyclopedia of American Quaker Genealogy.* 3 vols. Ann Arbor, Mich.: Genealogical Publishers, 1936–40.

KNIGHT, OLIVER. "Cherokee Society under the Stress of Removal, 1820–1846." *Chronicles of Oklahoma,* 32, no. 4 (Winter 1954–55), pp. 414–28.

LEVERING, J. MORTIMER. *A History of the Moravian Seminary for Young Ladies at Bethlehem.* Bethlehem, Pa.: New Era, 1901.

LITTON, GASTON. "The Principal Chiefs of the Cherokee Nation." *Chronicles of Oklahoma,* 15, no. 3 (September 1937), pp. 153–270.

MCNEIL, KENNETH. "Confederate Treaties in Indian Territory." *Chronicles of Oklahoma,* 42, no. 4 (Winter 1964), pp. 408–20.

MALONE, HENRY T. "*The Cherokee Phoenix*: Supreme Expression of Cherokee Nationalism." *Georgia Historical Quarterly,* 34, no. 3 (September 1950), pp. 163–88.

———. "Cherokee-White Relations on the Southern Frontier in the Early Nineteenth Century." *North Carolina Historical Review,* 34, no. 1 (June 1957), pp. 1–14.

———. "The Cherokees Become a Civilized Tribe." *Early Georgia,* 2, no. 2 (Spring 1957), pp. 12–15.

———. *Cherokees of the Old South: A People in Transition.* Athens: University of Georgia Press, 1956.

———. "The Early Nineteenth Century Missionaries in the Cherokee Country." *Tennessee Historical Quarterly,* 10, no. 2 (June 1951), pp. 127–39.

———. "Return Jonathan Meigs—Indian Agent Extraordinary." *East Tennessee Historical Society's Publications,* no. 28 (1956), pp. 3–22.

MESERVE, JOHN BARTLETT. "Chief John Ross." *Chronicles of Oklahoma,* 13, no. 4 (December 1935), pp. 421–37.

———. "Chief William Potter Ross." *Chronicles of Oklahoma*, 15, no. 1 (March 1937), pp. 21–29.

MILES, EDWIN A. "After John Marshall's Decision: *Worcester* v. *Georgia* and the Nullification Crisis." *Journal of Southern History*, 39, no. 4 (November 1973), pp. 519–44.

MONAGHAN, JAY. *Civil War on the Western Border, 1854–1865*. Boston: Little, Brown, 1955.

MOULTON, GARY E. "Cherokees and the Second Seminole War." *Florida Historical Quarterly*, 53, no. 3 (January 1975), pp. 296–305.

———. "Chief John Ross and Cherokee Removal Finances." *Chronicles of Oklahoma*, 52, no. 3 (Fall 1974), pp. 342–59.

———. "Chief John Ross during the Civil War." *Civil War History*, 19, no. 4 (December 1973), pp. 314–33.

PAINE, ROBERT. *Life and Times of Bishop McKendree*. 2 vols. Nashville, Tenn.: Southern Methodist Publishing House, 1869.

PASCHAL, GEORGE W. "The Trial of Stand Watie." Edited by Grant Foreman. *Chronicles of Oklahoma*, 12, no. 3 (September 1934), pp. 305–39.

PEAKE, ORA BROOKS. *A History of the United States Indian Factory System, 1795–1822*. Denver: Sage Books, 1954.

PRUCHA, F. P. "Andrew Jackson's Indian Policy: A Reassessment." *Journal of American History*, 56, no. 3 (December 1969), pp. 527–39.

REED, GERALD A. "The Ross-Watie Conflict: Political Factionalism in the Cherokee Nation, 1839–1865." Ph.D. diss., University of Oklahoma, 1967.

ROSS, MRS. WILLIAM P., ed. *The Life and Times of Honorable William P. Ross of the Cherokee Nation*. Fort Smith, Ark.: Weldon and Williams, 1893.

RUTLAND, ROBERT A. "Political Background of the Cherokee Treaty of New Echota." *Chronicles of Oklahoma*, 27, no. 4 (Winter 1949–50), pp. 389–406.

SATZ, RONALD N. *American Indian Policy in the Jacksonian Era*. Lincoln: University of Nebraska Press, 1975.

SCHWARZE, EDMUND. *History of the Moravian Missions among Southern Indian Tribes of the United States*. Bethlehem, Pa.: Times Publishing, 1923.

SMITH, JAMES F. *The Cherokee Land Lottery*. New York: Harper and Brothers, 1838.

SMITH, WILLIAM ROBERT LEE. *The Story of the Cherokees*. Cleveland, Tenn.: The Church of God Publishing House, 1928.

STARKEY, MARION L. *The Cherokee Nation*. New York: Alfred A. Knopf, 1946.

STARR, EMMET. *History of the Cherokee Indians*. Oklahoma City: Warden, 1921.

STEPHENSON, WENDELL HOLMES. *The Political Career of General James H. Lane.* Topeka: Kansas Printing Plant, 1930.

THOBURN, JOSEPH, ed. "The Cherokee Question." *Chronicles of Oklahoma,* 2, no. 2 (June 1924), pp. 141–242.

VAN HOEVEN, JAMES WILLIAM. "Salvation and Indian Removal: The Career Biography of John Freeman Schermerhorn, Indian Commissioner." Ph.D. diss., Vanderbilt University, 1972.

VIPPERMAN, CARL JACKSON. "Wilson Lumpkin and the Cherokee Removal." Master's thesis, University of Georgia, 1961.

WALKER, ROBERT SPARKS. *Lookout: The Story of a Mountain.* Kingsport, Tenn.: Southern Publishers, 1941.

———. *Torchlights to the Cherokees: The Brainerd Mission.* New York: Macmillan, 1931.

WARDELL, MORRIS L. *A Political History of the Cherokee Nation, 1838–1907.* Norman: University of Oklahoma Press, 1938.

WEST, ANSON. *A History of Methodism in Alabama.* Nashville, Tenn.: Publishing House, Methodist Episcopal Church, South, 1893.

WHITAKER, A. P. "Spain and the Cherokee Indians, 1783–98." *North Carolina Historical Review,* 4, no. 3 (July 1927), pp. 252–69.

WILKINS, THURMAN. *Cherokee Tragedy: The Story of the Ridge Family and of the Decimation of a People.* New York: Macmillan, 1970.

WILLIAMS, SAMUEL COLE, ed. "Christian Missions to the Overhill Cherokees." *Chronicles of Oklahoma,* 12, no. 1 (March 1934), pp. 66–73.

———, ed. *Early Travels in Tennessee Country, 1540–1800.* Johnson City, Tenn.: Watauga Press, 1928.

———, ed. "The Executive Journal of Governor John Sevier." *East Tennessee Historical Society's Publications,* no. 4 (1932), pp. 104–28.

WOODWARD, GRACE STEELE. *The Cherokees.* Norman: University of Oklahoma Press, 1963.

WOOTEN, JOHN MORGAN. *A History of Bradley County.* Nashville, Tenn.: Tennessee Historical Commission, 1949.

INDEX

DATE DUE
